C000047166

Nothing M
Than Reincarnation

Evidence of
Reincarnation in Early
Christianity

KEVIN R. WILLIAMS

DEDICATION

This book is dedicated to my grandmother, Marie Williams, who I took care of in her later years. Her descriptions of her father led me to understand how he was a past life of mine, my great grandfather Henry Bollinger, whose life paralleled my own in important ways.

CONTENTS

FOREWORD

Reincarnation has been called by some to be the greatest unknown scientific discovery today. In the last chapter of Dr. Ian Stevenson's book entitled Twenty Cases Suggestive of Reincarnation (1967), he provides rigorous scientific reasoning to show how reincarnation is the only viable explanation that fits the facts of his study. He considers every possible alternative explanation for his twenty cases of young children who were spontaneously able to describe a previous lifetime as soon as they learned to talk. He was able to rule out each alternative explanation using one or more aspects of these cases. Later research has even bolstered his case in favor of the existence of reincarnation. His study is also completely reproducible which means that anybody who doubts the validity of this study is perfectly welcome to repeat it for themselves. I believe it is only a short matter of time before his discovery of the existence of reincarnation is finally realized by the scientific community and the world to be accepted as one of the greatest scientific discoveries of all time.

CHAPTER 1:
REINCARNATION IN THE BIBLE (PART 1)

Human beings are the result of double evolution: the evolution of the body and the evolution of the soul (reincarnation). Reincarnation is the doctrine that human beings alive today have been on Earth many times before and will return many more times until their purpose of life is reached. In many documented near-death experiences (NDEs) involving Jesus, the concept of reincarnation appears. In the NDE testimony of Sandra Rogers resulting from a suicide attempt, for example, she was given two options by Jesus to choose from. She could return to life, resulting in an NDE, and overcome the problems she was currently having trouble facing. Obviously, this was the option she chose. Her other option was to remain in heaven with the agreement to reincarnate at a later time to overcome the problems she couldn't in her previous life. In another NDE example, this time not involving suicide, Jeanie Dicus was given the same option.

Reincarnation is not some "New Age" fad; and people have had misconceptions about reincarnation for thousands of years including Christians. Some people wrongly assume reincarnation means souls do not inhabit heavenly realms between Earth lives. The fact is that souls DO inhabit heavenly realms - and for as long as they desire. Some people wrongly assume reincarnation always happens immediately after death. Some people wrongly assume reincarnation means the soul never becomes a permanent resident of heaven. Even the reincarnational religions of the East do not support these misconceptions about reincarnation. Neither do NDE testimonies support these misconceptions. In every reincarnational religion, reincarnation is something a person must overcome. The goal for the soul is to become liberated from the need to reincarnate. And although reincarnation is always a choice - rather than a mandate - the benefits of reincarnating may prove to be "an offer too good for the soul to refuse."

There are options other than reincarnation available for the soul. But it is the Earth's "School of Hard Knocks" which provides the soul with best, quickest, and most efficient method of attaining its spiritual goal. Other options such as learning in a heavenly classroom where there is "no pain," and therefore "no gain," is not as real as "hands-on training" on Earth. Because despite what many Christians believe, heaven is all about deeds - not creeds - and in the afterlife, thoughts are deeds. Only in the physical realm, where darkness and light coexist, can a person say one thing while thinking another. In the afterlife there is nowhere to hide your thoughts because the spirit realm is the realm of thoughts and mind. Communication in the spirit realm is mediated by thought. This is why the major world religions teach the importance of having good thoughts and intentions - not just good words - because thoughts are deeds in the spirit world. This principle is what Jesus was referring to when he taught Nicodemus about the consequences of rejecting his message:

"This is the verdict: Light has come into the world, but people loved darkness instead of light because their deeds were evil. Everyone who does evil hates the light, and will not come into the light for fear that their deeds will be exposed. But whoever lives by the truth comes into the light, so that it may be seen plainly that what they have done has been done in the sight of God" (John 3:19-21).

The ultimate purpose of reincarnation is for the soul to learn enough spiritual lessons, gain enough enlightenment from Earth lives, so that the soul can qualify for even higher heavenly realms of the afterlife and dwell even closer to the light of God. And there are many realms - many heavens, many hells and many realms in between. The physical realm is just one of these realms in between. For example, the apostle Paul wrote about a man who had an NDE and journeyed to the "third heaven" (2 Corinthians 12:2-4). Jesus mentioned there were "many dwelling places" in his "Father's house" (John 14:2). Many sources reveal a cosmology of at least ten major afterlife realms. So reincarnation is God's "grand design" for souls, through good works, to "work their way up" through the afterlife hierarchy of realms toward the goal of becoming permanent citizens in God's highest heaven which is complete at-onement with the light of God. These Christian mysteries were once available during the first 500 years of early Christianity until the Church decided to declare them "heresy" for the sake of "orthodoxy." This article will reveal to you the mysteries of reincarnation as the lost doctrine in Christianity and the true interpretation of the end time Resurrection of the Dead.

NDE testimonies reveal how people have the free will to spend whatever amount of "time" they desire in afterlife realms before reincarnating to Earth again, if reincarnation is indeed their choice. This is because time does not exist in the afterlife realms like it does in the physical realm. NDE studies reveal time only exists in the physical realm, and according to Albert Einstein, time is relative and flexible. Upon entering the afterlife, you soon realize that you've been there before. You realize you existed before you were born and now you are returning to where you were before you were born. Returning to the afterlife feels as though you have been away for only a few moments. You feel as though your Earth experience was just a dream for which you are now waking up. This is because you have now entered eternity where time doesn't exist and cannot be measured. One moment can extend into a thousand years or vice versa. This principle agrees with the Bible: "With the Lord a day is like a thousand years, and a thousand years are like a day" (2 Peter 3:8)

One event follows another event in the afterlife, but there is no universal way to measure time. There is no sunrise to mark the start of the day, nor a sunset to mark the start of the night. And no need for sleep. There is no day or night - only the constant light source everywhere that is God. So clocks are relatively useless. When you are in heaven, you are happy and "time seems to fly" - events follow one another quickly. When you are in hell, or bored to tears, "time seems to drag on forever" - events seem to follow one another slowly. This is why people who have hellish NDEs often say their experience felt like it lasted an "eternity."

It's also understandable how a Christian would find the idea of reincarnation repulsive. After all, why would anyone want to leave heavenly paradise and return to this world of suffering and evil? Note that this is a question we might ask of Jesus himself. Why would he want to leave paradise to suffer and die a horrible death; and then promise he would return again in the future? Well, in Jesus' case, his reason for coming into this world was to save people. As someone once eloquently put it, "It was love, not nails, that held Jesus to the cross." So to better understand the answer to such questions, it helps to understand the nature of reincarnation itself and how it relates to life and the afterlife.

It all begins at birth when we are thrust from the womb onto the carousel of life, carried away in a blur of activities from childhood to adulthood and then old age. Day after day, life is busy. We have relationships, go to school, go to work, and we tend to not think about death. We have hints of a life after death. We have nightly dreams - a virtual reality that seems to exist only in our minds. We have religious experiences which gives us transcendental hints of an afterlife. Some people have NDEs which have revealed a wealth of information concerning what happens after death and the reality of an afterlife and reincarnation. When you die, the real "you" - your "soul body" - leaves your physical body and you can experience the physical world as you would expect a ghost would - having the ability to walk through walls, be invisible to the living, and fly through the air. Eventually, a "tunnel" appears and you are drawn into another realm. This other realm is part of the "soul realms" where you are greeted by the souls of your deceased loved ones and you have a kind of homecoming. At some point you will have a "life review" where you instantaneously "re-live" in your mind the life you lived on Earth with every memory and every second brought to mind. This life review process is for educational purposes and soul growth and may include revelations from past lives. Your life review also determines the next destination in the afterlife hierarchy you have earned. There are higher realms in the afterlife - the "spirit realms" - and the goal of everyone is to attain the highest spirit realm where there is no longer any reason to leave.

After each Earth experience and life review, you enter the spirit realm which you have earned. In the spirit realm, you meet and merge with your "spirit body" - your "higher self." In the spirit realm, you can also merge on a spirit level with God, remember your true origins, remember your true spiritual nature, realize your souls' shortcomings, and live forever with the spirits of all your loved ones you have known for all eternity. So your spirit actually never leaves

4

the spirit realms. Even while you live on Earth, your spirit within you exists in the spirit dimension. Humans are multidimensional beings living in multidimensional realms. Every time you reincarnate (if that is your choice), a particular aspect of your greater personality (your spirit) incarnates as a new soul. Depending upon which level in the spirit realms you have earned, you realize how close you are to complete at-onement with God and what is needed to attain the highest spirit heaven. You can choose soul growth without the need to reincarnate in lower realms, but there are great advantages in reincarnating into Earth's "School of Hard Knocks" as previously mentioned. A soul may choose to operate only in the soul realms for soul growth. The soul/spirit reincarnates into lower afterlife realms - not only for its own soul growth and goal to attain the highest realm of spirit - but to help loved ones in these realms, and to help further God's cosmic plan of salvation in these realms. As you grow into higher realms of soul and spirit, the closer you draw to God, the more you become like God, the more love you have for every soul, spirit, and body. Indeed, you are not a human being having a spiritual experience. You are spirit being having a human experience. Someday, all souls/spirits will be liberated from their "prison" of flesh which is the goal of reincarnation.

The relationship between the mind, the soul and the spirit, can be best understood as consciousness (mind), subconsciousness (soul) and superconsciousness or God Consciousness or Universal Consciousness (spirit). While you are awake, your conscious mind is in control and your subconscious mind (soul) recedes beyond your conscious awareness. Your spirit recedes even farther beyond your conscious awareness. When you sleep and dream, your conscious body sleeps and our subconscious mind "awakens" and becomes your conscious mind during which your soul/spirit body actually leaves your sleeping body and inhabits the "astral" realm near the physical realm. In the astral realm and in the soul realms, your superconscious mind (spirit) plays the same role that your subconscious mind plays while you are fully awake. Reincarnation allows multidimensional beings to ultimately attain the goal of at-onement with God which also means at-onement with your higher self and everyone else.

1. A Brief History of Reincarnation in Christian History

One of the reasons many Christians reject the validity of NDE testimony is because they sometimes appear to conflict with their interpretation of Christian doctrines. But Christians are usually surprised to learn that reincarnation, and its corresponding doctrine of preexistence, were beliefs held by a significant number of early Christians for the first 500 years of Christian history. As you will see in Part 5 of this article, the Bible mentions human beings preexisting as souls before the world began and having previous lifetimes. And as you will see in all parts of this article, the Bible is filled with references to reincarnation. The first great Father of the early Church, Origen of Alexandria (185-254 AD), was the first person since Paul to develop a system of theology around the teachings of Jesus. Origen was also an ardent defender of preexistence and reincarnation. Origen often expressly declared his stance against the transmigration of souls (or "metempsychosis") because it included the belief that humans could reincarnate into animals. Origen held a far more exalted reincarnational belief which was continued re-embodiment of the soul in the physical, destined for places of purification, but with the soul's ultimate goal of restoration to heaven and oneness with God. History shows how reincarnation was considered a mystery teaching and oral tradition handed down from the apostles only to those initiated into the Christian mysteries. St. Jerome (347-420 AD), Doctor of the Roman Catholic Church and no friend of Origen's doctrines, wrote how Origen's doctrines of preexistence and reincarnation were secretly taught within certain Christian sects in the past and in his day. According to the Catholic Encyclopedia article on Metempsychosis: "St. Jerome tells us that metempsychosis was a secret doctrine of certain sectaries in his day, but it was too evidently opposed to the Catholic doctrine of Redemption ever to obtain a settled footing."

According to Jerome's Letter 133 to Demetrias (414 AD), Jerome lamented that Origin's doctrines of preexistence and transmigration of souls (the "serpent's poison" according to Jerome) was formerly "ripe" within the churches in Egypt and the Middle East and continued to exist as a "secretly" as a teaching within these same churches: "In [Anastasius'] days a terrible storm of heresy (of the Origenists) came from the East and strove first to corrupt and then to undermine that simple faith which an apostle has praised (Romans

1:8). However the bishop (Anastasius), rich in poverty and as careful of his flock as an apostle, at once smote the noxious thing on the head, and stayed the hydra's hissing. Now I have reason to fear - in fact a report has reached me to this effect - that the poisonous germs of this heresy still live and sprout in the minds of some to this day. I think, therefore, that I ought to warn you, in all kindness and affection, to hold fast the faith of the saintly Innocent, the spiritual son of Anastasius and his successor in the apostolic see; and not to receive any foreign doctrine, however wise and discerning you may take yourself to be. Men of this type whisper in corners and pretend to inquire into the justice of God. Why, they ask, was a particular soul born in a particular province? What is the reason that some are born of Christian parents, others among wild beasts and savage tribes who have no knowledge of God? ... Now if God's judgments, they say, are "true and righteous altogether," (Psalm 19:9) and if "there is no unrighteousness in Him," (Psalm 92:15) we are compelled by reason to believe that our souls have pre-existed in heaven, that they are condemned to and, if I may so say, buried in human bodies because of some ancient sins, and that we are punished in this valley of weeping (Psalm 84:6) for old misdeeds. This according to them is the prophet's reason for saying: "Before I was afflicted I went astray," (Psalm 119:67) and again, "Bring my soul out of prison." (Psalm 142:7) They explain in the same way the question of the disciples in the gospel: "Who did sin, this man or his parents, that he was born blind?" (John 9:2) and other similar passages. This godless and wicked teaching was formerly ripe in Egypt and the East; and now it lurks secretly like a viper in its hole among many persons in those parts, defiling the purity of the faith and gradually creeping on like an inherited disease till it assails a large number ... However, I have defeated their wiles and counterworked their efforts to undermine the truth in a treatise (Jerome's Letter 124 to Avitus Concerning Origen)..." (Jerome's Letter 133 to Demetrias)

Origen was a disciple of Clement of Alexandria who was a disciple of Saint Mark, the author of the Gospel of Mark and disciple of the apostle Peter. Clement and Origen wrote about receiving secret teachings of Jesus handed down from the apostles. The doctrines of preexistence and reincarnation championed by Origen were eventually declared a heresy by the Roman Church in 553 A.D at the Second Council of Constantinople. It was at this time the Roman

Church aggressively destroyed competing teachings and so-called "heresies" within the Church. Along with the destruction of unorthodox teachings came the destruction of Jews and Christian Gnostics, and ultimately anyone who stood in the way of the Inquisition and Crusades: "If anyone asserts the fabulous pre-existence of souls, and shall assert the monstrous restoration which follows from it, let him be anathema [excommunicated]." - Decree of the Fifth Catholic Council, of the Second Council of Constantinople (553 AD), declaring preexistence and reincarnation to be heresy

From the time of this 6th century Council onward, reincarnation became a lost doctrine in Christianity. Lost was the mystery of Christ's teaching of a special "resurrection" - a rebirth as told to Nicodemus which was the following:

(1) A rebirth of the spirit into flesh ("born of water", childbirth, reincarnation) (John 3:5-6).

(2) A rebirth through the Holy Spirit ("born of the Spirit", spiritual regeneration, spiritual "resurrection") (John 3:6-8).

Evidently the mystery of reincarnation in Christianity was meant to remain mostly hidden for almost two thousand years until the 1945 discovery of the lost Christian Gnostic writings in northern Egypt and the 1946 discovery of the Dead Sea Scrolls around the time of the "rebirth" of the nation of Israel in 1948 which was a great fulfillment of Bible prophecy. Early Christian texts, such as the Gospel of Thomas and the Gospel of Philip, clearly show Jesus teaching reincarnation which is one reason they were declared heretical.

2. The Mystery of the Resurrection of the Dead

The "resurrection of the dead" (in Greek "anastasis ton nekron"), literally meaning "standing up again of the dead," is a term frequently used in the New Testament and in the writings and doctrine and theology in other religions to describe an event by which a person, or people are resurrected (brought back to life). The concept of resurrection originated with the Persian Zoroastrian religion (of Magi fame) which was then passed along to Judaism during their

Babylonian exile. As distinct from Judaism, the Zoroastrian resurrection concept is an endtime rise of all the dead to universal purification and renewal of the world. The early Hebrews had no notion of resurrection and thus no intermediate state after death. As with neighboring groups around Israel, the early Hebrews understood death to be the end of life. Their afterlife, Sheol (the Pit), was a dark place from which none return. By Jesus' time, however, the Book of Daniel (Daniel 12:1-4) and a prophecy in the Book of Isaiah (Isaiah 26:19) had made popular the idea that the dead in Sheol would be raised for a Last Judgment. According to the Book of Enoch, the righteous and wicked await the resurrection in separate divisions of Sheol, a teaching which may have influenced Jesus' Parable of the Rich Man and Lazarus (Luke 16:19-31). In the Septuagint and New Testament the authors used the Greek term Hades for the Hebrew Sheol. In the Parable of the Rich Man and Lazarus Jesus describes Hades along the lines of the Jewish understanding of a Sheol divided between the righteous, in the "bosom of Abraham," and the wicked "in torment."

According to Christian eschatology, some theological traditions, including most Protestants and Eastern Orthodox, teach that a particular judgment occurs immediately after death and an intermediate state exists as a disembodied foretaste of the final state before the final resurrection. Therefore, according to these traditions, those who die in Christ rest in peace in Hades while they await the final resurrection. Those who die unrepentant will experience torment in Gehenna while they await the resurrection and final condemnation on Judgment Day. So for thousands of years, Christians have believed that when a person dies their soul rests in peace until the final resurrection of the dead and the Last Judgment. The idea of people going immediately to heaven after death is a relatively new concept in orthodox Christianity. However, as previously mentioned, the suppressed early Christian teachings held reincarnation to be God's plan for the soul to "work its way up" the afterlife realms immediately after death with the goal of becoming permanent citizens in God's highest heaven. Early 20th century American preachers such as Billy Sunday epitomized the evangelical focus on "going to heaven" immediately after death in their sermons. Modern evangelists such as Sunday spoke of many aspects of the afterlife such as the nice weather and eternal health without any

9

mention of the resurrection of the dead. Billy Sunday would end his sermons with an illustration about a man who dies and goes to heaven exclaiming "Home, home at last!" as if he had arrived at the end of his eschatological journey. NDE studies and reincarnation research affirms that consciousness does indeed continue on in some afterlife dimension immediately after death. To people who understand early Christian Gnosticism, early esoteric Christianity, and early Christian mysticism, the doctrines of "soul sleep" and a final resurrection of corpses are the result of a gross misunderstanding of Christ's secret, mystery teachings concerning the "resurrection" of the spirit mentioned in the previous section. Part of this misunderstanding comes from the early Church's misunderstanding of the nature of Christ, the mystery of God in man, and of the nature of the soul in relation to the body. From this misunderstanding the Church erroneously concluded:

(1) Jesus was God in the flesh.
(2) The body and soul are inseparable and are of one substance.
(3) Only within Jesus does God uniquely reside meaning Jesus is the only son of God.
(4) The soul is not preexistent. It was created during conception and sleeps after death until the Resurrection of the Dead and Last Judgment.

So the traditional doctrine of the Resurrection of the Dead is based upon the unusual notion that the soul is inseparable from the physical body. As applied to the afterlife, this means the final resurrection process is simply the "reawakening" of the soul within the same body it belonged to in life. The official doctrine of the largest Christian church, the Catholic Church, reads the following in its Catechism (Part One: The Profession of Faith, Section Two I: The Creeds, Chapter Three: I Believe In The Holy Spirit, Article 11: "I Believe In The Resurrection Of The Body"):

The term "flesh" refers to man in his state of weakness and mortality. The "resurrection of the flesh" (the literal formulation of the Apostles' Creed) means not only that the immortal soul will live on after death, but that even our "mortal body" will come to life again.

As previously mentioned, the resurrection of corpses did not originate with Christianity, but with the Persian Zoroastrian religion. During the Babylonian exile in Old Testament times, the Jews were greatly influenced by many Zoroastrian concepts - not just resurrection. Other Zoroastrian influences in Judaism include: a final day of judgment, a dualism of good versus evil, a hierarchy of angels including fallen angels, and an arch rival of God in the form of a satanic being. Over time, these Zoroastrian concepts were incorporated into Judaism; and from those days forward, the concept of the resurrection of corpses competed with the much older concept of reincarnation and the concept of Sheol - concepts which can be found in the Hebrew scriptures. The first-century Jewish historian Flavius Josephus (31-100 AD) wrote about the Pharisees being believers in reincarnation. The Pharisees were the Jewish sect which Paul belonged to before conversion to Christianity. Josephus wrote about the Pharisees' belief of the souls of evil men being punished after death; but the souls of good men are "removed into other bodies" and they will have "power to revive and live again." From time to time throughout Jewish history, there was a persistent belief about dead prophets returning to life through reincarnation. But the Sadducees, a purist sect of Judaism, rejected Persian concepts of resurrection and all foreign influences involving reincarnation existing in Jesus' day. The Sadducees accepted only the ancient Hebrew belief in Sheol of which no one returned. History shows there were a variety of eschatological ideas existing in Jerusalem at the time of Jesus. Israel and the Middle East has always been the connection between Europe, Asia and Africa and its flow of ideas.

But the notion of a massive worldwide reanimation of corpses coming out of graves at the end of time seems bizarre, unnatural, repulsive, and against everything known in science. A better interpretation of a biblical "resurrection" is "live babies coming out of wombs" instead of "dead bodies coming out of tombs." Although "sleep" is a common metaphor in the Bible for "death", the idea of the soul sleeping after death until the resurrection is also an idea originating with Zoroastrianism. In the few instances in the Bible where corpses were reanimated, a mediator was needed to perform the miracle. Doctors today bring people back from the dead with modern technology as evidenced by NDEs. However, soul sleep is contradicted by the biblically supported idea of an immortal soul (or spirit) implying that it does not sleep after death nor can it be extinguished. By overcoming the flesh through spiritual rebirth (regeneration) by the Holy Spirit, the immortal soul need no longer be subjected to the cycle of physical birth-death and rebirth and can attain eternal life.

3. The Mystery of Rebirth Defined

As you will read in the next section of Part 1 in this article, the prophetic fulfillment of John the Baptist as a reincarnation of Elijah the prophet is the clearest biblical statement of the reality of reincarnation. When Jesus began his ministry, many people wondered if Jesus was the reincarnation of one of the prophets. Some people wondered the same thing concerning John the Baptist. Even Jesus affirmed to his disciples that John the Baptist was the reincarnation of the prophet Elijah. The Bible reveals John had both the spirit and power of Elijah - meaning his reincarnation. Skeptical objections to Elijah's reincarnation as John are debunked in this article. John and Elijah shared many similarities suggestive of reincarnation including appearance, diet, personality, relationships, life situations, ministry, locations they inhabited throughout in Israel, and karma. The evidence shows that if John was not the reincarnation of Elijah as prophecy foretold, then Jesus could not have been the Messiah as prophecy foretold. Elijah and Moses appeared transfigured with Christ at his first coming; and in the Book of Revelation, Elijah and Moses are implied to be reincarnated for Christ's second coming. This will also be shown in the next section.

As you will read in other Parts of this article, the Bible mentions the reincarnation of other prophets and other biblical personalities. The Bible even mentions the entire nation of Israel reincarnating. The Bible also mentions the apostles John and Paul reincarnating; and if you are willing to accept it, the Bible gives evidence of Jesus' past lives as Melchizedek, Joseph, Joshua, and Adam. Jesus mentioned to his followers they would be alive on Earth at his second coming implying their reincarnation. In other Parts of this article, you will read how some of the parables of Jesus only make sense if reincarnation is true. The Bible records Jesus himself teaching reincarnation to his followers. The Bible uses the Greek word "palingenesía" which translated means reincarnation. The Bible describes life as a cycle and how God brings everything to life again.

Some books of the Jewish and Christian Apocrypha mention reincarnation. You will also read in other Parts of this article where the Bible refers to angels as humans, humans as angels, and souls who "fell from heaven" long ago and are currently on a path back to God through reincarnation. The Bible mentions angels in "prisons" which is a Christian Gnostic metaphor meaning "flesh". The soul must free itself from this "prison" by following Christ in taking up one's own cross. The Bible also uses "prison" as a metaphor for hell. Both angels and humans are described in the Bible as being rescued from hell.

Another Part of this article describes God's law of divine justice as defined in the Bible as the law of karma which is reincarnation. Karma is the principle of "an eye for an eye" and "live by the sword, die by the sword." The assumption is if you live by the sword, and don't die by the sword, then you must die by the sword in some future lifetime. The law of karma and reincarnation can be found in the Hebrew Bible, the New Testament, the Gospels, the Epistles of Paul, and the parables of Jesus. All Hebrew and Christian scriptures support karma and reincarnation: the Dead Sea Scrolls, the Christian Gnostic gospels, the Torah, the Biblical Apocrypha, the New Testament Apocrypha, the Kabbalah and Zohar. Reincarnation was widely believed by the people throughout the Roman Empire in Jesus' day, throughout Israel, and by people all around the world. The Bible teaches how "bad karma" can extend into multiple lifetimes - to multiple generations. The Bible teaches how overcoming bad karma with good karma leads to eternal life and the end of the cycle of death and rebirth. The Bible also teaches how God's law of love, grace, and forgiveness can overcome bad karma.

4. The Real Resurrection of the Dead

In Part 2 of this article, you will read how, throughout his ministry, Jesus taught people about the true "resurrection" - a rebirth (regeneration) of the spirit within a living person. When Jesus declared he was "the resurrection and the life," he was teaching them a radical new principle apart from the well-known doctrine of the rebirth of the spirit into flesh (reincarnation). Jesus was teaching a new "resurrection" by the Holy Spirit which would liberate people from the cycle death and rebirth and bring eternal life. Reincarnation is the rebirth of a person's spirit into a new body to be born again as an infant. Spiritual "resurrection" is the rebirth of a person's spirit in a living person to be born again by the power of the Holy Spirit. You will read how Jesus taught Nicodemus of two births: one of the flesh, and the other of the spirit. To be "born of the flesh" means to be born of water, childbirth, and reincarnation. To be "born of the spirit" means spiritual regeneration by the Holy Spirit. Jesus taught how people must become spiritually reborn (regenerated) by the Holy Spirit or else they cannot attain eternal life. Those who are not spiritually reborn, and do not attain eternal life, must be physically reborn and continue the cycle of death and rebirth until they are spiritually reborn. The Bible often uses childbirth (reincarnation) as a metaphor for spiritual regeneration by the Holy Spirit. Along with the metaphor of childbirth is the use of baptism as a metaphor for spiritual regeneration. The Bible also often uses bodily resurrection as a metaphor for spiritual regeneration by the Holy Spirit.

In Part 3 of this article, you will read about many Judeo-Christian doctrines supporting reincarnation. The most obvious are the doctrines of: dot universal salvation, dot salvation by works, dot the preexistence of the soul, dot sanctification by the Holy Spirit, and dot glorification (divinization) of the saints. You will read how universal salvation defines God as having a plan of salvation after death for those who have not been spiritually regenerated. For the first 500 years of Christianity, Christians and Christian theologians were broadly Universalist. The mistranslation of the scriptures from Greek to Latin contributed to the reinterpretation of the eternal nature of hell. The merging of Church and State also fostered the corruption of Universalist thought. There are also plenty of Bible verses supporting universal salvation and how God's punishments are not eternal. Part 4 of this article shows how the doctrine of people being judged according to God's law is based upon their good and bad works and how this also supports reincarnation. People who have not overcome their bad works through good works must reincarnate until they do. The Bible is clear on how God's law, the Ten Commandments, has never been abrogated. Paul's writings tended to dismiss the law, perhaps because he erroneously believed Jesus was returning in his lifetime, but it is clear that Paul didn't believe salvation was based upon faith alone (Galatians 5:6). There are abundant Bible verses teaching salvation by good works according to God's law, especially in the teachings of Jesus. The few verses suggesting salvation by faith alone are either out of context or misinterpretations of Christ's teachings about the law. Salvation begins with repentance and the continual non-practice of sin. Those sinners who refuse to do so will not attain eternal life. They must instead continue the cycle of death and rebirth until they do. Everyone is working toward the goal of salvation whether they are awakened to the fact or not. Jesus has given us the way, the pattern to follow. We must take up our own crosses and follow his example.

Also in Part 4 of this article, you will read how the Bible refers to Christian perfection and glorification and how it implies reincarnation. The Bible is filled with teachings compelling people to be perfect and become sanctified through the Holy Spirit. Christians who are not perfected are reborn for more lifetimes until they are. The Bible reveals even Jesus needed to be perfected by suffering on the cross (Hebrews 2:10, Hebrews 5:9) proving he had a human nature subjected to temptation and reincarnation. As previously mentioned, the Christian mystery of the "resurrection of the dead" is that reincarnation is God's remedy for people to become permanent citizens in the highest heaven by "working their way up" the many afterlife realms immediately after death. The process of perfection and sanctification obviously takes more than one lifetime; and the Bible describes Jesus as the "firstborn" among those perfected. The goal for every human being is to become like Christ - to be transformed into his image. The mystery of God within human beings is an immortal human soul joined with a divine spirit encased in flesh. It is the flesh which must be overcome through reincarnation. As co-heirs with Christ, humans can attain at-onement with God as Christ did. Attaining perfection and at-onement with God requires a long period of time as the works of Christ show. For these reasons and more, reincarnation is a doctrine which can be accepted by every follower of Christ and should be a part of orthodox Christian doctrine today.

5. John the Baptist as Elijah Reincarnated

A. John the Baptist as Elijah is the Clearest Biblical Statement of Reincarnation

In many instances in the Bible, John the Baptist is identified as the reincarnation of Elijah the prophet. Often the person identifying John the Baptist as Elijah is Jesus himself. These instances are the clearest statements in the Bible declaring the reality of reincarnation. One example is during the "Transfiguration of Jesus" in the Gospel of Matthew:

Matthew 17:1-13: When Jesus took Peter, James and John to a high mountain where he transfigured before them. His face shone like the sun, and his clothes became as white as the light. Moses and Elijah also appeared and talked with Jesus. As they were coming down the mountain, the disciples asked Jesus, "The disciples asked him, 'Why then do the teachers of the law say that Elijah must come first?'

"Jesus replied, 'To be sure, Elijah comes and will restore all things. But I tell you, Elijah has already come, and they did not recognize him, but have done to him everything they wished. In the same way the Son of Man is going to suffer at their hands.'

"Then the disciples understood that he was talking to them about John the Baptist."

In very explicit language, Jesus identified John the Baptist as the reincarnation of Elijah. Even the disciples of Jesus understood what Jesus was saying.

The earliest New Testament Bibles began with the Gospel of Mark which opens by introducing John the Baptist as the return of Elijah, the greatest prophet of Israel:

Mark 1:1-2: "The beginning of the good news about Jesus the Messiah, the Son of God, as it is written in Isaiah the prophet: 'I will send my messenger ahead of you, who will prepare your way.'"

Because the Old Testament literally ends with the promise of Elijah's return, and the New Testament begins with the announcement of Elijah's return, this "John the Baptist as Elijah" information in the Bible seems to be extremely important. In the last book in the Old Testament, the final words are:

Malachi 4:5-6: "See, I will send the prophet Elijah to you before that great and dreadful day of the Lord comes. He will turn the hearts of the parents to their children, and the hearts of the children to their parents; or else I will come and strike the land with total destruction."

Also notice this "John the Baptist as Elijah" information is mentioned near the beginning of the rest of the gospels in Matthew

3:1-3, Luke 1:17, and John 1:6.

In the case of the beginning of the Gospel of John, we are given extra information about John the Baptist which is also very interesting. The verse in John 1:6 suggests John preexisted in the same way the Bible mentions Jesus preexisted:

John 1:6: "There was a man sent from God whose name was John [the Baptist]."

Notice John 1:6 says the Baptist was "sent from God" meaning his soul came from heaven before he was born. This means John preexisted before he was conceived. And because John the Baptist is identified as Elijah later on throughout the gospels, then his preexistence supports the fact he is Elijah. Not only this, James (the brother of Jesus) declared Elijah to be a human being "even as we are":

James 5:17: "Elijah was a human being, even as we are. He prayed earnestly it would not rain, and it did not rain on the land for three and a half years."

So, if Elijah was a just normal human being, then his reincarnation as John the Baptist was a normal human experience as well. And this indicates reincarnation is not uniquely human to Elijah alone.

B. John Had the Spirit and Power of Elijah

In the beginning of the Gospel of Luke, an angel appeared before Zacharias to announce his wife would bear a son who would be the embodiment of a prophet. The angel announced with total clarity the spirit manifested in the prophet would be Elijah; and he even quotes Malachi:

Luke 1:17: "And he will go on before the Lord, in the spirit and power of Elijah, to turn the hearts of the parents to their children and the disobedient to the wisdom of the righteous - to make ready a people prepared for the Lord."

Anti-reincarnationalists claim this Bible verse confirms John to be merely a prophet who performed the same ministry as Elijah - not as a reincarnation of Elijah. But this is not what the verse actually says. In fact, the verse gives a perfect definition of reincarnation: the return of a person's "spirit" and "power" into another body. It is the spirit and power of a person which reincarnates. Therefore this verse clearly states that John the Baptist had the spirit and power of Elijah.

And this is exactly what reincarnation means. It does not get much clearer than this.

Jesus not only identified the Baptist as the reincarnation of Elijah - the greatest of the Old Testament prophets - Jesus identified the Baptist as the fulfillment of all the prophets and the law:

Matthew 11:11-15: "Truly I tell you, among those born of women there has not risen anyone greater than John the Baptist; yet whoever is least in the kingdom of heaven is greater than he. From the days of John the Baptist until now, the kingdom of heaven has been subjected to violence, and violent people have been raiding it. For all the Prophets and the Law prophesied until John. And if you are willing to accept it, he is the Elijah who was to come. Whoever has ears, let them hear."

In the above passage, Jesus again clearly identifies John the Baptist as the reincarnation of Elijah the prophet. He also mentions there has not "risen" anyone greater than John the Baptist referring to reincarnation. But equally important, he identifies the Baptist with the prophecies concerning the coming of the Messiah and the one who precedes him. This identification of John to be the reincarnation of Elijah is very important when it comes to Bible prophecy. By identifying John with Elijah, Jesus identified himself as the Messiah. The Hebrew scriptures mentions specific signs would precede the coming of the Messiah. One of them is Elijah will return first:

Malachi 4:5: "Behold I will send you Elijah the prophet, before the coming of the great and dreadful day of the Lord."

C. If John Was Not Elijah, Then Jesus Was Not the Messiah

The above Bible verse in Malachi is one of the major Messianic prophecies from God found in the Bible. And these "John the Baptist is the reincarnation of Elijah" verses clearly demonstrate the reality of reincarnation. So there are two important conclusions we can draw from this:

(1) The Old Testament prophesied Elijah himself - not someone like him or someone in the same ministry as him - but Elijah himself would return before the advent of the Messiah. (Malachi 4:5)

(2) Jesus declared John to be Elijah when he stated Elijah has come.

18

(Matthew 17:10-13)

Based on the Bible verses in (1) and (2) alone, either (a) or (b) must be true:

(a) John was the reincarnation of Elijah the Prophet. Therefore, reincarnation must become once again a part of Judeo-Christian theology. It also means the current concept of the Resurrection of the Dead, the "reanimation" of corpses on "Judgment Day," can be discarded and replaced with:

I. Bodily "resurrection" (reincarnation); and

II. Spiritual "resurrection", which is the spiritual regeneration of spiritually dead LIVING people. In other words, becoming "born again" of the Holy Spirit.

Or else...

(b) John was not the reincarnation of Elijah the Prophet. Then this would mean Elijah himself had not returned. And if this were true, then we must conclude the following:

I. The Old Testament prophecy about Elijah returning before the coming of the Messiah failed to come to pass (meaning Biblical prophecy is fallible).

Or else ...

II. Jesus was not the Messiah.

So based upon the above logic, only one of the following can be true:

(1) Reincarnation is a reality, or else...
(2) Jesus was not the Messiah, or else...
(3) Bible prophecies are not reliable.

There are no other options. You must select one. And because Jesus' declaration of "John is Elijah" was overt and direct, then the only logical option is option (1) Reincarnation is a reality.

Had Elijah's spirit not reincarnated in the life and body of John the Baptist, the prophecies of Malachi 4:5 and Luke 1:17 would never have been fulfilled; and the Messiah - with Elijah yet to come - could not have possibly arrived! Therefore, Christian anti-reincarnationalists are inadvertently agreeing with Jewish Rabbis who, to this very day, await the return of Elijah before the Messiah. However, the fact that these prophecies were already fulfilled is self-evident when John identified himself to be "the voice crying in the wilderness preparing the way of the Lord."

D. Skeptical Objections to John as Elijah Answered

Some anti-reincarnationalists use 2 Kings 2:9-15 as evidence of John, having the "spirit" and "power" of Elijah, not referring to reincarnation:

2 Kings 2:9-15: "When they had crossed, Elijah said to Elisha, 'Tell me, what can I do for you before I am taken from you?' 'Let me inherit a double portion of your spirit,' Elisha replied. 'You have asked a difficult thing,' Elijah said, 'yet if you see me when I am taken from you, it will be yours - otherwise, it will not.' As they were walking along and talking together, suddenly a chariot of fire and horses of fire appeared and separated the two of them, and Elijah went up to heaven in a whirlwind. Elisha saw this and cried out, 'My father! My father! The chariots and horsemen of Israel!' And Elisha saw him no more. Then he took hold of his garment and tore it in two. Elisha then picked up Elijah's cloak that had fallen from him and went back and stood on the bank of the Jordan. He took the cloak that had fallen from Elijah and struck the water with it. 'Where now is the Lord, the God of Elijah?' he asked. When he struck the water, it divided to the right and to the left, and he crossed over. The company of the prophets from Jericho, who were watching, said, 'The spirit of Elijah is resting on Elisha.' And they went to meet him and bowed to the ground before him."

Anti-reincarnationalists claim Elijah didn't die, but was taken to heaven. Therefore, they claim it would be impossible for Elisha to receive Elijah's spirit. However, we have already established the fact that Elijah was a normal human being according to James 5:17. And, according to Paul: "Flesh and blood cannot inherit the kingdom of

God, nor does the perishable inherit the imperishable." (1 Corinthians 15:50)

So there should be no doubt that Elijah died the moment he was taken to heaven. Also, the fact that Elisha was an adult when he received the spirit of Elijah is not a conflict either according to reincarnation. According to all world religions teaching reincarnation, there is the phenomenon of the "walk-in reincarnation." This is when the spirit of a deceased person "possesses" the body of a living person. For example, after Herod had John the Baptist beheaded and began hearing about Jesus performing miracles, he thought Jesus was the "walk-in reincarnation spirit" of John the Baptist:

Mark 6:12-15: "They (the disciples) drove out many demons and anointed many sick people with oil and healed them. King Herod heard about this, for Jesus' name had become well known. Some were saying, 'John the Baptist has been raised from the dead, and that is why miraculous powers are at work in him.' Others said, 'He is Elijah.' And still others claimed, 'He is a prophet, like one of the prophets of long ago.'"

Matthew 14:1-2: "At that time Herod the tetrarch heard the reports about Jesus, and he said to his attendants, 'This is John the Baptist; he has risen from the dead! That is why miraculous powers are at work in him.'"

Luke 9:7-8: "Now Herod the tetrarch heard about all that was going on. And he was perplexed because some were saying that John had been raised from the dead, others that Elijah had appeared, and still others that one of the prophets of long ago had come back to life."

By "some" people in Israel assuming in the possibility of Jesus being one of the prophets of Israel from ancient times, they implicitly acknowledged their belief in reincarnation. Another reference of people believing Jesus had the "walk-in reincarnation" spirit of John the Baptist is in the Gospel of Matthew: "When Jesus came to the region of Caesarea Philippi, he asked his disciples, 'Who do people say the Son of Man is?' "They replied, 'Some say John the Baptist; others say Elijah; and still others, Jeremiah or one of the prophets.'" (Matthew 16:13-14)

Notice in the above Bible verse, Jesus asked his disciples who they believed he was in a past life. Also notice how the disciples knew exactly what Jesus was asking and gave reincarnational answers. The disciples' answer to Jesus, referring to John the Baptist, could only be true if Jesus was a "walk-in reincarnation" of John. The disciples' answer also referred to prophets who died a very long time ago. Although later in verse 16, Peter answers Jesus with, "You are the Messiah, the Son of the living God," Jesus does not deny reincarnation or correct them against the possibility of reincarnation. In many other instances, Jesus teaches reincarnation.

Now let's mention the final verse, John 1:19-27, used by anti-reincarnationalists to deny reincarnation which instead actually supports reincarnation: "Now this was John's testimony when the Jewish leaders in Jerusalem sent priests and Levites to ask him who he was. He did not fail to confess, but confessed freely, 'I am not the Messiah.' They asked him, 'Then who are you? Are you Elijah?' He said, 'I am not.' 'Are you the Prophet?' He answered, 'No.' Finally they said, 'Who are you? Give us an answer to take back to those who sent us. What do you say about yourself?' John replied in the words of Isaiah the prophet, 'I am the voice of one calling in the wilderness, 'Make straight the way for the Lord.' Now the Pharisees who had been sent questioned him, 'Why then do you baptize if you are not the Messiah, nor Elijah, nor the Prophet?' 'I baptize with water,' John replied, 'but among you stands one you do not know. He is the one who comes after me, the straps of whose sandals I am not worthy to untie.'" (John 1:19-27)

There are several items of interest in the above verse. First of all, notice how the Pharisees questioning John were expecting John to answer he was the reincarnation of an Old Testament prophet. And John did not refute the concept of reincarnation when he cleverly stated he was not Elijah - after all, he was John! Nevertheless, John's answer affirmed the fact of him being Elijah when he identified himself as "the voice of one calling in the wilderness" who "prepares the way" for the Messiah: "I am the voice of one calling in the wilderness, 'Make straight the way for the Lord.'" (John 1:23)

The above Bible verse (John 1:23) and its connection to Elijah, is so important, the Bible mentions it in six other instances in the Bible:

(1) Isaiah 40:3: "A voice of one calling: 'In the wilderness prepare the way for the Lord; make straight in the desert a highway for our God."

(2) Malachi 3:1: "'I will send my messenger, who will prepare the way

before me. Then suddenly the Lord you are seeking will come to his temple; the messenger of the covenant, whom you desire, will come,' says the Lord Almighty."

(3) Matthew 3:3: "This is he (the Baptist) who was spoken of through the prophet Isaiah: 'A voice of one calling in the wilderness, 'Prepare the way for the Lord, make straight paths for him.'"

(4) Mark 1:1-3: "The beginning of the good news about Jesus the Messiah, the Son of God, as it is written in Isaiah the prophet: 'I will send my messenger ahead of you, who will prepare your way;' 'a voice of one calling in the wilderness, 'Prepare the way for the Lord, make straight paths for him.'"

(5) Luke 3:3-4: "He (the Baptist) went into all the country around the Jordan, preaching a baptism of repentance for the forgiveness of sins. As it is written in the book of the words of Isaiah the prophet: 'A voice of one calling in the wilderness, 'Prepare the way for the Lord, make straight paths for him.'"

(6) Luke 7:27: "This is the one (the Baptist) about whom it is written: 'I will send my messenger ahead of you, who will prepare your way before you.'"

From the above verses we must conclude one of two options:

(1) John didn't know he was the reincarnation of Elijah.

(2) John knew he was the reincarnation of Elijah; but was being clever with the Pharisees.

Let's examine each option:

(1) John didn't know he was the reincarnation of Elijah. After all, John said he wasn't Elijah. But Jesus knew better. "He is the Elijah who was to come." (Matthew 11:14)

So Jesus revealed John to be Elijah; but John denied it. Which of the two people are right - Jesus or John? The answer should be very clear. John's denial of his own past identity as Elijah does not mean he did not have a past life as Elijah. This is especially true when Jesus claimed John was indeed Elijah. Although John carried the living spirit of Elijah, he did not carry Elijah's conscious mind and memory. Reincarnation involves only the higher consciousness of the spirit and not the conscious mind. With very few exceptions, nobody has a conscious memory of past lives. However, John did identify himself with an Old Testament prophecy about Elijah as being "the voice in the wilderness" (John 1:23): And if John did not have the conscious mind and past-life memories of Elijah, this would explain why John denied being Elijah.

(2) John knew he was the reincarnation of Elijah; but was being clever with the Pharisees.

This appears to be the only option because John did identify himself as being "the voice" (John 1:23) who is "preparing the way" in Isaiah 40:3 and Malachi 3:1. Although John may not have had the conscious memory of Elijah, his cleverness shows he carried the personality trait of Elijah. Personality traits do carry over from reincarnation. Elijah was certainly clever when he challenged the priests of Baal to a show of power by preparing two altars of sacrifice: one for them, and one for him. When the priests of Baal's sacrifice did not burn, Elijah told them to pray louder and made fun of them saying their "god" must be sleeping (1 Kings 18:27). Then Elijah had water poured over his sacrifice before he called upon God to send fire down from heaven to consume it (1 Kings 18:33–35).

So the anti-reincarnationalist argument of the Baptist's denial as evidence of him not being Elijah, doesn't necessarily mean he wasn't Elijah. It may simply been not aware of it. But the evidence shows he was aware of it.

E. The Similar Lives and Personalities of John and Elijah

When we compare the lives and personalities of Elijah and John the Baptist we find striking similarities. These similarities cannot be dismissed as mere coincidences. Believers in the concept of reincarnation know personality traits can be passed on from one life to the next, even though conscious memories are not passed along.

The following is a list of their similarities:

(1) Elijah and John where great prophets:

Elijah: "Then Elijah said to them, 'I am the only one of the Lord's prophets left, but Baal has four hundred and fifty prophets.'" (1 Kings 18:22)
John: "What did you go out to see? A prophet? Yes, I tell you, and more than a prophet." (Matthew 11:9)

(2) Elijah and John "turned the hearts of the parents to their children":

Elijah: "He will turn the hearts of the parents to their children, and the hearts of the children to their parents" (Malachi 4:6)
John: "And he will go on before the Lord, in the spirit and power of Elijah, to turn the hearts of the parents to their children and the disobedient to the wisdom of the righteous - to make ready a people prepared for the Lord." (Luke 1:17)

(3) Elijah and John had good relations with the Ruler of Israel:

Elijah: "Meanwhile a prophet came to Ahab king of Israel and announced, 'This is what the Lord says: 'Do you see this vast army? I will give it into your hand today, and then you will know that I am the Lord.'" (1 Kings 20:13)
John: "Herod feared John and protected him, knowing him to be a righteous and holy man. When Herod heard John, he was greatly puzzled; yet he liked to listen to him." (Mark 6:20)

(4) Elijah and John lived in the wilderness and had a bizarre diet:

Elijah: "The ravens brought him bread and meat in the morning and bread and meat in the evening, and he drank from the brook." (1 Kings 17:6)
John: "His food was locusts and wild honey." (Matthew 3:4)

(5) Elijah and John abstained from wine:

Elijah: "If a man or woman wants to make a special vow, a vow of dedication to the Lord as a Nazirite, they must abstain from wine and other fermented drink." (Numbers 6:2-3)

John: "He is never to take wine or other fermented drink, and he will be filled with the Holy Spirit even before he is born." (Luke 1:15)

(6) Elijah and John wore a garment of hair and a leather belt around his waist:

Elijah: "He had a garment of hair and had a leather belt around his waist." (2 Kings 1:8)

John: "John's clothes were made of camel's hair, and he had a leather belt around his waist." (Matthew 3:4)

(7) Elijah and John led multitudes of people to repentance:

Elijah: "Then Elijah said to all the people, 'Come here to me.' They came to him, and he repaired the altar of the Lord, which had been torn down." (1 Kings 18:30)

John: "People went out to him from Jerusalem and all Judea and the whole region of the Jordan." (Matthew 3:5)

(8) Elijah and John admonished Israel for demoralizing their religion:

Elijah: "Elijah went before the people and said, 'How long will you waver between two opinions? If the Lord is God, follow him; but if Baal is God, follow him.'" (1 Kings 18:21)

John: "John said to the crowds coming out to be baptized by him, 'You brood of vipers! Who warned you to flee from the coming wrath? Produce fruit in keeping with repentance. And do not begin to say to yourselves, 'We have Abraham as our father.' For I tell you that out of these stones God can raise up children for Abraham.'" (Luke 3:7-8)

(9) Elijah and John admonished the King of Israel:

Elijah: "So Obadiah went to meet Ahab and told him, and Ahab went to meet Elijah. When he saw Elijah, he said to him, 'Is that you, you troubler of Israel?' 'I have not made trouble for Israel,' Elijah replied. 'But you and your father's family have. You have abandoned the Lord's commands and have followed the Baals." (1 Kings 18:16-18)

John: "Now Herod had arrested John and bound him and put him in prison because of Herodias, his brother Philip's wife, for John had been saying to him: 'It is not lawful for you to have her.'" (Matthew 14:3-4)

(10) Elijah and John baptized a sacrifice to God with water:

Elijah: "Then he said to them, 'Fill four large jars with water and pour it on the offering and on the wood... Then the fire of the Lord fell and burned up the sacrifice, the wood, the stones and the soil, and also licked up the water in the trench. When all the people saw this, they fell prostrate and cried, 'The Lord - he is God! The Lord - he is God!'" (1 Kings 18:33;38-39)

John: (Paraphrased) After John baptized Jesus, the Lamb of God, heaven was opened and the Holy Spirit of fire descended upon Jesus in bodily form like a dove. And a voice came from heaven: "You are my Son, whom I love; with you I am well pleased." (Luke 3:21-22)

(11) Elijah and John were victims of the Ruler of Israel's evil wife:

Elijah: "So Jezebel sent a messenger to Elijah to say, 'May the gods deal with me, be it ever so severely, if by this time tomorrow I do not make your life like that of one of them.'" (1 Kings 19:2)

John: "On Herod's birthday the daughter of Herodias danced for the guests and pleased Herod so much that he promised with an oath to give her whatever she asked. Prompted by her mother, she said, 'Give me here on a platter the head of John the Baptist.'" (Matthew 14:6-8)

(12) Elijah and John were associated with Mount Carmel:

Elijah: Elijah established a school of prophets known as "the sons of the prophets" at Mount Carmel.

John: Josephus wrote that the Essenes were believers in baptism and reincarnation. The Essene community was located at Mount Carmel; and there is strong evidence that John the Baptist was an

Essene. (See "Reincarnation for the Christian" pp. 88-91)

(13) Elijah killed with the sword and John was killed with the sword:

Elijah: "Then Elijah commanded them, 'Seize the prophets of Baal. Don't let anyone get away!' They seized them, and Elijah had them brought down to the Kishon Valley and slaughtered there." (1 Kings 18:40) "Now Ahab told Jezebel everything Elijah had done and how he had killed all the prophets with the sword." (1 Kings 19:1)

John: "The king was distressed, but because of his oaths and his dinner guests, he ordered that her request be granted and had John beheaded in the prison." (Matthew 14:9-10)

F. John Had To Pay For Elijah's Bad Karma

Because Elijah killed the prophets of Baal with a sword; and John the Baptist himself was killed with a sword, this presents a major connection between the two men involving "karma". Although karma is often viewed as an Asian concept, it is practically a universal concept found throughout the world and throughout the Bible. In fact, Jesus himself taught it in the Gospel of Matthew:
Matthew 26:52: "Jesus said to him, 'for all who draw the sword will die by the sword.'"
Karma is divine justice; and karma is reincarnation. Karma means if those who "draw the sword" do not die by the sword in their lifetime, they must die by the sword in a future lifetime. In the case of Elijah, he killed the priests of Baal with the sword because their sacrifice failed to catch fire whereas his sacrifice did. Having all the priests of Baal beheaded was an incredible injustice on Elijah's part. And because John the Baptist was the reincarnation of Elijah, John had to "pay" Elijah's "karmic debt" for unjustly murdering the priests of Baal. John paid Elijah's debt by having his own head cut off. Jesus himself mentioned this karmic debt John paid as Elijah in the Gospel of Mark:
Mark 9:13: "But I tell you, Elijah has come, and they have done to him everything they wished, just as it is written about him."
What was written about Elijah is that he had Jezebel's prophets of Baal killed by the sword (1 Kings 18:40). In referring to John the

Baptist as Elijah - and everything they (Herod and his wife) had done to John (killed by the sword) "just as it is written about him (Elijah)" - Jesus associated John's death with what was written about Elijah concerning the killing of the prophets of Baal.

G. Elijah and Moses Appear at the First and Second Coming of Christ

The arrival of Elijah at the advent of the Messiah is a great fulfillment of Bible prophecy. So is the arrival of both Elijah and Moses. After John the Baptist was beheaded, when Jesus transfigured into a "Being of Light" at the Mount of Transfiguration (Matthew 17:1-13), he met with the spirits of Elijah and Moses. Afterward, Jesus identified John the Baptist to be the reincarnation of Elijah to his disciples. The description of Jesus' face "shining like the sun" and "his clothes becoming as white as the light" is remarkably similar to descriptions of Jesus in many NDE testimonies. The transfiguration of Jesus is just one of many events in the Bible corresponding with NDEs. Notice also how the appearance of Elijah and Moses in spirit with Jesus refutes the concept of people "resting in peace" until the Final Judgment.

The Bible also describes another reincarnation of Elijah occurring at the time of Jesus' Second Coming. Not only does Elijah reincarnate again, but Moses is reincarnated at Jesus' Second Coming as well. In the same way that John and Elijah appeared together on the Mount of Transfiguration, so they will appear together again at Jesus' return. Here is the biblical evidence:

Revelation 11:3-6: "And I will appoint my two witnesses, and they will prophesy for 1,260 days, clothed in sackcloth. They are 'the two olive trees' and the two lampstands, and 'they stand before the Lord of the Earth.' If anyone tries to harm them, fire comes from their mouths and devours their enemies. This is how anyone who wants to harm them must die. They have power to shut up the heavens so that it will not rain during the time they are prophesying; and they have power to turn the waters into blood and to strike the Earth with every kind of plague as often as they want."

While this passage in Revelation does not specifically identify the "two witnesses" as Elijah and Moses, the miraculous powers they perform suggest it is them. Just like one of the witnesses in this

29

Revelation passage, Elijah had the power to prevent rain from occurring for three and a half years (or 1,260 days)::

1 Kings 17:1: "Now Elijah the Tishbite, from Tishbe in Gilead, said to Ahab, 'As the Lord, the God of Israel, lives, whom I serve, there will be neither dew nor rain in the next few years except at my word.'"

James 5:17: "He (Elijah) prayed earnestly that it would not rain, and it did not rain on the land for three and a half years."

And just like the other witness in the Revelation passage, Moses had the power to turn water into blood and to bring plagues:

Exodus 7:17; 9:13-14: "This is what the Lord says: By this you will know that I am the Lord: With the staff that is in my hand I will strike the water of the Nile, and it will be changed into blood'...'This is what the Lord, the God of the Hebrews, says: Let my people go, so that they may worship me, or this time I will send the full force of my plagues against you and against your officials and your people."

The Bible prophecy in Revelation 11:3-6 describes two prophets who have the identical powers as Elijah and Moses. Is this a mere coincidence? You be the judge. And if Elijah and Moses are to reappear at Jesus' Second Coming, then the only realistic way for them to do so is through reincarnation. In the Book of Deuteronomy, Moses gives a prophecy about God reincarnating a prophet like him which can be interpreted to refer to Revelation 11:3-6:

Deuteronomy 18:15: "The Lord your God will raise up for you a prophet like me from among you, from your fellow Israelites. You must listen to him."

Because Elijah and Moses appeared at the First Coming of Christ, it no stretch of the imagination to believe Elijah and Moses will appear again at the Second Coming of Christ as well. The Malachi prophecy of Elijah's return may be references to reincarnations of Elijah at both the First and Second Coming of Christ:

Malachi 4:5: "Behold, I will send you Elijah the prophet, before the coming of the great and dreadful day of the Lord."

Because there are two advents of Jesus into the world, it is logical to assume there will be two advents of Elijah as well.

H. The Disciples Didn't Know What Spirit They Had

The next Bible verse describes the disciples asking Jesus if they should call down fire upon an unbelieving city as Elijah did. Jesus rebuked them by telling them they didn't know what spirit they had to accomplish the miracle. This is an important statement uttered from the lips of Christ concerning an aspect of reincarnation previously mentioned. People do not have a conscious awareness of the spirit they possess from a past life:

Luke 9:51-56: "Now it came to pass, when the time had come for him (Jesus) to be received up, that he steadfastly set his face to go to Jerusalem, and sent messengers before his face. And as they went, they entered a village of the Samaritans, to prepare for him. But they did not receive him, because his face was set for the journey to Jerusalem. And when his disciples James and John saw this, they said, 'Lord, do you want us to command fire to come down from heaven and consume them, just as Elijah did?'

"But he turned and rebuked them, and said, 'You do not know what manner of spirit you are of. For the Son of Man did not come to destroy men's lives but to save them.' And they went to another village."

The disciples wanted to call down fire upon the unbelievers just as Elijah did. Jesus rebuked them by telling them they didn't know "what manner of spirit" they had to accomplish this. The spirit of Elijah could call down fire from heaven; but this does not mean the disciples could. Also, in the original text, the phrase "manner of" was not part of the above original translation of the Bible verse or in the Vulgate version. The phrase "manner of" was added at the time when the Bible was being translated into English. Without the words "manner of" in the verse, it becomes an even clearer reference to reincarnation. The verse shows Jesus telling his disciples they "don't know what spirit they have." In a later translation of the Bible, this mistranslation was corrected:

Luke 9:54-56: "And turning, he rebuked them, saying: 'You know not of what spirit you are. The Son of man came not to destroy souls, but to save.' And they went into another town."

I. Summary

The mystery of the "resurrection of the dead" was a secret teaching passed on as an oral tradition only to those initiated into the

Christian mysteries. The mysteries of bodily resurrection (reincarnation) and spiritual resurrection (spiritual regeneration by the Holy Spirit) were misunderstood and eventually suppressed by the Church when it was seeking orthodoxy within the Roman Empire. Reincarnation allows people to "work their way up" through the afterlife realms immediately after death with the goal of becoming permanent citizens in God's highest heaven. The idea of a massive worldwide reanimation of corpses at the end of time is bizarre, unnatural, repulsive, and against science. Based upon the biblical evidence of John the Baptist as the reincarnation of Elijah alone, it can be easily declared that Jesus taught reincarnation. The prophetic fulfillment of John the Baptist as a reincarnation of Elijah the prophet is the clearest biblical statement of the reality of reincarnation. John had both the spirit and power of Elijah - meaning he was the reincarnation of Elijah. Skeptical objections to Elijah's reincarnation as John have been debunked. John and Elijah shared many similarities suggestive of reincarnation including appearance, diet, personality, relationships, life situations, ministry, locations inhabited throughout in Israel, and karma. If John was not the reincarnation of Elijah as prophecy foretold, then Jesus was not the Messiah as prophecy foretold. Elijah and Moses appeared transfigured with Christ at his First Coming. Elijah and Moses will become reincarnated for Christ's Second Coming. For these reasons and more, reincarnation must now be considered an official doctrine of Christianity as it was widely believed during the first 500 years of Christian history.

CHAPTER 2:
REINCARNATION IN THE BIBLE (PART 2)

1. Reincarnating Prophets and Other People

A. The Bible Mentions Reincarnating Prophets

In both Old and New Testament times, it was common knowledge for God to occasionally reincarnate prophets to warn the people of Israel. Here are a few Bible verses showing this:

Amos 2:11: "'I also raised up prophets from among your children and Nazirites from among your youths. Is this not true, people of Israel?' declares the Lord."

Jeremiah 29:14-15: "'I will be found by you,' declares the Lord, 'and will bring you back from captivity. I will gather you from all the nations and places where I have banished you,' declares the Lord, 'and will bring you back to the place from which I carried you into exile.' You may say, 'The Lord has raised up prophets for us in Babylon.'"

Matthew 16:13-14: "When Jesus came to the region of Caesarea Philippi, he asked his disciples, 'Who do people say the Son of Man is?' They replied, 'Some say John the Baptist; others say Elijah; and still others, Jeremiah or one of the prophets'"

B. The Bible Mentions Other Reincarnating People

Jesus taught how his followers would reincarnate in the future with good karma. The following Bible verse is a promise Jesus made to those who have forsaken everything to follow him:

Mark 10:29-30: "So Jesus answered and said, 'Assuredly, I say to you, there is no one who has left house or brothers or sisters or father or mother or wife or children or lands, for My sake and the gospel's, who shall not receive a hundredfold now in this time - houses and brothers and sisters and mothers and children and lands, with persecutions - and in the age to come, eternal life."

Without reincarnation and preexistence, this promise of Jesus is nonsensical and would be impossible to implement. For example, if people had only one life to live, these words of Jesus would mean those who leave their house and parents for Christ and the gospel's sake would receive a hundredfold houses and parents in heaven. It is self-evident that this promise of Jesus is intended to be fulfilled in future lifetimes on Earth defining eternal life.

The next Bible verse describes people who had an opportunity to return to Earth after death. This could only come about through reincarnation:

Hebrews 11:13-16: "All these people were still living by faith when they died. They did not receive the things promised; they only saw them and welcomed them from a distance, admitting that they were foreigners and strangers on Earth. People who say such things show that they are looking for a country of their own. If they had been thinking of the country they had left, they would have had opportunity to return. Instead, they were longing for a better country - a heavenly one. Therefore God is not ashamed to be called their God, for he has prepared a city for them."

Later in the same chapter it states:

Hebrews 11:35: "Women received back their dead, raised to life again. There were others who were tortured, refusing to be released so that they might gain an even better resurrection."

The above verse in Hebrews describes women receiving their dead - raised to life again. Unless some mediator performed a miracle - and none was mentioned - only through reincarnation can this happen. Otherwise it would take a miracle of bodily resurrection such as occurred at the resurrection of Lazarus (John 11:38-44) by Jesus. But the above verse isn't referring to bodily resurrection because the verse also mentions people refusing to die so they can live longer to do good works so they may obtain more favorable conditions in their next reincarnation - a "better resurrection."

Concerning a different Lazarus in the Bible, in Jesus' Parable of the Rich Man and Lazarus (Luke 16:19-31), there is another excellent reference to reincarnation. Jesus described the afterlife condition of a poor man named Lazarus and a rich man who are both dwelling in "Hades" (as previously mentioned, the Greek for the Hebrew "Sheol") which was the intermediate state after death for both the righteous and the unrighteous. Lazarus was resting in "Abraham's bosom," the righteous part of Sheol; and the rich man was in torment in the unrighteous part of Sheol. Beginning in verse 27, the rich man finally pleads to Abraham:

Luke 16:27-31: "I beg you, father, send Lazarus to my family, for I have five brothers. Let him warn them, so that they will not also come to this place of torment." Abraham replied, "They have Moses and the Prophets; let them listen to them." "No, father Abraham," he said, "but if someone from the dead goes to them, they will repent." He said to him, "If they do not listen to Moses and the Prophets, they will not be convinced even if someone rises from the dead."

Because this parable isn't a "Last Day" reference to the "Resurrection of the Dead" on "Judgment Day", the rich man is asking Abraham to do a remarkable thing: to "resurrect" Lazarus to warn his five brothers about the torment of Sheol. Now unless Jesus is applying his own miracle experience of raising another Lazarus from the dead in this parable, the rich man is asking Abraham to perform a miracle. And the only way for Lazarus to "resurrect" and warn the rich man's brothers, short of a Jesus-type miracle, would be through reincarnation. If the rich man needed to warn his brothers immediately, Lazarus would have to do so through a "walk-in reincarnation" which was covered in Part 1.2d of this article. Notice that it has already been established that "rising from the dead" and "resurrection" in Jesus' day were often references to reincarnation. Notice also that Abraham did not inform the rich man of the impossibility of the "resurrection" of Lazarus in the same way that Abraham informed the rich man of the impossibility of sending Lazarus "to dip the tip of his finger in water" to cool his tongue because of his agony in the fire (Luke 16:24-26).

Here is a Bible verse which describes God bringing up the dead from Sheol, and bringing those in heaven back down to Earth which is a perfect description of reincarnation:

Amos 9:2: "Though they dig into Sheol, from there shall my hand take them; though they climb up to heaven, from there I will bring them down."

The following is a list of more Bible verses referencing reincarnation:

1 Samuel 2:6-8: "The Lord brings death and makes alive; he brings down to the grave and raises up. The Lord sends poverty and wealth; he humbles and he exalts. He raises the poor from the dust and lifts the needy from the ash heap; he seats them with princes and has them inherit a throne of honor."

Job 1:20-21: "Then Job arose, tore his robe, shaved his head, and fell on the ground and worshiped. He said, 'Naked I came from my mother's womb, and naked shall I return there; the Lord gave, and the Lord has taken away; blessed be the name of the Lord.'"

Job 19:25-27: "I know that my redeemer lives, and that in the end he will stand on the Earth. And after my skin has been destroyed, yet in my flesh I will see God; I myself will see him with my own eyes - I, and not another. How my heart yearns within me!"

Job 33:29-30: "God indeed does all these things, twice, three times, with mortals, to bring back their souls from the Pit, so that they may see the light of life."

Psalm 90:2-6: "Before the mountains were brought forth or ever You had formed and given birth to the Earth and the world, even from everlasting to everlasting You are God. You turn man back to dust and corruption, and say, Return, O sons of the Earthborn to the Earth! For a thousand years in Your sight are but as yesterday when it is past, or as a watch in the night. You carry away these disobedient people, doomed to die within forty years as with a flood; they are as a sleep vague and forgotten as soon as they are gone. In the morning they are like grass which grows up - In the morning it flourishes and springs up; in the evening it is mown down and withers."

Psalm 116:7-9: "Return to your rest, my soul, for the Lord has been good to you. For you, Lord, have delivered me from death, my eyes from tears, my feet from stumbling, that I may walk before the Lord in the land of the living."

Lamentations 5:19-22: "You, Lord, reign forever; your throne endures from generation to generation. Why do you always forget us? Why do you forsake us so long? Restore us to yourself, Lord, that we may return; renew our days as of old unless you have utterly rejected us and are angry with us beyond measure."

Psalm 102:21-28: "So the name of the Lord will be declared in Zion and his praise in Jerusalem when the peoples and the kingdoms assemble to worship the Lord. In the course of my life he broke my strength; he cut short my days. So I said: 'Do not take me away, my God, in the midst of my days; your years go on through all generations...They will perish, but you remain; they will all wear out like a garment. Like clothing you will change them and they will be discarded. But you remain the same, and your years will never end. The children of your servants will live in your presence; their descendants will be established before you.'"

Isaiah 35:8-10: "And a highway will be there; it will be called the Way of Holiness; it will be for those who walk on that Way. The unclean will not journey on it; wicked fools will not go about on it. No lion will be there, nor any ravenous beast; they will not be found there. But only the redeemed will walk there, and those the Lord has rescued will return. They will enter Zion with singing; everlasting joy will crown their heads."

The biblical writer of the Book of Isaiah clarifies how the return of the Jews to Zion, through "resurrection," will be through childbirth and therefore reincarnation:

Isaiah 66:3-14: "'They have chosen their own ways, and they delight in their abominations; so I also will choose harsh treatment for them and will bring on them what they dread. For when I called, no one answered, when I spoke, no one listened. They did evil in my sight and chose what displeases me.' Hear the word of the Lord, you who tremble at his word: 'Your own people who hate you, and exclude you because of my name, have said, 'Let the Lord be glorified, that we may see your joy!' Yet they will be put to shame. Hear that uproar from the city, hear that noise from the temple! It is the sound of the Lord repaying his enemies all they deserve. Before she goes into labor, she gives birth; before the pains come upon her, she delivers a son. Who has ever heard of such things? Who has ever seen things like this? Can a country be born in a day or a nation be brought forth in a moment? Yet no sooner is Zion in labor than she gives birth to her children. Do I bring to the moment of birth and not give delivery?' says the Lord. 'Do I close up the womb when I bring to delivery?' says your God. 'Rejoice with Jerusalem and be glad for her, all you who love her; rejoice greatly with her, all you who mourn over her. For you will nurse and be satisfied at her comforting breasts; you will drink deeply and delight in her overflowing abundance.' For this is what the Lord says: 'I will extend peace to her like a river, and the wealth of nations like a flooding stream; you will nurse and be carried on her arm and dandled on her knees. As a mother comforts her child, so will I comfort you; and you will be comforted over Jerusalem.' When you see this, your heart will rejoice and you will flourish like grass; the hand of the Lord will be made known to his servants, but his fury will be shown to his foes."

Here is another verse in Isaiah where people "rising" from the dead is equated with childbirth implying reincarnation:

Isaiah 26:17-19: "As a pregnant woman about to give birth writhes and cries out in her pain, so were we in your presence, Lord. We were with child, we writhed in labor, but we gave birth to wind. We have not brought salvation to the Earth, and the people of the world have not come to life. But your dead will live, Lord; their bodies will rise - let those who dwell in the dust wake up and shout for joy - your dew is like the dew of the morning; the Earth will give birth to her dead."

In the Book of Job, Job wonders if he will live again after death:

Job 14:14: "If someone dies, will they live again? All the days of my hard service I will wait for my renewal to come."

Job answers his own question by saying he will live again when he is renewed. According to the Hebrew dictionary, the word translated "renewal" is "chaliyphah" (pronounced "khal-ee-faw"). In the 12 occurrences of this word in the Bible, 8 times it is used to mean a "change in garments." In 2 occurrences, including Job 14:14, it is used in reference to death which are obvious references to a "change in bodies" or reincarnation.

C. Some of Jesus' Contemporaries Will Be Alive on Earth at His Second Coming

Jesus told the people responsible for his death that they will be alive on Earth and see him when he returns. This can only happen through reincarnation:

Matthew 26:63-64: "The high priest said to him (Jesus), 'I charge you under oath by the living God: Tell us if you are the Messiah, the Son of God.' 'You have said so,' Jesus replied. 'But I say to all of you: From now on you will see the Son of Man sitting at the right hand of the Mighty One and coming on the clouds of heaven.'"

John the Revelator made the same claim which is beyond dispute:

Revelation 1:7: "'Look, he is coming with the clouds,' and 'every eye will see him, even those who pierced him'; and all peoples on Earth 'will mourn because of him.' So shall it be! Amen."

The prophet Zechariah made the same claim which is also beyond dispute:

Zechariah 12:10: "And I will pour out on the house of David and the inhabitants of Jerusalem a spirit of grace and supplication. They will look on me, the one they have pierced, and they will mourn for him as one mourns for an only child, and grieve bitterly for him as one grieves for a firstborn son."

Given the fact that the people who killed Jesus have been dead for thousands of years, the only possible way these prophecies to be fulfilled is for the killers to be reincarnated before Jesus returns.

In the Book of Acts, Peter confronted those who killed Jesus and told them to repent so that Jesus the Messiah can return and the Kingdom of Heaven can be established. By confronting Jesus' killers, Peter affirmed the truthfulness of the previous prophecies just mentioned:

Acts 3:14-15; 3:19-21: "But you rejected the Holy and Righteous One and asked to have a murderer given to you, and you killed the Author of life, whom God raised from the dead. To this we are witnesses... Repent therefore, and turn to God so that your sins may be wiped out, so that times of refreshing may come from the presence of the Lord, and that he may send the Messiah appointed for you, that is, Jesus, who must remain in heaven until the time of universal restoration that God announced long ago through his holy prophets."

There is a lot to be mentioned in the above verse. First of all, we know those who killed Jesus will be forgiven because Jesus requested they be forgiven while on the cross when he said, "Father, forgive them, for they do not know what they are doing" (Luke 23:34). But Peter told those who killed Jesus they must repent and he told them they would receive forgiveness at the "times of refreshing" and the "time of universal restoration" when Jesus returns. But why do they have to wait until then? Because no one can be forgiven until they first realize they are wrong and then repent. And as we have already mentioned, the Bible informs us that Jesus' killers would not realize they were wrong until they see Jesus' Second Coming (Revelation 1:7). Also, the reference to "universal restoration" - or "apokatastasis" in Greek - refers to the thousand year reign of Christ on Earth (Revelation 20:1-6) and the universal salvation of all souls resulting from it. This will be explained later in Part 6 of this article as it deals with the "first resurrection" and reincarnation.

Another verse supporting reincarnation is where Jesus described two different groups of people entering heaven at different times. This contradicts "corpse resurrection" on the "Last Day" which assumes everyone will be judged and enter heaven at the same time:

Matthew 21:31-32: "Jesus said to them, 'Truly I tell you, the tax collectors and the prostitutes are entering the kingdom of God ahead of you (the Pharisees). For John came to you to show you the way of righteousness, and you did not believe him, but the tax collectors and the prostitutes did. And even after you saw this, you did not repent and believe him.'"

The above statement by Jesus is a clear refutation of a final resurrection of corpses resting in peace in graves until "Judgment Day." The so-called "Resurrection of the Dead" assumes everyone will be bodily resurrected and enter heaven on the same day at the same time. But reincarnation assumes a person's judgment day occurs on the last day of their life when their soul leaves their body and enters the afterlife immediately after death. Reincarnation implies that those people who die, and are not yet ready for the Kingdom of God, will be reincarnated until they are ready. People who die, and are ready for the Kingdom, do not need to reincarnate unless they choose to do so. For example, some Christians choose to reincarnate to continue to be perfected and to work in "the Harvest" to advance the Kingdom of God on Earth. And by applying this correct interpretation of "resurrection" to Matthew 21:31-32 above, the only way the tax collectors and prostitutes could enter the Kingdom of God at a different time before the Pharisees, is if the tax collectors and prostitutes had overcome the cycle of reincarnation before the Pharisees. Otherwise, if a final resurrection of corpses on Judgment Day were true, those who would be entering heaven would do so at the same time. Entering heaven at different times would be impossible.

In another instance, John the Revelator described a future event when God's judgment will be "poured out" as "blood to drink" upon the people who killed God's holy people and the biblical prophets. This implies the killers of the biblical prophets will be alive on Earth when God's judgment occurs. This can only occur through reincarnation:

Revelation 16:4-6: "The third angel poured out his bowl on the rivers and springs of water, and they became blood. Then I heard the angel in charge of the waters say: 'You are just in these judgments, O Holy One, you who are and who were; for they have shed the blood of your holy people and your prophets, and you have given them blood to drink as they deserve"

Jesus gave another prophecy about his Second Coming which can be fulfilled only if reincarnation is a fact:

Matthew 24:30-34: "Then will appear the sign of the Son of Man in heaven. And then all the peoples of the Earth will mourn when they see the Son of Man coming on the clouds of heaven... Truly I tell you, this generation will certainly not pass away until all these things have happened."

Jesus told his followers they would be alive on Earth when the signs of the times have been fulfilled and he returns to Earth again. Without reincarnation this prophecy uttered by Jesus would be a false prophecy. In fact, this prophecy was partly responsible for many Christians in the first century to believe the Second Coming would occur in their lifetime. And the historical evidence shows how disappointing it was for the early Christians when they and the apostles were dying off and the hopes for an imminent return of Jesus were dashed.

There are two other verses in the Bible similar to Matthew 24:30-34:

Matthew 16:28 and Luke 9:27: "Truly I tell you, some who are standing here will not taste death before they see the Son of Man coming in his kingdom."

Again, if reincarnation was not a reality, these words uttered by Jesus would be a false prophecy.

In another verse, Jesus told those around him that he would be with them in Spirit "to the very end of the age" while they make disciples of all nations, baptizing and teaching them:

Matthew 28:19-20: "Therefore go and make disciples of all nations, baptizing them in the name of the Father and of the Son and of the Holy Spirit, and teaching them to obey everything I have commanded you. And surely I am with you always, to the very end of the age."

The above statement by Jesus implies the people he was talking to would be alive on Earth until the end of the age, making disciples of all nations, baptizing and teaching them. This can happen only through reincarnation.

The final words of the Bible give a warning which has implications of reincarnation:

Revelation 22:18: "I warn everyone who hears the words of the prophecy of this scroll: If anyone adds anything to them, God will add to that person the plagues described in this scroll."

This warning was written somewhere between 81-96 AD and is directed at anyone who reads the prophecy. And because this warning is over a thousand years old, violators of the warning would have to be reincarnated to experience "the plagues described in the scroll."

D. The Greek Word "Palingenesía" in the Bible is Translated "Reincarnation"

When the ancient Greeks referred to reincarnation, they sometimes used the word "palingenesía." Wuest's "Word Studies from the Greek New Testament" (pp. 89-90) says of palingenesia:

"In the Pythagorean [a school of Greek philosophy] doctrine of the transmigration of souls [reincarnation], their reappearance in new bodies was called their palingenesia. The Stoics used this word to speak of the periodic renovation of the Earth in the springtime when it budded and blossomed again, awaking from its winter sleep, and in a sense, revived from its winter death. The word palingenesia is made up of the Greek words "palin" and "genesis." Palin is a Greek word meaning "back again." Genesis is a noun used in the Bible, in the sense of "origin, race, and birth." It is rendered "birth" in Matthew 1:18: "This is how the birth of Jesus the Messiah came about..." The word palingenesia therefore means to be born again [reincarnated].

According to Strong's Exhaustive Concordance 3824, the word palingenesia (a transliteration of "paliggenesia") is found twice in the Bible; however it is mistranslated "regeneration" or "rebirth". The following are the two verses with the word translated from "palingenesia" in bold font:

(1) Palingenesía Use #1: Matthew 19:27-29: "Then Peter answered and said to Him, 'See, we have left all and followed You. Therefore what shall we have?' So Jesus said to them, 'Assuredly I say to you, that in the REGENERATION, when the Son of Man sits on the throne of His glory, you who have followed Me will also sit on twelve thrones, judging the twelve tribes of Israel. And everyone who has left houses or brothers or sisters or father or mother or wife or children or lands, for My name's sake, shall receive a hundredfold, and inherit eternal life.'"

The word mistranslated as "regeneration" is the Greek word "palingenesía" which refers to reincarnation. In the above verse, Peter asked Jesus what he and the other apostles would receive for following Jesus. Jesus answered Peter's question by saying, in essence, "You won't rule and reign with me in this incarnation; but in a future incarnation, you will. And you'll not only be richly rewarded at that time for what you've had to forego and forsake at this time - but you will also judge the twelve tribes of Israel and inherit eternal life." The idea of the twelve apostles judging the twelve tribes of Israel leads one to wonder if the twelve apostles were the reincarnation of the twelve sons of Jacob who fathered the twelve tribes of Israel.

So the event Jesus is referring to in the above verse is the biblical "first resurrection" - the first reincarnation of souls into the Kingdom of Heaven on Earth at the beginning of the thousand year reign of Christ as described in the Book of Revelation:

Revelation 20:4-6: "I saw thrones on which were seated those who had been given authority to judge. And I saw the souls of those who had been beheaded because of their testimony about Jesus and because of the word of God. They had not worshiped the beast or its image and had not received its mark on their foreheads or their hands. They came to life (on Earth)* and reigned with Christ a thousand years. The rest of the dead did not come to life until the thousand years were ended. This is the first resurrection. Blessed and holy are those who share in the first resurrection. The second death has no power over them, but they will be priests of God and of Christ and will reign with him for a thousand years."

More about the "first resurrection," the "second death," and the thousand year reign of Christ will be described in Part 6 of this article.

(2) Palingenesía Use #2: Titus 3:5: "He saved us, not because of righteous things we had done, but because of his mercy. He saved us through the washing of REBIRTH and renewal by the Holy Spirit."

According to all reincanationalist religions, reincarnation is not a goal to be achieved. Reincarnation is something to be avoided. Reincarnation is something to be overcome through enlightenment and the performing good works and good karma. Overcoming bad karma and overcoming the cycle of death-and-rebirth means obtaining eternal life. This is the true meaning behind the Christian idea of receiving "eternal life." For example, Jesus told the believers of the Church of Philadelphia that once they overcome the world, they will never again have to leave heaven:

Revelation 3:12: "The one who is victorious I will make a pillar in the temple of my God. Never again will they leave it."

The above statement by Jesus is a clear reference affirming the preexistence of the soul and its partner concept of reincarnation. The verse also implies those people who do not overcome the world must leave the heavenly temple and return to Earth until they do overcome the world.

According to Strong's Concordance, the following Greek words in the Bible refer to resurrection: anastasis (a rising again), anistémi (raise up), egeiró (to waken), egersis (a waking up), exanastasis (a rising again), exegeiró (to raise up), and sunegeiró (to raise together). However, many of these words in the Bible can also be references to reincarnation. Then there are Greek words in the Bible used as metaphors for reincarnation such as "changing garments" and "metamorphosis" such as the wordfs: allassó (to change), metaschématizó (to change in fashion or appearance), metathesis (a change), and summorphos (to be conformed to).

E. The Bible Describes Life as a Cycle

The Jewish Kabbalists interpreted the following Bible verse to mean a generation dies and subsequently returns through reincarnation:

Ecclesiastes 1:4-9: "A generation goes, and a generation comes, but the Earth remains forever. The sun rises and the sun goes down, and hurries to the place where it rises. The wind blows to the south, and goes around to the north; round and round goes the wind, and on its circuits the wind returns. All streams run to the sea, but the sea is not full; to the place where the streams flow, there they continue to flow. All things are wearisome; more than one can express; the eye is not satisfied with seeing, or the ear filled with hearing. What has been is what will be, and what has been done is what will be done; There is nothing new under the sun."

In context of the other cycles mentioned: the sun, the wind, the streams, etc., the cycle of generations as the reincarnation of generations, is an obvious interpretation. In a normal cycle of reincarnating souls, the same generation of souls cannot reincarnate until the previous generation of the same souls have passed away. The key to this passage of scripture is verse 9 where it states: "What has been is what will be." Due to the fact that verse 9 applies to the "generation" of people, this can only be a reference to reincarnation.

Also notice in verse 6 the Greek translation of the Hebrew word for wind, "pneuma", is the same for the Hebrew word for spirit.

Ecclesiastes 1:6: "The wind blows to the south, and goes around to the north; round and round goes the wind, and on its circuits the wind returns."

The verse following Ecclesiastes 1:4-9 yields yet another reference to reincarnation:

Ecclesiastes 1:10-11: "Is there a thing of which it is said, 'See, this is new?' It has already been, in the ages before us. The people of long ago are not remembered, nor will there be any remembrance of people yet to come by those who come after them."

In the above verse, the writer of the Book of Ecclesiastes makes an important reference to reincarnation when describing the "veil of memory" which causes people to not remember their previous lifetimes. This shows the entire verse in Ecclesiastes 1:4-11 is using the cycle of reincarnation as the most important cycle of life in God's natural creation.

In yet another verse, the writer of Ecclesiastes again mentions God's cycle of life:

Ecclesiastes 3:15: "What is happening now has happened before, and what will happen in the future has happened before, because God makes the same things happen over and over again."

In the New Testament, James refers to this cycle as the "wheel of birth" which is another clear reference to reincarnation:

James 3:6: "And the tongue is a fire. [The tongue is a] world of wickedness set among our members, contaminating and depraving the whole body and setting on fire the wheel of birth (the cycle of man's nature), being itself ignited by hell (Gehenna)."

This verse in James is one of the clearest references to reincarnation in the entire Bible. And because the author is James, the brother of Jesus, this makes it even more significant. James actually used the phrase translated in Greek "trochos tes geneseos" which had a special meaning in those days. It literally translates to "wheel of birth." By using this phrase, James gave this statement a specific technical reference to reincarnation. The revolution of the wheel symbolizes the cycle of successive lives. The comparison of life to a wheel and the symbol of the wheel itself was, and is, a common symbol in many religions and civilizations referring to reincarnation. According to Flavius Josephus, the second Jewish temple at Jerusalem had the wheel of the Zodiac inlaid in its floor. The wheel of the zodiac is also mentioned in the Bible:

Job 38:32: "Can you lead forth the signs of the zodiac in their season? Or can you guide the stars of the Bear with her young?"

The "wheel" is also related to the mythical wheel of fortune which is another reference to reincarnation. For thousands of years, orthodox Jews have been believers in reincarnation and their scriptures, the Zohar, is a book of great authority among them. It states the following:

Zohar, Mishpatim 32: "All souls come in reincarnation (literally "wheeling") and humans don't know the ways of the Lord and how the Scales stand and how people are judged every day and time. How the souls are judged before entering this world and how they are judged after leaving it."

So the above verse in James referring to the "wheel of birth" is declaring how harsh the consequences can be when words are used inappropriately. While on the cycle of birth and death, peoples' own words can condemn them. It can set their whole life "on fire" causing them to cycle through the fire of hell and having consequences in their next cycle of life as well. Peoples' own words can condemn them to the extent that they can cause people to continually cycle through unpleasant circumstances, not just in one life, but in successive lives. The Hebrew word for reincarnation is "gilgul," a word which comes from a verb meaning "turning in a circle" or "turning a wheel." Many of James' followers would have known this, and therefore would have understood exactly what he was telling them in James 3:6. James warning about words mirrors the teachings of Jesus:

Matthew 12:36-37: "But I tell you that everyone will have to give account on the day of judgment for every empty word they have spoken. For by your words you will be acquitted, and by your words you will be condemned."

F. The Apocrypha Mentions Reincarnating Humans

The books constituting the Bible mean different things to different Christians. The Protestant Bible has fewer books than the Catholic Bible. Therefore, the Jerusalem Bible has a part of the Old Testament which was not included in Protestant versions of the Bible. They are the Book of Tobit, Book of Judith, 1 Maccabees, the Book of Wisdom (also called the "Wisdom of Solomon"), Ecclesiasticus (also called the "Wisdom of Jesus", the "Son of Sirach", or just "Sirach"), and the Book of Baruch. These seven additions are also called Deuterocanonical Books. The Greek Orthodox Church's Bible has, in addition to the Catholic Bible, the following books: 1 Esdras, Psalm 151 (the last Psalm in the Roman Catholic and Protestant Bibles is Psalm 150), the Prayer of Manasseh, and 3 Maccabees. Another book, 4 Maccabees, is added in the Appendix. Slavonic Bibles, approved by the Russian Orthodox Church, have in addition to the Catholic Bible: 1 Esdras and 2 Esdras, Psalm 151, and 3 Maccabees. Eleven other books, together with the Deuterocanonical Books, form the Apocrypha. The full Apocrypha is normally available as a separate publication from the Bible; but it is included in some interfaith versions of the Bible, such as the Expanded Edition of the Revised Standard Version published by Oxford University Press. So the books constituting the Protestant Bible are first and second different from those of the Catholic Church which are in turn different from those of the Greek and Russian Orthodox Churches. Furthermore, for the same book, there may be differences in the text because of the different original sources (manuscripts) used for the translations from ancient into modern languages. With these clarifications in mind, let's proceed to review the evidence of reincarnation from some of these Apocryphal books. Here is a list of them:

Tobit 13:1-2: "Then Tobit said: 'Blessed be God who lives forever, because his kingdom lasts throughout all ages. For he afflicts, and he shows mercy; he leads down to Hades in the lowest regions of the Earth, and he brings up from the great abyss, and there is nothing that can escape his hand."

Sirach 41:8-10: "Woe to you, the ungodly, who have forsaken the law of the Most High God! If you have children, calamity will be theirs; you will beget them only for groaning. When you stumble, there is lasting joy; and when you die, a curse is your lot. Whatever comes from Earth returns to Earth; so the ungodly go from curse to destruction."

2 Maccabees 7:22-23: "I do not know how you came into being in my womb. It was not I who gave you life and breath, nor I who set in order the elements within each of you. Therefore the Creator of the world, who shaped the beginning of humankind and devised the origin of all things, will in his mercy give life and breath back to you again, since you now forget yourselves for the sake of his laws."

2 Maccabees 7:28-29: "I beg you, my child, to look at the heaven and the Earth and see everything that is in them, and recognize that God did not make them out of things that existed. And in the same way the human race came into being. Do not fear this butcher, but prove worthy of your brothers. Accept death, so that in God's mercy I may get you back again along with your brothers."

2 Maccabees 12:39-45: "On the next day, as had now become necessary, Judas and his men went to take up the bodies of the fallen and to bring them back to lie with their kindred in the sepulchres of their ancestors. Then under the tunic of each one of the dead they found sacred tokens of the idols of Jamnia, which the law forbids the Jews to wear. And it became clear to all that this was the reason these men had fallen. So they all blessed the ways of the Lord, the righteous judge, who reveals the things that are hidden; and they turned to supplication, praying that the sin that had been committed might be wholly blotted out. The noble Judas exhorted the people to keep themselves free from sin, for they had seen with their own eyes what had happened as the result of the sin of those who had fallen. He also took up a collection, man by man, to the amount of two

thousand drachmas of silver, and sent it to Jerusalem to provide for a sin offering. In doing this he acted very well and honorably, taking account of the resurrection. For if he were not expecting that those who had fallen would rise again, it would have been superfluous and foolish to pray for the dead. But if he was looking to the splendid reward that is laid up for those who fall asleep in godliness, it was a holy and pious thought. Therefore he made atonement for the dead, so that they might be delivered from their sin."

Wisdom 8:19-20: "As a child I was naturally gifted, and a good soul fell to my lot; or rather, being good, I entered an undefiled body."

The following verse in Wisdom describes life as the ungodly view it - who also don't believe in reincarnation:

Wisdom 1:16-2:22: "But the ungodly by their words and deeds summoned death... For they reasoned unsoundly, saying to themselves, 'Short and sorrowful is our life, and there is no remedy when a life comes to its end, and no one has been known to return from Hades. For we were born by mere chance, and hereafter we shall be as though we had never been, for the breath in our nostrils is smoke, and reason is a spark kindled by the beating of our hearts; when it is extinguished, the body will turn to ashes, and the spirit will dissolve like empty air. Our name will be forgotten in time, and no one will remember our works; our life will pass away like the traces of a cloud, and be scattered like mist that is chased by the rays of the sun and overcome by its heat. For our allotted time is the passing of a shadow, and there is no return from our death, because it is sealed up and no one turns back...' Thus they reasoned, but they were led astray, for their wickedness blinded them, and they did not know the secret purposes of God, nor hoped for the wages of holiness, nor discerned the prize for blameless souls."

G. The Parables of Jesus and Reincarnation

Jesus also gave several parables having a reincarnation interpretation. The first parable to consider is the so-called "Parable of the Weeds (Tares)":

Matthew 13:24-30: "Jesus told them another parable: 'The kingdom of heaven is like a man who sowed good seed in his field. But while everyone was sleeping, his enemy came and sowed weeds among the wheat, and went away. When the wheat sprouted and formed heads, then the weeds also appeared. The owner's servants came to him and said, 'Sir, didn't you sow good seed in your field? Where then did the weeds come from?' 'An enemy did this,' he replied. The servants asked him, 'Do you want us to go and pull them up?' 'No,' he answered, 'because while you are pulling the weeds, you may uproot the wheat with them. Let both grow together until the harvest. At that time I will tell the harvesters: First collect the weeds and tie them in bundles to be burned; then gather the wheat and bring it into my barn.'"

An eschatological interpretation of this parable is provided by Jesus in Matthew:

Matthew 13:36-43: "Then he left the crowd and went into the house. His disciples came to him and said, 'Explain to us the parable of the weeds in the field.' He answered, 'The one who sowed the good seed is the Son of Man. The field is the world, and the good seed stands for the people of the kingdom. The weeds are the people of the evil one, and the enemy who sows them is the devil. The harvest is the end of the age, and the harvesters are angels. As the weeds are pulled up and burned in the fire, so it will be at the end of the age. The Son of Man will send out his angels, and they will weed out of his kingdom everything that causes sin and all who do evil. They will throw them into the blazing furnace, where there will be weeping and gnashing of teeth. Then the righteous will shine like the sun in the kingdom of their Father. Whoever has ears, let them hear."

The literal interpretation of the parable given by Jesus describes how people of God's Kingdom live alongside with other people until the time the Kingdom of Heaven arrives on Earth. This interpretation has a reincarnation reference because it shows the Kingdom of Heaven growing on Earth until the "harvest" occurs at the end times. It's also possible this interpretation needs another interpretation because of the phrase Jesus used, "He who has ears to hear, let him hear" following his interpretation of the parable. This phrase appears after other sayings by Jesus having a hidden meaning. See these search results. According to a metaphorical interpretation of Jesus' parable, "the children of the evil one" and "the children of the kingdom" are something other than human beings. In other Bible verses, the "seed" always represents the application of the "Word of God" and not people (See Luke 8:11, Luke 17:6, Mark 4:30-32, 1

Corinthians 9:11, 1 Peter 1:23, 1 John 3:9). According to the first Church Father Origen (184-253 AD), an ardent defender of preexistence and reincarnation in early Christianity, there is a metaphorical interpretation of the Parable of the Weeds which is more suggestive of reincarnation:

Origen: "Good things in the human soul are the offspring of the kingdom of God and have been sown by God the Word so that wholesome words about anything are children of the kingdom. But while men are asleep who do not act according to the command of Jesus, 'Watch and pray that you enter not into temptation,' (Matthew 26:41) the devil sows tares - that is, evil opinions - over and among natural conceptions. And according to this the whole world might be called a field, for in the whole world the Son of man sowed the good seed, but the wicked one tares - that is, evil words. And at the end of things there will be a harvest, in order that the angels may gather up the bad opinions that have grown upon the soul, and may give them over to fire. Then those who become conscious that they have received the seeds of the evil one in themselves shall wail and be angry against themselves; for this is the gnashing of teeth. (Acts 7:54) Then above all shall the righteous shine, no longer differently as at the first, but all 'as one sun in the kingdom of their Father.' (Matthew 13:43) Daniel, knowing that the multitudes of the righteous differ in glory, said this, 'And the intelligent shall shine as the brightness of the firmament, and from among the multitudes of the righteous as the stars for ever and ever.' (Daniel 12:3) And in the passage, 'There is one glory of the sun, and another glory of the moon, and another glory of the stars: for one star differs from another star in glory: so also is the resurrection of the dead,' (1 Corinthians 15:41-42) the apostle says the same thing. I think, then, that at the beginning of the blessedness enjoyed by those who are being saved the difference connected with the light takes place. Perhaps the saying, 'Let your light shine before men,' (Matthew 5:16) can be written upon the table of the heart in a threefold way; so that even now the light of the disciples of Jesus shines before the rest of men, and after death before the resurrection, and after the resurrection until 'all shall attain unto a full-grown man,' (Ephesians 4:13) and all become one sun." (Origen, Commentary on Matthew, Book X, Newadvent.org)

This interpretation by Origen becomes even more apparent when you consider a similar parable by Jesus - the "Parable of the Sower."

This parable is important because it appears in all three Synoptic Gospels in Matthew 13:1-23, Mark 4:1-20, and Luke 8:1-15. The following is the Parable of the Sower in the Gospel of Mark:

Mark 4:1-9: "Again Jesus began to teach by the lake. The crowd that gathered around him was so large that he got into a boat and sat in it out on the lake, while all the people were along the shore at the water's edge. He taught them many things by parables, and in his teaching said: 'Listen! A farmer went out to sow his seed. As he was scattering the seed, some fell along the path, and the birds came and ate it up. Some fell on rocky places, where it did not have much soil. It sprang up quickly, because the soil was shallow. But when the sun came up, the plants were scorched, and they withered because they had no root. Other seed fell among thorns, which grew up and choked the plants, so that they did not bear grain. Still other seed fell on good soil. It came up, grew and produced a crop, some multiplying thirty, some sixty, some a hundred times.' Then Jesus said, 'Whoever has ears to hear, let them hear.'"

Once again, Jesus gave an eschatological interpretation of the above parable in the Gospel of Mark:

Mark 4:10-20: "When he was alone, the Twelve and the others around him asked him about the parables. He told them, 'The secret of the kingdom of God has been given to you. But to those on the outside everything is said in parables so that: 'They may be ever seeing but never perceiving, and ever hearing but never understanding; otherwise they might turn and be forgiven!' Then Jesus said to them, 'Don't you understand this parable? How then will you understand any parable? The farmer sows the word. Some people are like seed along the path, where the word is sown. As soon as they hear it, Satan comes and takes away the word that was sown in them. Others, like seed sown on rocky places, hear the word and at once receive it with joy. But since they have no root, they last only a short time. When trouble or persecution comes because of the word, they quickly fall away. Still others, like seed sown among thorns, hear the word; but the worries of this life, the deceitfulness of wealth and the desires for other things come in and choke the word, making it unfruitful. Others, like seed sown on good soil, hear the word, accept it, and produce a crop - some thirty, some sixty, some a hundred times what was sown.'"

So in Jesus' Parable of the Sower, the soil represents a person's "heart" in which the "seed" of the Word of God is planted. Jesus described how a person on the right path whose "heart" is not overcome by persecution, nor consumed with the worries of this life, when the Word of God is heard and heeded, can produce many "harvests" of good works for the Kingdom of Heaven. And because the "harvest" represents the end times, we can assume the person who has the Word of God planted in "good soil" will continue to produce good works no matter how many times they reincarnate (produce a crop) until the end time "harvest" when the Kingdom of Heaven appears on Earth.

H. Summary

The mystery of the "resurrection of the dead" was a secret teaching passed on as an oral tradition; but was misunderstood and suppressed by the Church. But based upon the Biblical evidence of John the Baptist as the reincarnation of Elijah alone, it is evident both the Bible and Jesus taught reincarnation. The Bible also mentions the reincarnation of other prophets and biblical personalities including the future reincarnation of Jesus' followers and enemies at his Second Coming. The Bible uses the Greek word "palingenesía" which translated means reincarnation. The Bible describes life as a cycle and how God brings everything to life again. Some of the parables of Jesus make sense if reincarnation is true. Some books of the Jewish and Christian Apocrypha mention reincarnation. Therefore, reincarnation must now become a doctrine of Christianity as it was widely believed during the first 500 years of Christian history.

2. Jesus Said, "You Must Be Born Again"

A. Why Humans Need To Be Spiritually Reborn

To understand the nature of bodily and spiritual rebirth, it is necessary to briefly mention how the fallen spiritual condition of humanity originated. A literal interpretation of the Bible, from the Garden of Eden in the Book of Genesis to the Book of Revelation, tells a bizarre tale of how sin entered the world roughly 6,000 years ago when the world and humanity was created and how humans fell away from God. In summary:

Genesis describes how a talking snake tricked a woman, who was created from a man's rib, into eating some mysterious fruit. This event unleashed the horrible satanic legions of apocalyptic abomination of desecration and damnation from the dark abyss and into the hearts of all humanity bringing unspeakable sin, evil, death, oblivion, holocaust, and Armageddon.

However, if we give this bizarre story a metaphorical interpretation, as one would do with a parable or dream interpretation; then we can view the Bible to be an archetypal account of humanity's fall from the spiritual universe to its ultimate restoration. The "Garden of Eden" represents our heavenly origin. The "apple" represents our free will. Our "banishment from Eden" represents how souls left the divine origins of heaven to explore their free will and the physical cosmos. Not coincidentally, a large group of early Christian Gnostics believed this was the real story behind Genesis. Accordingly, the "fall of souls" from heaven to Earth, and their entrapment into flesh, resulted in humanity's "spiritual death" as recorded in Genesis:

Genesis 3:1-5: "He (Satan) said to the woman, 'Did God really say, 'You must not eat from any tree in the garden'?' The woman said to the serpent, 'We may eat fruit from the trees in the garden, but God did say, 'You must not eat fruit from the tree that is in the middle of the garden, and you must not touch it, or you will die.' 'You will not certainly die,' the serpent said to the woman. For God knows that when you eat from it your eyes will be opened, and you will be like God, knowing good and evil.'"

The metaphorical interpretation of the Fall describes how free will, which led to the fall of souls from heaven to Earth, resulted in humanity's spiritual "death". According to the doctrine of original sin, everyone is born spiritually dead with a sinful nature, being separated from God (Romans 5:12-21). For a person to be restored to heaven and attain eternal life, the condition of spiritual death must be reversed which requires the person's spirit to be "made alive" or "reborn" by the Holy Spirit. According to reincarnation principles, a person is born with the karma of their previous lives still intact; but do not maintain a memory of them.

Also in Genesis, appears the first prophecy concerning the coming of a Savior Messiah. After humanity's fall from Paradise, God judged

Satan by declaring how a woman would give birth to a son who would "strike" Satan, although Satan will "strike" her son's "heel":

Genesis 3:15: "And I will put enmity between you (Satan) and the woman, and between your offspring (Satan's) and hers (the Messiah); he (the Messiah) will strike your (Satan's) head, and you (Satan) will strike his (the Messiah's) heel."

The "offspring" of Satan are revealed in the Gospel of John as the ones who killed Jesus:

John 8:44: "You (those trying to kill Jesus) belong to your father, the devil, and you want to carry out your father's desires. He was a murderer from the beginning, not holding to the truth, for there is no truth in him. When he lies, he speaks his native language, for he is a liar and the father of lies."

So until a person is "spiritually reborn" by the Holy Spirit, they remain "spiritually dead" and have not attained eternal life.

B. The Man From Above Explains How To Be Born From Above

The Gospel of John describes a Pharisee named Nicodemus, a secret follower of Jesus, who had a revealing discussion with Jesus concerning the Kingdom of God and how to enter into it. Nicodemus began his discussion with Jesus by addressing the miracles Jesus performed and how these miracles demonstrated Jesus' preexistence:

John 3:1-2: "Now there was a Pharisee, a man named Nicodemus who was a member of the Jewish ruling council. He came to Jesus at night and said, 'Rabbi, we know that you are a teacher who has come from God. For no one could perform the signs you are doing if God were not with him.'"

This first statement by Nicodemus is very important and often overlooked. Nicodemus affirmed Jesus must have "come from God" (preexisted before birth) because of the "signs" he displayed. Jesus' response to Nicodemus is equally important and relevant:

John 3:3: "Jesus replied, 'Very truly I tell you, no one can see the kingdom of God unless they are born again.'"

The Greek word for "again" (anothen), as in "born again," also means "from above," as in "born from above" which is why so many other translations of the Bible say "born from above." So Nicodemus acknowledged that Jesus had "come from above" (paraphrased) to which Jesus replied, "Unless you are born from above, you cannot see the kingdom of God." This initial exchange between the two men is often overlooked; but is the key to understanding the rest of the discussion between them. By Jesus telling Nicodemus how no one can see the kingdom of God unless they are "born again" (from above) Jesus is referring to spiritual "rebirth" or regeneration by the Holy Spirit as a requirement to entering the Kingdom. As a Pharisee, Nicodemus was well aware of the meaning of physical "rebirth" - the rebirth of the spirit into a fetus - but Nicodemus obviously didn't understand this new version of spiritual rebirth - the regeneration of the spirit in an adult through the Holy Spirit. This confusion becomes apparent with Nicodemus' next statement:

John 3:4: "'How can someone be born when they are old?' Nicodemus asked. 'Surely they cannot enter a second time into their mother's womb to be born!'"

Jesus answered Nicodemus by explaining the difference between rebirth of the spirit into flesh ("born of water", childbirth, reincarnation) and rebirth through the Holy Spirit ("born of the Spirit", spiritual regeneration, spiritual "resurrection"):

John 3:5-7: "Jesus answered, 'Very truly I tell you, no one can enter the kingdom of God unless they are born of water and the Spirit. Flesh gives birth to flesh, but the Spirit gives birth to spirit. You should not be surprised at my saying, 'You must be born again.'"

Paul also mentioned these two types of rebirth - of the flesh and of the Spirit - when referring to Ishmael (Abraham's first son, born of the flesh) and Isaac (Abraham's second son, born by the Spirit):

Galatians 4:28-29: "Now you, brothers and sisters, like Isaac, are children of promise. At that time the son born according to the flesh persecuted the son born by the power of the Spirit. It is the same now."

So Jesus explained to Nicodemus that the way to enter the Kingdom of God; the way to overcome spiritual death, the way to attain eternal life, is through spiritual rebirth through the Holy Spirit. Unless a person is spiritually "reborn" by the Holy Spirit, they cannot attain eternal life and must be physically reborn (reincarnated).

In other instances in the gospels, Jesus taught this "bodily rebirth" until "spiritual rebirth" salvation principle:

Matthew 18:1-5: "At that time the disciples came to Jesus and asked, 'Who, then, is the greatest in the kingdom of heaven?' He called a little child to him, and placed the child among them. And he said: 'Truly I tell you, unless you change and become like little children, you will never enter the kingdom of heaven. Therefore, whoever takes the lowly position of this child is the greatest in the kingdom of heaven. And whoever welcomes one such child in my name welcomes me.'"

Jesus recognized children's souls are preexistent and therefore closer to "the Source" than adults. And although conscious memories do not transfer from lifetime to lifetime, spiritual growth does. This explains Jesus' implication of the innocence and wisdom of children. The following Bible passage is a reference by Jesus to "resurrection" as a process where the dead become "like the angels" - as immortal spirits - who become "children of the resurrection" or children of reincarnation:

Luke 20:27-40 and Mark 12:18-27: "Some of the Sadducees, who say there is no resurrection, came to Jesus with a question. 'Teacher,' they said, 'Moses wrote for us that if a man's brother dies and leaves a wife but no children, the man must marry the widow and raise up offspring for his brother. Now there were seven brothers. The first one married a woman and died childless. The second and then the third married her, and in the same way the seven died, leaving no children. Finally, the woman died too. Now then, at the resurrection whose wife will she be, since the seven were married to her?' Jesus replied, 'The people of this age marry and are given in marriage. But those who are considered worthy of taking part in the age to come and in the resurrection from the dead will neither marry nor be given in marriage, and they can no longer die; for they are like the angels. They are God's children, since they are children of the resurrection. But in the account of the burning bush, even Moses showed that the dead rise, for he calls the Lord 'the God of Abraham, and the God of Isaac, and the God of Jacob.' He is not the God of the dead, but of the living, for to him all are alive.' Some of the teachers of the law responded, 'Well said, teacher!' And no one dared to ask him any more questions."

In the Mark 12:18-27 version of the above incident, the phrase "rise again" is used twice. According to Strong's Concordance, the phrase "rise again" is translated "egeirontai" which means repeated embodiments which also negates a one-time resurrection. It's also important to note that of all the verses in the New Testament containing the word "resurrection," all but two of them contain the Greek word "egeiro" - "rising again" - (1) Matthew 27:53 referencing Jesus' resurrection, and (2) Philippians 3:11 referencing a final "resurrection from the dead." And this is why Jesus says God is the God of Abraham, Isaac and Jacob. Their souls were not "resting in peace" until "Judgment Day," but they continued to live, continued to rise into new bodies. Moreover, in all the verses in the New Testament where the word "resurrection" is a translation of the Greek word "anastasis" - according to Strong's Concordance - the word can mean either a one-time "resurrection" or repeated embodiments of "rising again." And there are multiple Bible verses contradicting a superficial understanding of Hebrews 9:27 which teach the preexistence of souls from the dawn of creation; thereby making it clear that Jesus accepted and taught reincarnation. Also, in the above Bible passage, Jesus taught the Sadducees how "resurrection" involves living souls becoming "like angels" and then as children - the child of Abraham, the child of Isaac, the child of Jacob, etc. By replying in this manner, Jesus affirmed "bodily rebirth until spiritual rebirth salvation."

The following is a list of more instances of Jesus teaching about children of reincarnation:

Matthew 19:14, Mark 10:14, and Luke 18:16: "Jesus said, 'Let the little children come to me, and do not hinder them, for the Kingdom of Heaven belongs to such as these.'"

Luke 9:48 and Mark 9:37: "Whoever welcomes this little child in my name welcomes me; and whoever welcomes me welcomes the one who sent me. For it is the one who is least among you all who is the greatest."

Luke 18:17 and Mark 10:15: "Truly I tell you, anyone who will not receive the Kingdom of God like a little child will never enter it."

John 12:36: "Believe in the light while you have the light, so that you may become children of light."

Luke 10:21: "At that time Jesus, full of joy through the Holy Spirit, said, 'I praise you, Father, Lord of heaven and Earth, because you have hidden these things from the wise and learned, and revealed them to little children. Yes, Father, for this is what you were pleased to do.'"

C. Reincarnation as a Metaphor For Spiritual Rebirth by the Holy

Spirit

Other biblical writers used physical rebirth (reincarnation) as a metaphor for the transformation from spiritual death to spiritual rebirth by the Holy Spirit:

James 1:18: "He chose to give us birth through the word of truth, that we might be a kind of first fruits of all he created."

1 Peter 1:3: "Praise be to the God and Father of our Lord Jesus Christ! In his great mercy he has given us new birth into a living hope through the resurrection of Jesus Christ from the dead ..."

1 John 2:29: "If you know that he is righteous, you know that everyone who does what is right has been born of him."

1 John 3:9-10: "No one who is born of God will continue to sin, because God's seed remains in them; they cannot go on sinning, because they have been born of God. This is how we know who the children of God are and who the children of the devil are: Anyone who does not do what is right is not God's child, nor is anyone who does not love their brother and sister."

1 John 4:7-8: "Dear friends, let us love one another, for love comes from God. Everyone who loves has been born of God and knows God. Whoever does not love does not know God, because God is love."

John 1:11-13: "He came to that which was his own, but his own did not receive him. Yet to all who did receive him, to those who believed in his name, he gave the right to become children of God - children born not of natural descent, nor of human decision or a husband's will, but born of God."

1 John 5:3-4: "In fact, this is love for God: to keep his commands. And his commands are not burdensome, for everyone born of God overcomes the world."

1 John 5:18: "We know that anyone born of God does not continue to sin; the One who was born of God keeps them safe, and the evil one cannot harm them."

D. Christ's Resurrection as a Metaphor For Spiritual Rebirth by the Holy Spirit

The Bible contains many references to Christ's resurrection as a metaphor for the transformation from spiritual death to spiritual rebirth by the Holy Spirit. However, these references are literally more of a "walk-in incarnation" of the risen Christ into the "spiritually dead" body of the Christian - a form of reincarnation. Here are some of these references:

Galatians 2:20: "I have been crucified with Christ and I no longer live, but Christ lives in me."

Romans 6:11: "In the same way, count yourselves dead to sin but alive to God in Christ Jesus."

Colossians 2:13: "When you were dead in your sins and in the uncircumcision of your sinful nature, God made you alive with Christ."

Colossians 3:1: "Since, then, you have been raised with Christ, set your hearts on things above, where Christ is, seated at the right hand of God."

Ephesians 2:4-6: "But because of his great love for us, God, who is rich in mercy, made us alive with Christ even when we were dead in transgressions - it is by grace you have been saved. And God raised us up with Christ and seated us with him in the heavenly realms in Christ Jesus."

E. Baptism as a Metaphor For Spiritual Rebirth by the Holy Spirit

The Bible contains several references to baptism as a metaphor for childbirth (and by extension, physical rebirth, reincarnation) and spiritual rebirth. Baptism is a ritual symbolizing a person's transformation from spiritual death to spiritual rebirth and regeneration by the Holy Spirit. The Christian ritual of water baptism is performed as a symbol for birth by: (1) the flesh, and (2) the Spirit (John 3:5). The nakedness of water baptism (the second birth), for which baptism was originally performed without clothes, paralleled the condition of one's original birth. The removal of clothing also represented the image of "putting off the old man with his deeds" as mentioned by Paul. Here are a few verses:

Colossians 3:9-10: "Do not lie to one another, since you have put off the old man with his deeds, and have put on the new man who is renewed in knowledge according to the image of Him who created him."

Ephesians 4:21-24: "If indeed you have heard him and have been taught by him, as the truth is in Jesus: that you put off, concerning your former conduct, the old man which grows corrupt according to the deceitful lusts, and be renewed in the spirit of your mind, and that you put on the new man which was created according to God, in true righteousness and holiness."

Romans 6:3-6: "Or don't you know that all of us who were baptized into Christ Jesus were baptized into his death? We were therefore buried with him through baptism into death in order that, just as Christ was raised from the dead through the glory of the Father, we too may live a new life. For if we have been united together in the likeness of His death, certainly we also shall be in the likeness of His resurrection, knowing this, that our old man was crucified with Him, that the body of sin might be done away with, that we should no longer be slaves of sin."

Galatians 3:26-27: "For you are all sons of God through faith in Christ Jesus. For as many of you as were baptized into Christ have put on Christ."

F. Jesus and Nicodemus on Earthly and Heavenly Things

Another point to make is the phrase "born again" which literally means "reincarnation". There is nothing in the Bible to warrant putting only a metaphorical interpretation on the phrase "you must be born again" although we know Jesus meant it to be understood both metaphorically (born again by the Holy Spirit) and literally (born again into flesh). So traditional Christianity's exclusive metaphorical interpretation of "born again by the Holy Spirit" is unsupportable.

In the next verse in the Gospel of John, Jesus tells Nicodemus he shouldn't be surprised at his words:

John 3:7: "You should not be surprised at my saying, 'You must be born again.'"

In the discussion between Jesus and Nicodemus about the Kingdom of God, and how to enter into it, Jesus described what it's like to be metaphorically "born again" by the Holy Spirit:

John 3:7-12: "'The wind blows wherever it pleases. You hear its sound, but you cannot tell where it comes from or where it is going. So it is with everyone born of the Spirit.' 'How can this be?' Nicodemus asked. 'You are Israel's teacher,' said Jesus, 'and do you not understand these things? Very truly I tell you, we speak of what we know, and we testify to what we have seen, but still you people do not accept our testimony. I have spoken to you of earthly things and you do not believe; how then will you believe if I speak of heavenly things?"

The amazing part of the above statement by Jesus is the revelation that he was speaking of earthly things all along and not of heavenly things. He was speaking of the Kingdom of God on Earth, the rebirth of the flesh, and the rebirth of the spirit. He was speaking of how to attain eternal life, how to end the cycle of death and physical rebirth, and how to enter the Kingdom of God. Jesus spoke of the Kingdom of God in the following verse:

Luke 17:20-21: "Now when he (Jesus) was asked by the Pharisees when the kingdom of God would come, he answered them and said, 'The kingdom of God does not come with observation; nor will they say, 'See here!' or 'See there!' For indeed, the kingdom of God is within you.'"

So Jesus has been talking to Nicodemus about earthly things all along. Finally, at the end of his discussion with Nicodemus, Jesus shared the gospel with him and how Nicodemus can overcome death and enter into the Kingdom of God within:

John 3:13-21: "No one has ever gone into heaven except the one who came from heaven - the Son of Man. Just as Moses lifted up the snake in the wilderness, so the Son of Man must be lifted up, that everyone who believes may have eternal life in him. For God so loved the world that he gave his one and only Son, that whoever believes in him shall not perish but have eternal life. For God did not send his Son into the world to condemn the world, but to save the world through him. Whoever believes in him is not condemned, but whoever does not believe stands condemned already because they have not believed in the name of God's one and only Son. This is the verdict: Light has come into the world, but people loved darkness instead of light because their deeds were evil. Everyone who does evil hates the light, and will not come into the light for fear that their deeds will be exposed. But whoever lives by the truth comes into the light, so that it may be seen plainly that what they have done has been done in the sight of God."

Near-death experience testimonies confirm the fact that some souls are not willing to enter into the light immediately after death. Such souls are allowed to remain in darkness until they are ready and willing to see the light - something which all souls will eventually do according to NDE studies and Christian Universalism as revealed in the Bible. Also notice in the above Bible verse, Jesus mentioned his mission was to "save the world" implying universal salvation and, by implication, reincarnation.

G. Summary

Jesus taught Nicodemus of two rebirths: one of the flesh, and the other of the spirit. To be "born of the flesh" means to be born of water, childbirth, and reincarnation. To be "born of the spirit" means spiritual regeneration by the Holy Spirit. Jesus taught how people must become spiritually reborn by the Holy Spirit or else they cannot attain eternal life - permanent citizenship in God's heaven. Those who are not spiritually reborn and do not attain eternal life must be physically "reborn of the flesh" and continue the cycle of death and rebirth until they are spiritually reborn by the Holy Spirit. There are many biblical references using metaphors describing the transformation from spiritual death to spiritual rebirth by the Holy Spirit including water baptism, reincarnation, and Christ's resurrection. For all these reasons and more, reincarnation must now become a doctrine of Christianity as it was widely believed during the first 500 years of Christian history.

CHAPTER 3:
REINCARNATION IN THE BIBLE (PART 3)

1. God Wants Everyone Saved Implies Reincarnation

A. Universal Salvation in the First 500 Years of Christianity

Universal salvation, or Christian Universalism, is the doctrine of universal reconciliation - the view that all human beings will ultimately be restored to a right relationship with God. It is the belief that God's infinite love and mercy is such that God is not willing for anyone to be lost. Therefore, God has a plan of salvation for everyone - even after death. One major plan involves reincarnation which allows people to "work their way up" through the afterlife realms immediately after death with the goal of becoming permanent citizens once again in the highest heaven - the soul's original home. Universalism is a doctrine supported by numerous Bible verses. According to religious studies scholar, Dr. Ken R. Vincent, the number of Bible verses supporting universal salvation is second in number only to those advocating salvation by "good works." One example is 1 John 2:6 which states, "Whoever claims to live in him must live as Jesus did." Universal salvation does not assume the nonexistence of hell; but assumes hell to be a spiritual condition of purification which doesn't last forever (1 Corinthians 3:10-15). In this sense, hell is more like the Catholic notion of Purgatory. History shows for the first 500 years of Christianity, Christians and Christian theologians believed in the doctrine of universal salvation. Modern archeological findings and Biblical scholarship has confirmed Universalist thought among early Christians. Contemporary Christian scholars, such as the Jesus Seminar, found Universalist theology was most authentic to Jesus. The translation and mistranslation of the Bible from Greek to Latin contributed significantly to the later reinterpretation of the eternal nature of hell. The merging of Church and State under Emperor Constantine (272-337 AD) encouraged the corruption of Universalist teachings as the Church sought more political control over the people through the fear of eternal damnation and salvation only through Church priests. Later in Christian history, when the Church claimed hell was a place for eternal torment and punishment, the so-called Universalist "heretics" countered with their conviction of God being too good, loving and merciful to condemn anyone to eternal torture. With today's world news replete with the horrors resulting from religions which insist on their own "exclusive" path to God, universal salvation is making a comeback - assisted by the proliferation of information concerning spiritual experiences such as near-death experiences (NDEs).

Dr. Ken R. Vincent recommends the works of three scholars for further examination of the first 500 years of universal salvation in Christianity:

(1) Ballou, H. (1842). Ancient history of Universalism: From the time of the apostles to the Fifth General Council. Forgotten Books. (Original work published in 1878).

(2) Beecher, E. (2007). History of opinions on the scriptural doctrine of retribution. Kessinger Publishing, LLC.

(3) Hanson, J.W. (2012). Universalism, the prevailing doctrine of the Church for its first 500 years with authorities and extracts. Forgotten Books. (Original work published in 1899).

In this Part of this article, the biblical case will be made that it is God's will for everyone to be saved; and how this implies God has a plan of salvation for people after their death; and how this implies the reality of reincarnation.

B. God's Punishment is Not Eternal

Webster's Dictionary defines the word "punishment" as: "suffering, pain, or loss, that serves as retribution" and "a penalty inflicted on an offender through judicial procedure." Divine retribution in the Bible establishes how punishment must correspond in kind and degree to the offense as authorized by God's law:

Leviticus 24:19-21: "Anyone who injures their neighbor is to be injured in the same manner: fracture for fracture, eye for eye, tooth for tooth. The one who has inflicted the injury must suffer the same injury. Whoever kills an animal must make restitution, but whoever kills a human being is to be put to death."

Because of this, a case can be made for the injustice of eternal damnation as retribution upon any person for sin(s) - especially in those cases where the person's lifetime was very short. Retribution in a just judicial system must use punishment in the context of correction. Sentences of "life in prison" and the "death penalty" can be viewed as corrective punishment because the punishment is of limited duration. Because all punishment has a corrective aim, it is necessarily of limited duration. On the other hand, eternal damnation is neither corrective nor limited; so it is therefore not punishment. The purpose of punishment is to correct human behavior toward the goal of not repeating the offense for which the offender is being punished. Therefore, eternal damnation does not fit into any punitive or judicial system.

We also know God is love, and whoever lives in love lives in God, and God in them (1 John 4:16). And we know Jesus taught us to be merciful, just as our Father in heaven is merciful (Luke 6:36). So if we, as human beings, would not want to see someone tortured for eternity, how much more would God not want it. Jesus himself expressed this principle when he said, "Which of you, if your son asks for bread, will give him a stone? ... If you, then, though you are evil, know how to give good gifts to your children, how much more will your Father in heaven give good gifts to those who ask him" (Matthew 7:9-11). The following Bible verses describe God's mercy while refuting the concept of eternal damnation. And because the Bible does so, it also implies God gives people opportunities of salvation after death:

Lamentations 3:31-33: "For no one is cast off by the Lord forever. Though he brings grief, he will show compassion, so great is his unfailing love. For he does not willingly bring affliction or grief to anyone."

Isaiah 57:16: "I will not accuse them forever, nor will I always be angry, for then they would faint away because of me - the very people I have created."

In the following parables, Jesus uses the metaphor of a "prison" for hell and a "judge" for God:

Matthew 5:25-26: "Settle matters quickly with your adversary who is taking you to court. Do it while you are still together on the way, or your adversary may hand you over to the judge, and the judge may hand you over to the officer, and you may be thrown into prison. Truly I tell you, you will not get out until you have paid the last penny."

Matthew 18:34-35: "In anger his master handed him over to the jailers to be tortured, until he should pay back all he owed. This is how my heavenly Father will treat each of you unless you forgive your brother or sister from your heart."

The interesting aspect about the above parables is how they declare a person will not get out of "prison" (hell) until their "debt" (transgressions) have been paid in full. Because these parables imply people getting out of hell, one wonders where they would go? It would be reasonable to assume they would be reincarnated. Also, as you will see in Part 6.12g of this article, the very words in the Bible translated in the Greek for "eternal" and "forever" are mistranslations of the word "eon" which means "a long period of time" but not forever. This is important because "eon" should be properly translated in verses dealing with "eternal" damnation and to "forever" as the measurement of time that people spend in hell. The word "eon" also applies to the "Lake of Fire" as a temporary place for purification before reincarnation - not a place of eternal torture.

C. God Wills Everyone To Be Saved

The following Bible verse clearly states it is God's will for everyone to be saved:

1 Timothy 2:3-4: "For this is good and acceptable in the sight of God our Savior; who will have all men to be saved, and to come unto the knowledge of the truth."

And there should be no doubt about this: nothing can thwart

God's will from being accomplished:

Job 42:2: "I know that you (God) can do all things; no purpose of yours can be thwarted"

Daniel 4:35: "He (God) does as he pleases with the powers of heaven and the peoples of the Earth. No one can hold back his hand or say to him: 'What have you done?'"

So the question is not, "Will everyone be saved?" because 1 Timothy 2:3-4 says it is God's will that everyone be saved. And because nothing can thwart God's will, the only logical conclusion is that everyone will be saved. These combined Bible verses prove beyond doubt the reality of universal salvation. So the real question is, "How is everyone saved?," because it is obvious that a countless number of people have died without salvation. Therefore, God must have a plan of salvation for such people after their death. Obviously, one such plan of salvation is through reincarnation. Given enough opportunities and lifetimes, as Jesus' Parable of the Prodigal Son implies, everyone will return to the Father. The following are more Bible verses supporting the doctrine of universal salvation implying an "after death" plan of salvation such as reincarnation:

Romans 11:32: "For God has bound everyone over to disobedience so that he may have mercy on them all."

Matthew 18:12-14: "What do you think? If a man owns a hundred sheep, and one of them wanders away, will he not leave the ninety-nine on the hills and go to look for the one that wandered off? And if he finds it, truly I tell you, he is happier about that one sheep than about the ninety-nine that did not wander off. In the same way your Father in heaven is not willing that any of these little ones should perish."

The next verse is not only a statement of God wanting everyone saved, it is a statement that makes the most sense if reincarnation is true. Peter is dealing with scoffers who no longer believe Jesus is returning. But Peter reassures his audience that the Lord is patiently waiting for everyone to be saved. And if this is true, it can only come about through reincarnation:

2 Peter 3:3-9: "Above all, you must understand that in the last days scoffers will come, scoffing and following their own evil desires. They will say, 'Where is this coming he promised? Ever since our ancestors died, everything goes on as it has since the beginning of creation.' But they deliberately forget that long ago by God's word

the heavens came into being and the Earth was formed out of water and by water. By these waters also the world of that time was deluged and destroyed. By the same word the present heavens and Earth are reserved for fire, being kept for the day of judgment and destruction of the ungodly. But do not forget this one thing, dear friends: With the Lord a day is like a thousand years, and a thousand years are like a day. The Lord is not slow in keeping his promise, as some understand slowness. Instead he is patient with you, not wanting anyone to perish, but everyone to come to repentance."

Part 2 of this article describes Jesus telling some of his followers they would be alive when he returns, and how this meant they would be reincarnated before he returns, not that he would return in their current lifetime. This misunderstanding, among other things, led early Christians to expect Jesus' return in their lifetime and the non-occurrence of Jesus' return surprised the early Christian communities of the 1st century. And as the decades continued on without the return of Jesus, scoffers began to doubt he would ever return. So in the above verse, Peter dealt with these scoffers by reminding his audience of similar scoffers in Noah's day at his building the ark until the very day of their destruction by the flood. Peter mentioned a similar "day of judgment" is coming when Jesus will return resulting in the death of "the ungodly." Peter also informed his Christian audience how humanity's timetable is not equivalent to God's timetable by suggesting it may be a "thousand years" before Jesus returns. Peter continued his line of reasoning to justify the Lord's "patience" on the grounds the Lord is trying to save "everyone" because he does "not want anyone to perish." So if we try to understand Peter's words of universal salvation, without the context of reincarnation, they makes little sense because at that time many people have already died without salvation and there would have been no hope for them. And the Lord would be disappointed because his wanting of everyone's salvation would perish along with the people who died unsaved. But if we understand Peter's words with the context of reincarnation, Peter's words of universal salvation make perfect sense. The Lord is patiently waiting for everyone to be saved; and this can only occur through reincarnation.

D. Everyone Will Be Saved

Now that it's been established through scripture that God wills everyone to be saved, it will be established through scripture that everyone will be saved and this implies reincarnation. The following list of Bible verses compares the results of Adam's original sin - the condemnation of the entire human race - with the results of Jesus paying the "karmic debt" for Adam's sin through his crucifixion and death, resulting in the justification of the entire human race:

Romans 5:18: "Consequently, just as one trespass resulted in condemnation for all people, so also one righteous act resulted in justification and life for all people."

1 Corinthians 15:22: "For as in Adam all die, so in Christ all will be made alive."

1 Corinthians 15:27-28: "For he 'has put everything under his feet.' Now when it says that 'everything' has been put under him, it is clear that this does not include God himself, who put everything under Christ. When he has done this, then the Son himself will be made subject to him who put everything under him, so that God may be all in all."

Think of the enormity of the above statements by Paul: in Christ all will be made alive; and God will be "all in all." These verses are two of the most explicit Universalist verses in the entire Bible and cannot be refuted.

The following Bible verses describe all people turning (repenting) to the Lord and seeing God's salvation which can only be accomplished through reincarnation:

Luke 3:5-6: "Every valley shall be filled in, every mountain and hill made low. The crooked roads shall become straight, the rough ways smooth. And all people will see God's salvation."

Psalm 65:2-3: "You who answer prayer, to you all people will come. When we were overwhelmed by sins, you forgave our transgressions."

Psalm 22:27: "All the ends of the Earth will remember and turn to the Lord, and all the families of the nations will bow down before him."

Isaiah 52:10: "The Lord will lay bare his holy arm in the sight of all the nations, and all the ends of the Earth will see the salvation of our God."

Psalm 86:9: "All the nations you have made will come and worship before you, Lord; they will bring glory to your name."

The following Bible verses reveal Jesus to be the Savior of "all men", "all people", the "whole world" and "everyone":

1 Timothy 4:10: "That is why we labor and strive, because we have put our hope in the living God, who is the Savior of all people, and especially of those who believe."

1 John 2:2: "He is the atoning sacrifice for our sins, and not only for ours but also for the sins of the whole world."

1 John 4:14: "And we have seen and testify that the Father has sent his Son to be the Savior of the world."

Hebrews 2:9: "But we do see Jesus, who was made lower than the angels for a little while, now crowned with glory and honor because he suffered death, so that by the grace of God he might taste death for everyone."

John 1:7: "The same came for a witness, to bear witness of the Light, that all men through him might believe."

John 12:32: "And I, if I be lifted up from the Earth, will draw all men unto me."

Some of the parables of Jesus have a Universalist interpretation which can only occur through reincarnation:

Luke 15:3-7, Parable of the Lost Sheep: "Then Jesus told them this parable: 'Suppose one of you has a hundred sheep and loses one of them. Doesn't he leave the ninety-nine in the open country and go after the lost sheep until he finds it? And when he finds it, he joyfully puts it on his shoulders and goes home. Then he calls his friends and neighbors together and says, 'Rejoice with me; I have found my lost sheep.' I tell you that in the same way there will be more rejoicing in heaven over one sinner who repents than over ninety-nine righteous persons who do not need to repent.'"

Luke 15:8-10, Parable of the Lost Coin: "Or suppose a woman has ten silver coins and loses one. Doesn't she light a lamp, sweep the house and search carefully until she finds it? And when she finds it, she calls her friends and neighbors together and says, 'Rejoice with me; I have found my lost coin.' In the same way, I tell you, there is rejoicing in the presence of the angels of God over one sinner who repents."

Luke 15:21-24, Parable of the Prodigal Son: "The son said to him, 'Father, I have sinned against heaven and against you. I am no longer worthy to be called your son.' But the father said to his servants, 'Quick! Bring the best robe and put it on him. Put a ring on his finger and sandals on his feet. Bring the fattened calf and kill it. Let's have a feast and celebrate. For this son of mine was dead and is alive again; he was lost and is found.'"

The greatest biblical scholar of early Christianity, Origen, considered Jesus' Parable of the Prodigal Son to be a perfect example of how God's love would not allow anyone to be lost forever or destroyed. According to Kurt Eggenstein's chapter entitled "The Prodigal Son: Preexistential Origin of Man from the Fallen First-Created Spirits," from his book, Origen believed the soul leaves the place of purification, again and again; but punishment does not go on forever:

Origen: "Perfection will have been achieved when all souls have found salvation in becoming angels. All creation returns to God. The universal resolve to achieve salvation is a revelation of the all-compassionate God." (Origen, The Book on Heretics, Walter Nigg, p.56-57)

In his Contra Celsus 92-97, Origen equated Adam with the primal unit of human nature, which fell from heaven in the beginning of time as a whole. Origen refers to the words of the prophet Joshua upon reaching the Promised Land:

Origen: "Far indeed my soul has been wandering. Comprehend, therefore, if you are able, what are these wanderings of the soul, to continue on which she laments with sighs and sorrows. For, of course, for as long as she is wanderings insight into these things is halted and is veiled, only when she has reached her homeland, her peace, paradise, shall she be enlightened more truly on this, and see more clearly which has been the way and meaning of her wanderings." (Origen, Contra Celsus 92-97)

E. The Time of Universal Restoration

Paul mentioned a time of "universal reconciliation" in his Epistle to the Colossians:

Colossians 1:19-20: "For God was pleased to have all his fullness dwell in him, and through him to reconcile to himself all things, whether things on Earth or things in heaven, by making peace through his blood, shed on the cross."

Peter also mentioned a time of "universal restoration." As previously mentioned, Peter confronted those who killed Jesus and told them to repent so the "times of refreshing" may come, so Jesus can return, and the time of universal restoration happen:

Acts 3:14-15; 3:19-21: "But you rejected the Holy and Righteous One and asked to have a murderer given to you, and you killed the Author of life, whom God raised from the dead. To this we are witnesses... Repent therefore, and turn to God so that your sins may be wiped out, so that times of refreshing may come from the presence of the Lord, and that he may send the Messiah appointed for you, that is, Jesus, who must remain in heaven until the time of universal restoration that God announced long ago through his holy prophets."

Peter's reference to a "time of universal restoration" becomes clear when we read of Jesus' words in Matthew:

Matthew 19:28: "Jesus said to them, 'Truly I tell you, at the renewal of all things, when the Son of Man sits on his glorious throne, you who have followed me will also sit on twelve thrones, judging the twelve tribes of Israel.'"

The reference to "universal restoration," or "apokatastasis" in Greek, refers to the thousand year reign of Christ on Earth and the universal salvation of all souls resulting from it mentioned in Revelation 20:1-6. More information about the thousand year reign of Christ will be given in Part 6 of this article. Origen, the writer most commonly associated with "apokatastasis panton," although not the first writer on the subject, saw an end to the cycle of successive reincarnations predicted by the final restoration of all souls to God. Clement of Alexandria (150-215 AD), the first Christian to write on the subject, described the fire of hell as a "wise" fire, the means by which sinners are purified, reincarnated, and ultimately saved. Origen's cosmological scheme starts with the creation of angels who, after falling away from God, underwent an ontological change to become souls. It ends with the return of all the souls to God. In De Principiis1 VI 3, Origen argued how even the demons, souls who are most remote from God, could ascend to the human condition and from there ascend to the angelic. Origen's argument follows naturally after two assumptions:

(1) The power of free will remains with the soul after death.
(2) God has not created an eternal place of damnation.

Origen saw the entrapment of the souls in matter, as well as the flames of hell, existing as both a punishment and as a means of rehabilitation for souls to be encouraged to return to God. Furthermore, Origen writes elsewhere of the nature of hell not being eternal. The ancient as well as the late Byzantine position, was that nothing evil can come from God, not even punishment. The punishment and torments of hell are only inflicted upon ourselves, both in this world and in the next one. Hell and its fire are not different, essentially, from the benevolent purifying Spirit of God, when experienced by the sinners (Hebrews 12:29, Acts 15:8-9).

Gregory of Nyssa (335-395 AD), in "On the Soul and the Resurrection" and in the "Catechism Oration," followed Origen in writing how the fire of hell plays a purifying role and is, therefore, not eternal. He goes even further in his argument however: because evil has no real existence, its "relative" existence will be completely annihilated at the end times. He stated his belief in the final restoration of all:

Gregory of Nyssa: "When, after long periods of time, the evil of our nature... has been expelled, and when there has been a restoration of those who are now lying in sin to their primal state, a harmony of thanksgiving will arise from all creation, as well from those who in the process of the purgation have suffered chastisement, as from those who needed not any purgation at all." (Gregory of Nyssa, Catechism Oration 26)

Gregory of Nyssa: The main role of divine judgment, according to Gregory, is not to punish sinners. Instead, it: "...operates by separating good from evil and pulling the soul towards the fellowship of blessedness." (Gregory of Nyssa, On the Soul and the Resurrection)

More than merely "separating," the purifying fire will melt away evil so what is left is only good. We have to keep in mind, in several of the writings of Gregory of Nyssa on the Fall and the nature of evil, Satan is not presented as the adversary of God, but as the adversary of man. In this sense, the "relative" existence of evil does not diminish God's power or goodness. Evil is directly connected with the pain experienced by sinners after the last judgment, when they are given to torture "until they pay back all that they owe" according to the parables of Jesus:

Matthew 18:34-35, Parable of the Unforgiving Servant: "In anger his master handed him over to the jailers to be tortured, until he should pay back all he owed. This is how my heavenly Father will treat each of you unless you forgive your brother or sister from your heart."

According to Gregory, after their punishment, they will "enter into freedom and confidence" and "God will be all in all."

The Christian Gnostic text, the Gospel of Philip (180-350 AD), also contains the word "apokatastasis" and associates it with reincarnation which implies universal salvation:

Gospel of Philip: "There is a rebirth and an image of rebirth. It is certainly necessary to be born again through the image. Which one? Resurrection. The image must rise again through the image. The bridal chamber and the image must enter through the image into the truth: this is the restoration (apokatastasis). Not only must those who produce the name of the Father and the Son and the Holy Spirit, do so, but have produced them for you. If one does not acquire them, the name ("Christian") will also be taken from him."

The above verse agrees with New Testament verses concerning the two rebirths mentioned in Part 2: of the flesh and of the spirit. Spiritual rebirth comes when we share in Christ's resurrection by taking up our own crosses in self-denial and self-sacrifice to follow Jesus in putting into practice his teachings toward spiritual perfection:

Matthew 10:38: "Whoever does not take up their cross and follow me is not worthy of me."

Romans 7:4: "So, my brothers and sisters, you also died to the law through the body of Christ, that you might belong to another, to him who was raised from the dead."

As members of the "Bride of Christ", his followers must make themselves ready through good works for the "wedding of the Lamb":

Revelation 19:7: "For the wedding of the Lamb has come, and His bride has made herself ready."

Everyone's goal is to be transformed into the image of the Logos - the image of God in man:

2 Corinthians 3:18: "We all, who with unveiled faces contemplate the Lord's glory, are being transformed into his image with ever-increasing glory, which comes from the Lord, who is the Spirit."

So if Christians must take up their own cross, follow Jesus, make themselves ready and be transformed into his image with "ever-increasing glory", then we know this is much more than a single lifetime process - especially when you consider how life is often cut short for so many people.

F. Summary

Jesus taught Nicodemus of two rebirths: one of the flesh, and the other of the spirit. To be "born again of the flesh" means to be reborn of water, childbirth, and reincarnation. To be "born again of the spirit" means spiritual regeneration by the Holy Spirit. Those who are not spiritually regenerated, who have not transformed into Christ's image, who have not attained eternal life, must be reincarnated and continue the cycle of death and rebirth until they do. The biblical teaching of universal salvation means God has a plan of salvation after death for those who have not been spiritually regenerated, and that plan involves reincarnation. For the first 500 years of Christianity, Christians and Christian theologians were broadly Universalists and reincarnationalists. The mistranslation of the scriptures from Greek to Latin and the merging of Church and State fostered the corruption of Universalist and reincarnationalist thought. Universal salvation is an important doctrine because it shows how God is indeed infinite in love and mercy. It shows God is not willing that even one soul fall into some "crack in the universe" to be lost forever. Universal salvation shows God giving people as many opportunities as necessary to attain salvation. Universal salvation is not only suggestive of the reality of reincarnation, as we will see in the next section, God's law demands it. For all these reasons, reincarnation must now become a doctrine of Christianity as it was widely believed during the first hundred years of Christian history.

2. God's Law of Divine Justice as the Law of Reincarnation

A. The Law of Divine Justice Defined as Karma and Reincarnation

We have already mentioned in Part 1 about the law of divine justice in the case of John the Baptist as a reincarnation of the prophet Elijah. Elijah killed with a sword the prophets of Baal who were associated with the King's wife Jezebel. And although Elijah may have repented and God forgiven him, divine justice demands "life for life, eye for eye, tooth for tooth" to satisfy divine justice (Exodus 21:23-25). So when Elijah reincarnated as John the Baptist, his life had to end by being killed by the sword. This law of divine justice, karma, is taught elsewhere in the Bible:

Matthew 26:52: "All who draw the sword will die by the sword."

Revelation 13:10: "He who kills with the sword must be killed with the sword."

As previously mentioned, this law of divine justice is known by eastern religions as "karma" and is practically a universal religious concept. It is a law which implies reincarnation and can be found throughout the Bible. And in such cases as John the Baptist and Elijah, people who "kill with the sword" and do not "die by the sword" in their lifetime (as is often the case), must do so in a future lifetime. In fact, the law of karma is reincarnation. Every action has an equal and opposite reaction according to the law of karma (causality). Karma is the law of cause and effect - action and reaction. There is in this universe a strict balancing process steadily at work which deals justly with everyone "according to their works."

"Bad karma" is not the "sin" or transgression itself. Bad karma is a state of imbalance in the equilibrium of divine justice in the negative direction in a person's life because of particular sins committed which have yet to occur to the sinner. According to the biblical concept of "original sin," Adam's sin created "bad karma" for himself and for his descendants - spiritual death - which was "paid" by Christ at the cross (1 Corinthians 15:22). Christ's atonement for sins and the redemption of sinners does not nullify karma. Karmic debts against other people are separate from our karmic debts to God for sin because God's law was not nullified at the cross (Matthew 5:17-20). God may forgive a man for killing another man; but God's forgiveness of his sins doesn't nullify the murderer's obligation to seek forgiveness, pay restitution, and restore the karmic "balance" with his victims. Otherwise, people such as Adolf Hitler could have "accepted Jesus" as Savior before he killed himself and it would be his "ticket" to heaven. Sure, God would have forgiven him. But what about the millions of people he ordered killed? Hitler has a lot of things to set right. And although God's forgiveness could spare Hitler a very, very long time of purification in hell, everyone is still judged according to their works - both good and bad. It is easy for a God of infinite love and mercy to forgive even the worst of sinners, but unless the sinner seek (and get) forgiveness, pay restitution, and give good karma to his victims, then a karmic debt still remains. So the salvific work of Christ on the cross doesn't necessarily nullify the effect of all sin or karma. To be sure, God has forgiven us of our sins - our sins against God unto death. God forgives the murderer for murdering his victims. But only the victims can forgive (or not forgive) the murderer for the murderous act against them. If, as Jesus taught, the victim is of a pious nature and forgives the murderer, then that karma is paid and ends there. Else, the cycle of karma continues and the murderer faces the possibility of being murdered.

When it comes to karma there are many different kinds of karma. Besides personal karma, there is group karma, family karma, relationship karma, organization karma, nation karma, etc. As a perfect example of nation karma, the Christian psychic Edgar Cayce revealed that many of the Jews who suffered in the Holocaust were the reincarnation of Jews who lived in Jesus' day and chose to reincarnate and suffer to pay the karmic debt for Israel's rejection of their Messiah. Cayce also revealed that Hitler was the reincarnation of Pontius Pilate. So although Christ's sacrifice applies to our justification with God, and our justification with God is not necessarily mutually exclusive with justification from sins committed against God's Law, there are aspects to God's Law which concerns only human-to-human relationships which demand justification. In other words, there are aspects to God's Law which are relevant to human relationships and are mutually exclusive to aspects of God's Law which are only relevant to God's relationship to humans.

A person's accumulation of "bad" and "good" karma determines which heaven or hell in God's hierarchy of afterlife realms they dwell in between Earth lifetimes. As Jesus said, there are many abodes in his Father's house (John 14:2), and there are many levels of heaven and hell. Everyone is on a path moving up God's "corporate ladder of success" (see "Jacob's Ladder"). Everyone's goal is the highest heaven which is permanent citizenship there (Revelation 3:12). In fact, the physical universe is just one of the Father's abode - one level of heaven - out of many. According to many sources I've come across, the physical realm is somewhere in the middle between the highest heavenly realm and the lowest hell realm. So, in essence, we are halfway to heaven while in the physical. But we are actually spiritual beings having a physical experience which means we come from higher spirit realms with missions from God to further God's Kingdom in the physical.

B. The Law of Karma in the Old Testament

The Old Testament is filled with references to karma; and therefore, reincarnation. Here is a list of some of them:

Genesis 9:6: "Whoever sheds human blood, by humans shall their blood be shed; for in the image of God has God made mankind."

Ecclesiastes 11:1: "Cast your bread upon the waters, for you will find it after many days."

Hosea 8:7: "They sow the wind and reap the whirlwind."

Hosea 10:12-13: "Sow righteousness for yourselves, reap the fruit of unfailing love, and break up your unplowed ground; for it is time to seek the Lord, until he comes and showers his righteousness on you. But you have planted wickedness, you have reaped evil, you have eaten the fruit of deception."

Job 4:8: "As I have observed, those who plow evil and those who sow trouble reap it."

Obadiah 1:15: "As you have done, it will be done to you; your deeds will return upon your own head."

Proverbs 10:16: "The wages of the righteous is life, but the earnings of the wicked are sin and death."

Proverbs 11:27: "Whoever seeks good finds favor, but evil comes to one who searches for it."

Proverbs 20:22: "Do not say, 'I'll pay you back for this wrong!' Wait for the Lord, and he will avenge you."

Proverbs 22:8: "Whoever sows injustice reaps calamity, And the rod they wield in fury will be broken."

Proverbs 26:27: "Whoever digs a pit will fall into it; if someone rolls a stone, it will roll back on them."

Proverbs 28:18: "The one whose walk is blameless is kept safe, but the one whose ways are perverse will fall into the pit."

Psalm 7:16: "The trouble they cause recoils on them; their violence comes down on their own heads."

C. The Law of Karma Taught By Paul

The Apostle Paul (5-67 AD) was a Pharisee; and according to Josephus, the Pharisees were believers in reincarnation and karma. This fact can be seen in the Epistles of Paul:

Galatians 6:7-10: "Do not be deceived: God cannot be mocked. A man reaps what he sows. Whoever sows to please their flesh, from the flesh will reap destruction; whoever sows to please the Spirit, from the Spirit will reap eternal life. Let us not become weary in doing good, for at the proper time we will reap a harvest if we do not give up. Therefore, as we have opportunity, let us do good to all people, especially to those who belong to the family of believers."

2 Corinthians 9:6: "Whoever sows sparingly will also reap sparingly, and whoever sows generously will also reap generously."

Only reincarnation can satisfy God's divine justice of reaping what we sow; an eye for an eye; living by the sword and dying by the sword. This universal law of God explains why some people are born into favorable conditions and others are born into unfavorable conditions. Some people are born into unfavorable conditions because of "bad karma" from a previous lifetime. This can be seen in the story of Jacob and Esau as described by Paul:

Romans 9:13-21: "Just as it is written: 'Jacob I loved, but Esau I hated.' What then shall we say? Is God unjust? Not at all! For he says to Moses: 'I will have mercy on whom I have mercy, and I will have compassion on whom I have compassion.' It does not, therefore, depend on human desire or effort, but on God's mercy. For Scripture says to Pharaoh: 'I raised you up for this very purpose, that I might display my power in you and that my name might be proclaimed in all the Earth.' Therefore God has mercy on whom he wants to have mercy, and he hardens whom he wants to harden. One of you will say to me: 'Then why does God still blame us? For who is able to resist his will?' But who are you, a human being, to talk back to God? Shall what is formed say to the one who formed it, 'Why did you make me like this?' Does not the potter have the right to make out of the same lump of clay some pottery for special purposes and some for common use?"

The Book of Genesis describes the story of how Abraham's son Isaac and his wife Rebekah had twins named Jacob and Esau and how God preferred Jacob over Esau even before they were born:

Genesis 25:22-23: "The babies (Jacob and Esau) jostled each other within her (Rebekah), and she said, 'Why is this happening to me?' So she went to inquire of the Lord. The Lord said to her, 'Two nations are in your womb, and two peoples from within you will be separated; one people will be stronger than the other, and the older will serve the younger.'"

We now understand it was divine justice, Jacob's and Esau's karma, determining the twin's destiny and Esau's unfavorable life conditions. This is why Paul could safely ask and answer:

Romans 9:14: "Is God unjust? Not at all!"

In referring to Esau's apparent unjust and unfavorable life conditions, Paul asks then answers:

Romans 9:19: "Then why does God still blame us? For who is able to resist his will? But who are you, a human being, to talk back to God?"

Paul doesn't argue any further; but simply lays Esau's karma at God's feet and divine justice. The potter has a right to do as he pleases with his clay. And of course, we know the potter is infinite in divine justice and mercy. Paul's metaphor of the potter (God) and clay (flesh) to describe the perfection process of how God creates, destroys and recreates better pots (people) is an excellent description of the preexistence of souls and reincarnation which originally can be found in the Book of Jeremiah:

Jeremiah 18:1-6: "This is the word that came to Jeremiah from the Lord, 'Go down to the potter's house, and there I will give you my message.' "So I went down to the potter's house, and I saw him working at the wheel. But the pot he was shaping from the clay was marred in his hands; so the potter formed it into another pot, shaping it as seemed best to him. Then the word of the Lord came to me, 'O house of Israel, can I not do with you as this potter does?' declares the Lord."

By comparing the sovereignty of God over humans with the sovereignty a potter has with clay, Paul is also affirming both the preexistence and karma of Jacob and Esau. The central point Paul makes is that God created Esau as an object of wrath because of his so-called "hatred" for him before he was even born. God must have "hated" Esau because of a past incarnation displeasing to Him which can only explain why God reincarnated him as an "object of wrath." The opposite destiny of Esau was the destiny of Jacob. Because Jacob had led a previous life pleasing to God, Jacob was reincarnated as an object of God's mercy. So the story of Jacob and Esau is rich with hidden knowledge concerning divine justice, the sovereignty of God, preexistence, reincarnation, predestination, and free will.

Origen also wrote of the "karma" of Jacob and Esau:

Origen: "'Is there unrighteousness with God? God forbid.' (Romans 9:14) As, therefore, when the Scriptures are carefully examined regarding Jacob and Esau, it is not found to be unrighteousness with God that it should be said, before they were born, or had done anything in this life, 'the elder shall serve the younger;' and as it is found not to be unrighteousness that even in the womb Jacob supplanted his brother, if we feel that he was worthily beloved by God, according to the merits of his previous life, so as to deserve to be preferred over his brother." (Origen, On First Principles 2.9.7)

The following is a list of more Bible verses by Paul on how to deal with the God's just law of karma:

Romans 12:17-19: "Do not repay anyone evil for evil. Be careful to do what is right in the eyes of everyone. If it is possible, as far as it depends on you, live at peace with everyone. Do not take revenge, my dear friends, but leave room for God's wrath, for it is written: 'It is mine to avenge; I will repay,' says the Lord."

2 Thessalonians 1:6: "God is just: He will pay back trouble to those who trouble you."

2 Corinthians 5:10: "For we must all appear before the judgment seat of Christ, so that each of us may receive what is due us for the things done while in the body, whether good or bad."

Hebrews 10:30: "For we know him who said, 'It is mine to avenge; I will repay,' and again, 'The Lord will judge his people.'"

D. The Law of Karma Taught By Jesus

Reincarnation and karma are the missing links, the long lost doctrines, of Christianity. They are the keys to understanding the secret, mystery teachings of Jesus and his parables. A good example is the beginning of Jesus' Parable of the Talents:

Matthew 25:14-15: "It (the kingdom of heaven) is as if a man, going on a journey, summoned his slaves and entrusted his property to them; to one he gave five talents, to another two, to another one, to each according to his ability. Then he went away."

This idea of God giving people varying amounts of abilities at birth - each according to his ability - is the heart of reincarnation and the law of divine justice. Origen used this very parable to teach preexistence and reincarnation. Here is an excellent summary of Origen's position on preexistence and reincarnation based upon his work "On First Principles":

Origen: "Every soul has existed from the beginning; it has therefore passed through some worlds already, and will pass through others before it reaches final consummation. It comes into this world strengthened by its victories or weakened by the defeats of its previous life. Its place in this world as a vessel appointed to honor or to dishonor is determined by its previous merits or demerits. Its work in this world determines its place in the world which is to follow." (Hatch, Edwin, and A M. Fairbairn. The Influence of Greek Ideas and Usages Upon the Christian Church. London: Williams and Norgate. page 235)

The above summary comes from the following writings of Origen:

Origen: "The soul, as we have frequently said, is immortal and eternal, it is possible that, in the many and endless periods of duration in the immeasurable and different worlds, it may descend from the highest good to the lowest evil, or be restored from the lowest evil to the highest good. (Origen, On First Principles 3.1.21)

Origen: "If they (souls) had a beginning such as the end for which they hope, they existed undoubtedly from the very beginning in those (ages) which are not seen, and are eternal." (Origen, On First Principles 3:5:4)

Origen: "The cause of each one's actions is a pre-existing one; and then everyone, according to his merits, is made by God either a vessel unto honor or dishonor ... it is due to previous causes." (Origen, On First Principles 3:1:20)

Origen: "At the consummation and restoration of all things, those who make a gradual advance, and who ascend (in the scale of improvement), will arrive in due measure and order at that land." (Origen, On First Principles 3.6.9)

When Origen used the Parable of the Talents to refer to reincarnation and preexistence, he was not introducing some foreign religious concept into Christianity. He was merely expressing what is described throughout the Bible and believed by early Christians to be one of the secret teachings of Jesus. At the end of the Parable of the Unforgiving Servant in Matthew 18, Jesus mentioned karmic divine justice which can also be viewed as a Universalist parable denying eternal damnation:

Matthew 18:34-35: "In anger his master handed him over to the jailers to be tortured, until he should pay back all he owed. This is how my heavenly Father will treat each of you unless you forgive your brother or sister from your heart"

The following are more Bible verses of Jesus teaching karma:

Matthew 7:1-2: "Do not judge, or you too will be judged. For in the same way you judge others, you will be judged, and with the measure you use, it will be measured to you."

Matthew 7:8: "For everyone who asks receives; the one who seeks finds; and to the one who knocks, the door will be opened."

Matthew 7:12: "So in everything, do to others what you would have them do to you, for this sums up the Law and the Prophets."

Matthew 16:27: "For the Son of Man is going to come in his Father's glory with his angels, and then he will reward each person according to what they have done."

Matthew 18:7: "Woe to the world because of the things that cause people to stumble! Such things must come, but woe to the person through whom they come!"

Matthew 23:12, Luke 14:11, and Luke 18:14: "For those who exalt themselves will be humbled, and those who humble themselves will be exalted."

Mark 4:24: "Consider carefully what you hear," he continued. "With the measure you use, it will be measured to you - and even more."

Mark 11:25-26: "And when you stand praying, if you hold anything against anyone, forgive them, so that your Father in heaven may forgive you your sins."

Luke 6:37-38: "Do not judge, and you will not be judged. Do not condemn, and you will not be condemned. Forgive, and you will be forgiven. Give, and it will be given to you. A good measure, pressed down, shaken together and running over, will be poured into your lap. For with the measure you use, it will be measured to you."

Luke 10:25-28: "On one occasion an expert in the law stood up to test Jesus. 'Teacher,' he asked, 'what must I do to inherit eternal life?' 'What is written in the Law?' he replied. 'How do you read it?' He answered, 'Love the Lord your God with all your heart and with all your soul and with all your strength and with all your mind; and,

Love your neighbor as yourself.' 'You have answered correctly,' Jesus replied. 'Do this and you will live.'"

Luke 11:4 and Matthew 6:12: "Forgive us our sins, for we also forgive everyone who sins against us."

The brother of Jesus, James the Just, wrote this karmic verse:

James 3:18: "Peacemakers who sow in peace reap a harvest of righteousness."

Jesus also taught how to stop and reverse the cycle of bad karma when it happens to you:

Luke 6:27-36: "But to you who are listening I say: Love your enemies, do good to those who hate you, bless those who curse you, pray for those who mistreat you. If someone slaps you on one cheek, turn to them the other also. If someone takes your coat, do not withhold your shirt from them. Give to everyone who asks you, and if anyone takes what belongs to you, do not demand it back. Do to others as you would have them do to you. If you love those who love you, what credit is that to you? Even sinners love those who love them. And if you do good to those who are good to you, what credit is that to you? Even sinners do that. And if you lend to those from whom you expect repayment, what credit is that to you? Even sinners lend to sinners, expecting to be repaid in full. But love your enemies, do good to them, and lend to them without expecting to get anything back. Then your reward will be great, and you will be children of the Most High, because he is kind to the ungrateful and wicked. Be merciful, just as your Father is merciful."

The Apostle Peter described how Jesus practiced what he preached in stopping bad karma instead passing it along:

1 Peter 2:21–23: "To this you were called, because Christ suffered for you, leaving you an example, that you should follow in his steps. 'He committed no sin, and no deceit was found in his mouth.' When they hurled their insults at him, he did not retaliate; when he suffered, he made no threats. Instead, he entrusted himself to him who judges justly."

E. Bad Karma Can Extend Into Multiple Lifetimes

As Paul taught, using the story of Jacob and Esau, knowing the divine justice of karma allows us to ask and answer, "Is God unjust? Not at all." It also allows us to understand some of the apparent injustices in the Old Testament. Here is one of them:

Genesis 4:14-15: "'Today you (God) are driving me (Cain) from the land, and I will be hidden from your presence; I will be a restless wanderer on the Earth, and whoever finds me will kill me.' But the Lord said to him, 'Not so; anyone who kills Cain will suffer vengeance seven times over.' Then the Lord put a mark on Cain so that no one who found him would kill him."

Many Bible versions of verse 14 are translated as Cain saying "everyone who finds me will kill me" suggesting Cain believed he would be killed by many people in many lifetimes implying reincarnation. God's reply to Cain also implies reincarnation and karma when God declared "anyone who kills Cain will suffer vengeance seven times over" meaning the killer of Cain will have to be killed seven times implying seven lifetimes.

Consider the next apparently injustices in the Old Testament:

Exodus 20:5 and Deuteronomy 5:9: "You shall not bow down to them (idols) or worship them; for I, the Lord your God, am a jealous God, punishing the children for the sin of the parents to the third and fourth generation of those who hate me."

Numbers 14:18: "The Lord is slow to anger, abounding in love and forgiving sin and rebellion. Yet he does not leave the guilty unpunished; he punishes the children for the sin of the parents to the third and fourth generation."

According to Strong's Exhaustive Concordance 1755, the Hebrew word translated "generation" is "dor" meaning "a revolution of time" - also "a dwelling." The latter is especially significant, as our human bodies are characterized in Scripture as temporary dwellings. So with this understanding, it is consistent with sound interpretation to also translate this verse, "he punishes the children for the sins of the parents to the third and fourth reincarnation (bodily dwelling) of those who hate me." A literal interpretation of the above verses describe God punishing the children and great-grandchildren for the sins of the parents. The obvious question again is: "Is God unjust?" The only answer can be: "Not at all." And the reason is because of divine justice, karma, and reincarnation. God punishes the parent when they reincarnate as one of their own grandchildren or great grandchildren - the third and fourth generation. And it is common knowledge in reincarnation studies how people tend to reincarnate within their own families; for example, a father may reincarnate as their own grandchild or great grandchild.

F. Is There an End To Reincarnation?

Because a person's karma carries over from one lifetime to the next, the question then arises, "Is there an end to reincarnation; and if so, how does it end?" Thankfully, the Bible has an answer for this question as well. The short answer is bad karma can be overcome through good karma or good works:

Galatians 6:8: "Whoever sows to please the Spirit, from the Spirit will reap eternal life."

A careful study of relevant scriptures reveals a metaphorical interpretation of spiritual "resurrection" as the beginning of the state of liberation from the cycle reincarnation and its corollary, liberation from death, and the freedom to eventually ascend to Paradise from which Adam and Eve originally fell. In the Nicene Creed (325 AD) we find the expression the "Resurrection of the Dead." The "dead" are those who are subject to the law of sowing and reaping of the cycle of birth, death and rebirth. They are those who are caught in the wheel of the relentless law of karma until Christ opened the way to liberation, to spiritual "resurrection," and the restoration to Paradise:

Revelation 2:2-7: "I (Jesus) know your deeds, your hard work and your perseverance. I know that you cannot tolerate wicked people... You have persevered and have endured hardships for my name, and have not grown weary... Whoever has ears, let them hear what the Spirit says to the churches. To the one who is victorious, I will give the right to eat from the tree of life, which is in the paradise of God."

The above words of Christ are an obvious reference to reincarnation. By doing good works, persevering, and standing firm until the end times, this ensures a person has attained Paradise as Jesus taught in the following verse in the Gospel of Matthew. Notice how Jesus told the people around him that they will be persecuted at his Second Coming:

Matthew 10:21-22: "Brother will betray brother to death, and a father his child; children will rebel against their parents and have them put to death. You will be hated by everyone because of me, but the one who stands firm to the end will be saved."

In Jesus' great Sermon on the Mount, he mentioned more ways to overcome the world through good karma such as:

Matthew 5:5: "Blessed are the meek, for they will inherit the Earth."

The above teaching also begs the following question: when and how will the meek inherit the Earth? For millions of years, the principle has always been that only the aggressive and strong rule the world. The law of evolution is the physical correlation to the law of "spiritual evolution" or reincarnation. Evolution means only the fittest survive - certainly not those who are meek. So Jesus' promise of the meek inheriting the Earth can only be fulfilled in some future reincarnation when the meek reincarnate into a world ruled by meek people. And this can only be a reference to the thousand year reign of Christ on Earth described in Revelation 20. The following list of Bible verses are more promises of how good karma (good works) can ultimately lead to the end of reincarnation and the beginning of eternal life in God's Kingdom:

Matthew 5:7-10: "Blessed are the merciful, for they will be shown mercy. Blessed are the pure in heart, for they will see God. Blessed are the peacemakers, for they will be called children of God. Blessed are those who are persecuted because of righteousness, for theirs is the kingdom of heaven."

Luke 16:9: "Use worldly wealth to gain friends for yourselves, so that when it is gone, you will be welcomed into eternal dwellings."

Luke 18:18-22: "A certain ruler asked him (Jesus), 'Good teacher, what must I do to inherit eternal life?' 'Why do you call me good?' Jesus answered. 'No one is good - except God alone. You know the commandments: 'You shall not commit adultery, you shall not murder, you shall not steal, you shall not give false testimony, honor your father and mother.' 'All these I have kept since I was a boy,' he said. 'When Jesus heard this, he said to him, 'You still lack one thing. Sell everything you have and give to the poor, and you will have treasure in heaven. Then come, follow me.'"

G. Other Ways To Overcome Bad Karma and Reincarnation

Jesus taught another way to overcome bad karma through simply not responding to bad behavior or through responding with righteous behavior. Here are some examples of such teachings:

Matthew 5:38-39: "You have heard that it was said, 'Eye for eye, and tooth for tooth.' But I tell you, do not resist an evil person. If anyone slaps you on the right cheek, turn to them the other cheek also."

Matthew 5:44-45: "You have heard that it was said, 'Love your neighbor and hate your enemy.' But I tell you, love your enemies and pray for those who persecute you, that you may be children of your Father in heaven."

Although all our actions have repercussions, not everything happening to us is the result of previous karma. Here is a good Biblical example presented by Christ:

Luke 13:1-5: "Now there were some present at that time who told Jesus about the Galileans whose blood Pilate had mixed with their sacrifices. Jesus answered, 'Do you think that these Galileans were worse sinners than all the other Galileans because they suffered this way? I tell you, no! But unless you repent, you too will all perish. Or those eighteen who died when the tower in Siloam fell on them - do you think they were more guilty than all the others living in Jerusalem? I tell you, no! But unless you repent, you too will all perish."

In the above verse, the people around Jesus assumed the Galileans were killed because of bad karma; but Jesus explained this was not the case. Bad things can happen because of bad karma, and bad things can happen without karmic origins. One thing we know for certain is that the persecution of those Galileans will result in their gaining good karma. And as for Pilate's unjust actions, they will certainly result in his own bad karma.

In a different incident, Jesus did refer to how bad karmic actions can result in bad karmic consequences. After Jesus healed the invalid of thirty-eight years near the Sheep Gate pool, he later told him:

John 5:1-15: "See, you are well again. Stop sinning or something worse may happen to you."

As previously mentioned, the law of karma is also called the law of cause and effect (causality). This law is so universal it can even be found in science. Isaac Newton (1642-1726) established the well-known third law in physics: for every action there always opposed an equal reaction. What goes up must come down. In fact, the law of divine justice is very similar in principle to the law of gravity. Both laws are impersonal. Breaking both of these laws are like breaking the laws of nature. We cannot blame God for the apparent injustices happening to us in life. Like the law of gravity, if we go against the law of divine justice, it is completely our fault and due to our ignorance of divine justice. However, there are even greater divine laws which can overcome bad karma. They are God's law of love, the law of forgiveness, and the law of grace.

H. The Law of Karma and the Law of Grace

Some Christians deny the law of karma based on certain passages in Paul's epistles which emphasize salvation by faith and grace alone. Such Christians claim good works are no guarantee of salvation though they believe good works are an important part of Christian life. They claim we are not required to perform good works, such as seek forgiveness and pay restitution to those we've transgressed against, because Christ paid for all our transgressions. But Jesus taught differently:

Matthew 5:25-26: "Settle matters quickly with your adversary who is taking you to court. Do it while you are still together on the way, or your adversary may hand you over to the judge, and the judge may hand you over to the officer, and you may be thrown into prison. Truly I tell you, you will not get out until you have paid the last penny."

Matthew 18:34-35: "In anger his master handed him over to the jailers to be tortured, until he should pay back all he owed. This is how my heavenly Father will treat each of you unless you forgive your brother or sister from your heart."

Matthew 10:38 and Luke 14:27: "Whoever does not take up their cross and follow me is not worthy of me."

Matthew 16:24, Mark 8:34, and Luke 9:23: "Whoever wants to be my disciple must deny themselves and take up their cross and follow me."

So while it's true that people are saved by the grace of God, it means God's grace allows us the time and space through reincarnation to follow Jesus, carry our own cross, and pay for our karmic transgressions against others as God has forgiven our transgressions against Him. As Paul stated:

1 Corinthians 6:19-20: "You were bought at a price."

So Christ paid the karmic debt of Adam's transgression as the great burden-bearer of our bad karma against God. But inherent in

God's grace is our obligation to follow Christ, take up our own cross, pay our karmic debts against others, become transformed into his image, and attain at-onement with God. And because of this, we can say along with Paul:

Romans 8:17: "Now if we are children, then we are heirs - heirs of God and co-heirs with Christ, if indeed we share in his sufferings in order that we may also share in his glory."

More arguments will be presented in Part 4 about salvation based upon good works versus salvation based upon faith alone.

I. Summary

God's law of divine justice as the law of karma is mentioned many times throughout the Bible. The biblical teaching of universal salvation implies reincarnation and is also mentioned many times throughout the Bible. Reincarnation, universal salvation, and the law of karma are doctrines which can be found in the Old and New Testaments, the Gospels, the Epistles of Paul, the parables of Jesus, all Hebrew and Christian writings, the Dead Sea Scrolls, the Christian Gnostic gospels, the Torah, the Apocrypha, the Kabbalah and Zohar. The Bible teaches how bad karma can extend into multiple lifetimes; and how overcoming bad karma with good karma ultimately leads to eternal life - the end of reincarnation. The Bible also teaches how God's law of love, grace, and forgiveness overcomes bad karma. Reincarnation is God's plan for people to "work their way up" through the afterlife realms immediately after death, through earning good karma and paying for bad karma on Earth, with the goal of becoming permanent citizens in God's Kingdom. For all these reasons and more, reincarnation must now become a doctrine of Christianity as it was widely believed during the first 500 hundred years of Christian history.

CHAPTER 4:
REINCARNATION IN THE BIBLE (PART 4)

1. God's Demand For Human Perfection Implies Reincarnation

A. The Perfection Process of Sanctification Defined

Sanctification is the perfecting process by the Holy Spirit working together with the soul of the person toward becoming transformed into Christ's image. Paul mentioned sanctification:

2 Thessalonians 2:13: "But we ought always to thank God for you, brothers and sisters loved by the Lord, because God chose you as firstfruits to be saved through the sanctifying work of the Spirit and through belief in the truth."

Jesus called upon people to be perfect:

Matthew 5:48: "Be perfect, therefore, as your heavenly Father is perfect."

It should be self-evident that this perfection process takes much longer than one lifetime to accomplish. All human beings need perfecting; and even Jesus, as a human being, needed perfecting:

Hebrews 2:10: "In bringing many sons and daughters to glory, it was fitting that God, for whom and through whom everything exists, should make the pioneer of their salvation perfect through what he suffered."

Hebrews 5:9: "Once made perfect, he (Jesus) became the source of eternal salvation for all who obey him."

Just how perfect are people supposed to become to attain eternal life? Well, perfect is perfect:

Matthew 5:8: "Blessed are the pure in heart, for they will see God."

1 John 3:9: "No one who is born of God will continue to sin, because God's seed remains in them; they cannot go on sinning, because they have been born of God."

1 Thessalonians 5:23: "May God himself, the God of peace, sanctify you through and through. May your whole spirit, soul and body be kept blameless at the coming of our Lord Jesus Christ."

Notice in the above verse, the Holy Spirit inspired Paul to write about the sanctification process occurring until the Second Coming of Christ which implies reincarnation. The following are more verses about the perfecting sanctification process:

Romans 6:1-2: "What shall we say, then? Shall we go on sinning so that grace may increase? By no means! We are those who have died to sin; how can we live in it any longer?"

James 1:25: "But whoever looks intently into the perfect law that gives freedom, and continues in it - not forgetting what they have heard, but doing it - they will be blessed in what they do."

Hebrews 6:1: "Therefore leaving the principles of the doctrine of Christ, let us go on unto perfection; not laying again the foundation of repentance from dead works, and of faith toward God."

Jesus expected people to do even greater works than he performed:

John 14:12: "Very truly I tell you, whoever believes in me will do the works I have been doing, and they will do even greater things than these, because I am going to the Father."

Becoming perfected is defined in the Bible as becoming like Christ - to be made into his image - in other words, to become without sin; to become one with the Father. By extension, I would include having psychic abilities; being able to perform miracles such as walk on water and raise the dead. I submit to you that for humans to become like Christ is the equivalent to humanity attaining to the next stage of human evolution of which Jesus was the first. Perhaps the Kingdom of Heaven and the Second Coming of Christ will appear on Earth when the world is filled with Christs, Moseses, and Buddhas. Who can say this is not possible? With God all things are possible. Humanity has come a long way since the first century. Christianity has been preached throughout the entire world as Jesus foretold. A tremendous amount of scientific knowledge has been learned. Millions of people have come back from the dead through NDEs to tell us what life after death is like. Psychic phenomena has become common knowledge. Reincarnation studies have provided an abundant amount of evidence. In the 20th century alone, rapid technological change has taken place and it looks like the 21st century will be no different.

B. God Requires People To Become Perfect and Holy

In many instances in the Bible, we are told we must be perfect, holy and sanctified. This is a very high standard and implies a multiple-lifetime process. The following is a list of Bible verses which deal with Christian perfection:

Hebrews 12:14: "Make every effort to live in peace with everyone and to be holy; without holiness no one will see the Lord."

1 Thessalonians 4:3: "It is God's will that you should be sanctified."

James 4:8: "Come near to God and he will come near to you. Wash your hands, you sinners, and purify your hearts, you double-minded."

1 Peter 1:15-16, Leviticus 11:45, Leviticus 19:2, Leviticus 20:26: "But just as he who called you is holy, so be holy in all you do; for it is written: 'Be holy, because I am holy.'"

2 Corinthians 7:1: "Let us purify ourselves from everything that contaminates body and spirit, perfecting holiness out of reverence for God."

Galatians 4:19: "My dear children, for whom I am again in the pains of childbirth until Christ is formed in you."

Hebrews 8:10-13 and Jeremiah 31:33: "For this is the covenant that I will make with the house of Israel after those days, says the Lord: I will put My laws in their mind and write them on their hearts."

Ephesians 4:11-13: "And He Himself gave some to be apostles, some prophets, some evangelists, and some pastors and teachers, for the equipping of the saints for the work of ministry, for the edifying of the body of Christ, till we all come to the unity of the faith and of the knowledge of the Son of God, to a perfect man, to the measure of the stature of the fullness of Christ."

C. The Requirement For Perfection Implies Reincarnation

God's requirement for people to become perfect and holy implies the perfecting process takes more than one lifetime. Even Paul admitted he was not yet perfected in his Epistle to the Philippians:

Philippians 3:10-12: "That I may know Him and the power of His resurrection, and the fellowship of His sufferings, being conformed to His death, if, by any means, I may attain to the resurrection from the dead. Not that I have already attained, or am already perfected; but I press on, that I may lay hold of that for which Christ Jesus has also laid hold of me."

Concerning the great personalities of the Old Testament, such as Abraham, Isaac and Jacob, the Bible gives the reason why they did not remain in heaven (the promise). It was so they could be reincarnated along with everyone else to attain spiritual perfection:

Hebrews 11:39-40: "These were all commended for their faith, yet none of them received what had been promised, since God had planned something better for us so that only together with us would they be made perfect."

Concerning those end times, an angel told the prophet Daniel in a vision in the Book of Daniel:

Daniel 11:35: "Some of the wise will stumble, so that they may be refined, purified and made spotless until the time of the end, for it will still come at the appointed time."

Daniel 12:8-10: I asked, 'My lord, what will the outcome of all this be?' He replied, 'Go your way, Daniel, because the words are rolled up and sealed until the time of the end. Many will be purified, made spotless and refined, but the wicked will continue to be wicked.'"

So what happens when people overcome their bad karma and reincarnation, and become perfected? In the Book of Revelation, Jesus himself said they will never have to leave heaven again implying reincarnation:

Revelation 3:12: "The one who is victorious I will make a pillar in the temple of my God. Never again will they leave it."

The following Bible verses also teach Christian perfection and sanctification:

Philippians 1:6: "Being confident of this, that he who began a good work in you will carry it on to completion until the day of

Christ Jesus."

Notice the above verse is another instance where the Holy Spirit inspired Paul to write about the sanctification process occurring until the Second Coming of Christ which implies reincarnation. Here are more Bible verses teaching Christian perfection and sanctification:

Ephesians 5:1-2: "Follow God's example, therefore, as dearly loved children and walk in the way of love, just as Christ loved us and gave himself up for us as a fragrant offering and sacrifice to God."

2 Corinthians 3:18: "But we all, with unveiled face, beholding as in a mirror the glory of the Lord, are being transformed into the same image from glory to glory, just as by the Spirit of the Lord."

John 13:15: "I (Jesus) have set you an example that you should do as I have done for you."

1 Peter 2:21: "To this you were called, because Christ suffered for you, leaving you an example, that you should follow in his steps."

D. Reincarnation Nullifies the Need for an End Time Corpse Resurrection

A unique point about Jesus' resurrection was it took place very soon after his death without waiting until the end times. And according to Paul, the "resurrection" happens immediately after physical death:

2 Corinthians 5:1-4: "For we know that if the earthly tent we live in is destroyed, we have a building from God, an eternal house in heaven, not built by human hands. Meanwhile we groan, longing to be clothed instead with our heavenly dwelling, because when we are clothed, we will not be found naked. For while we are in this tent, we groan and are burdened, because we do not wish to be unclothed but to be clothed instead with our heavenly dwelling, so that what is mortal may be swallowed up by life."

2 Corinthians 5:8: "We are confident, yes, well pleased rather to be absent from the body and to be present with the Lord."

So it's reasonable to assume the "Resurrection of the Dead" takes place immediately after a person's physical death. As Paul mentioned in 1 Corinthians 15:35-54, the resurrection body is a spirit body - not of flesh - because flesh and blood cannot inherit the Kingdom of God in heaven. And if a worldwide reanimation of corpses at the end times were true, there would be a long period of time of "resting in peace" from the moment of death until Christ's Second Coming. Such a situation would make any personal identity of the soul impossible which makes quite a strong case against a worldwide corpse resurrection at the end times. And this is an important point which the traditional interpretations of the Abrahamic religions seem to have a considerable difficulty in addressing - salvation and personal spiritual growth after death. But the Bible does mention Jesus descending to Hades to preach to the "imprisoned spirits" for their possible salvation after his death, an event previously mentioned as "the Harrowing of Hell":

1 Peter 3:18-20: "For Christ also suffered once for sins, the righteous for the unrighteous, to bring you to God. He was put to death in the body but made alive in the Spirit. After being made alive, he went and made proclamation to the imprisoned spirits - to those who were disobedient long ago when God waited patiently in the days of Noah while the ark was being built.."

But most Christian denominations believe death means the end of spiritual growth and the end of possible salvation for the unsaved. They believe a particular judgment occurs immediately after death and an intermediate state exists as a disembodied foretaste of the final state before the final resurrection. Therefore, according to these traditions, those who die in Christ rest in peace in the "bosom of Abraham" in Hades while they await the final resurrection. Those who die unrepentant will experience torment in Hades while they await the resurrection and final condemnation on Judgment Day. So for thousands of years, Christians have believed that when a person dies their soul rests in peace until the final resurrection of the dead and the Last Judgment. The only exceptions are Purgatory as understood by the Catholic Church and reincarnation as understood by the Christian Gnostics. Only reincarnation offers continued personal identity and further spiritual growth after death. And only reincarnation offers the unsaved more opportunities toward spiritual growth and possible salvation which is consistent with a God of infinite love and mercy. In an effort to justify the love of God, many modern Christian thinkers have adopted reincarnation to their theology such as the Unitarian Universalists.

E. Summary

Universal salvation, Christian perfection and reincarnation are mentioned many times throughout the Bible. The Bible is filled with teachings compelling people to be perfect and become sanctified through the Holy Spirit. Those people who are not perfected must be reincarnated until they are perfected. The Bible mentions Jesus needed to be perfected by suffering on the cross implying he had a human nature subjected to reincarnation. Life is short; and for many people, very short. It is self-evident that the process of sanctification takes more than one lifetime. The goal for every human is to become like Christ - to be transformed into his image. Only reincarnation offers continued personal identity, further spiritual growth, and the opportunity for the unsaved to receive many opportunities for salvation after death. For all these reasons and more, reincarnation must now become a doctrine of Christianity as it was widely believed during the first 500 hundred years of Christian history.

2. God's Judgment According To Works Implies Reincarnation

A. God's Law Has Not Been Nullified and Still Remains in Effect

There are a multitude of Bible verses supporting the Biblical principle that everyone will be judged "according to their works." Here are several:

Matthew 16:27: "For the Son of Man is going to come in his Father's glory with his angels, and then he will reward each person according to what they have done."

Romans 2:13: "For it is not those who hear the law who are righteous in God's sight, but it is those who obey the law who will be declared righteous."

Philippians 2:12: "Therefore, my dear friends, as you have always obeyed - not only in my presence, but now much more in my absence - continue to work out your salvation with fear and trembling."

James 2:14-18: "What good is it, my brothers and sisters, if someone claims to have faith but has no deeds? Can such faith save them? Suppose a brother or a sister is without clothes and daily food. If one of you says to them, "Go in peace; keep warm and well fed," but does nothing about their physical needs, what good is it? In the same way, faith by itself, if it is not accompanied by action, is dead.

But someone will say, "You have faith; I have deeds." Show me your faith without deeds, and I will show you my faith by my deeds."

James 2:26: "As the body without the spirit is dead, so faith without deeds is dead."

Revelation 20:12-13: "And I saw the dead, great and small, standing before the throne, and books were opened. Another book was opened, which is the book of life. The dead were judged according to what they had done as recorded in the books. The sea gave up the dead that were in it, and death and Hades gave up the dead that were in them, and each person was judged according to what they had done."

Every Bible verse about people being judged and "saved according to their works" proves God's law (the Ten Commandments) remains in effect and has not been abrogated. Such verses also support the existence of a perfecting sanctification process involved in God's plan of salvation which implies reincarnation. Such verses assume one lifetime is not enough time for a person to become Christ-like and implies many lifetimes are required to accomplish this. The following Bible verses prove God's law has not been nullified:

Matthew 5:17-18: "Do not think that I have come to abolish the Law or the Prophets; I have not come to abolish them but to fulfill them. For truly I tell you, until heaven and Earth disappear, not the smallest letter, not the least stroke of a pen, will by any means disappear from the Law until everything is accomplished."

Matthew 7:12: "So in everything, do to others what you would have them do to you, for this sums up the Law and the Prophets."

Matthew 22:36-40: "'Teacher, which is the greatest commandment in the Law?' Jesus replied: 'Love the Lord your God with all your heart and with all your soul and with all your mind.' This is the first and greatest commandment. And the second is like it: 'Love your neighbor as yourself.' All the Law and the Prophets hang on these two commandments.'"

B. Everyone Is Judged According To God's Law

The following list of Bible verses prove everyone will be judged according to God's law and that salvation is based upon performing good works of faith which implies a perfecting process exists based upon reincarnation:

James 2:12-13: "Speak and act as those who are going to be judged by the law that gives freedom, because judgment without mercy will be shown to anyone who has not been merciful. Mercy triumphs over judgment."

Romans 2:13: "For it is not those who hear the law who are righteous in God's sight, but it is those who obey the law who will be declared righteous."

Luke 10:25-28: "On one occasion an expert in the law stood up to test Jesus. 'Teacher,' he asked, 'what must I do to inherit eternal life?' 'What is written in the Law?' he replied. 'How do you read it?' He answered, 'Love the Lord your God with all your heart and with all your soul and with all your strength and with all your mind'; and, 'Love your neighbor as yourself.' 'You have answered correctly,' Jesus replied. 'Do this and you will live.'"

One of the problems concerning the apparent debate about whether or not Christians must by live by "good works of faith" according "to the law," or by "faith alone" without "works of the law" is distinguishing which "law" is being referenced. Biblical law in Judaism and Christianity is divided between the following laws (in this order):

(1) The seven laws of Noah which applies to both Jews and Gentiles.

(2) The Ten Commandments given to Moses which applies to both Jews and Gentiles.

(3) The hundreds of commandments in the Torah (mitzvot) given to Moses such as the commandment of circumcision which applies only to Jews.

In the 1st century, Jews believed every Jew must follow the Torah's hundreds of Mosaic laws of mitzvot of which circumcision was of the most important. Jewish Christians in Jerusalem were Jews whose only difference between other Jews was that they believed Jesus was their Messiah. So in Acts 15:1-29, when Paul met with the Jerusalem apostles, there was a conflict concerning whether new Gentile converts should follow all the Torah's Mosaic laws of mitzvot and be circumcised. It was ultimately decided that Paul and the Gentile Christians did not need to follow all the Torah's Mosaic Laws which in Judaism would be heretical. This Jerusalem Council resulted in the "Apostolic Decree" which stated that Gentiles did not need to be circumcised. But it was also agreed that Gentiles should:

(a) Abstain from things offered to idols.
(b) Abstain from eating food with blood in it.
(c) Abstain from eating animals not properly killed.
(d) Abstain from sexual immorality.

Nevertheless, following the Ten Commandments and the Noahide laws remained in effect because there was no debate concerning them. The obligation of both Jews and Gentiles to follow these laws were beyond dispute. In other words, Paul's dispute with the Jews between "following the law" and "faith in Christ" salvation had to do with whether Christians needed to follow the hundreds of Jewish Mosaic laws of mitzvot - not the Ten Commandments. So the apparent historic debate between salvation based upon "good works of faith" by the Ten Commandments, and not salvation based upon "faith alone," can be seen in James position:

James 2:24: "You see then that a man is justified by works, and not by faith only."

And salvation based upon "faith alone" without the "works of the law" - the hundreds of Jewish Mosaic laws of mitzvot - was Paul's position:

Romans 3:28: "For we account a man to be justified by faith, without the works of the law."

So Paul was not referring to "the law" - the Ten Commandments - as many Christians historically have thought. Paul is referring to the Mosaic law of mitzvot which has been abrogated by Christ for Christians. This is why some scholars, according to the "new perspectives on Paul," believe this historic Christian debate between "good works" and "faith alone" salvation may be more of a misunderstanding in interpretation between Paul's actual position. For example, Paul does not claim "the law" - the Ten Commandments - have been abrogated as some Christians have historically claimed. Paul only claimed "the law" - the Mosaic law of mitzvot of the Jews - had been abrogated. And Paul does give some indication that faith in Jesus alone is not enough for salvation:

Galatians 5:6: "For in Christ Jesus neither circumcision nor uncircumcision avails anything, but faith working through love."

So the Christian can rightly claim that neither "good works" alone, nor "faith alone," can save anyone. Rather it is through performing "good works of faith" through Christ and the joint work with the perfection process of sanctification through the Holy Spirit that we are saved. And as Jesus taught in the Bible verses previously mentioned, the Ten Commandments remain in effect and must be followed of which love for God and neighbor are the greatest laws:

Matthew 22:36-40: "'Teacher, which is the greatest commandment in the Law?' Jesus replied: 'Love the Lord your God with all your heart and with all your soul and with all your mind.' This is the first and greatest commandment. And the second is like it: 'Love your neighbor as yourself.' All the Law and the Prophets hang on these two commandments.

C. Everyone Is Judged According To Their Works Both Good and Bad

So the Ten Commandments have always remained in effect, demanding bad karma among people be paid, and people be judged according to their works both good and bad. And a perfecting process exists where people are saved by good works of faith whereby people spiritually evolve into Christ's image through the Holy Spirit in a multiple-lifetime reality of reincarnation. The following is a list of Bible verses from Paul describing how people are judged according to their works both good and bad:

Romans 2:6: "God will repay each person according to what they have done."

2 Corinthians 5:10: "For we must all appear before the judgment seat of Christ, so that each of us may receive what is due us for the things done while in the body, whether good or bad."

Philippians 2:12: "Therefore, my dear friends, as you have always obeyed - not only in my presence, but now much more in my absence - continue to work out your salvation with fear and trembling."

1 Corinthians 3:8: "The one who plants and the one who waters have one purpose, and they will each be rewarded according to their own labor."

1 Corinthians 3:12-15: "If anyone builds on this foundation using gold, silver, costly stones, wood, hay or straw, their work will be shown for what it is, because the Day will bring it to light. It will be revealed with fire, and the fire will test the quality of each person's work. If what has been built survives, the builder will receive a reward. If it is burned up, the builder will suffer loss but yet will be saved - even though only as one escaping through the flames."

Several Church Fathers regarded the above verse in 1 Corinthians 3:12-15 as evidence for the existence of an intermediate state called "Purgatory" where the dross of lighter transgressions will be burnt away, and the soul thus purified will be saved. This, of course, suggests a path of salvation after death. In Judaism, "Gehenna" is a place of purification where, according to Rabbinical Judaism, the maximum amount of time spent there is a year before release.

Jesus mentioned several times of judgment according to works. Here is a list of them:

Matthew 12:36-37: "But I tell you that everyone will have to give account on the day of judgment for every empty word they have spoken. For by your words you will be acquitted, and by your words you will be condemned."

Matthew 16:27: "For the Son of Man is going to come in his Father's glory with his angels, and then he will reward each person according to what they have done."

Revelation 22:12: "Look, I am coming soon! My reward is with me, and I will give to each person according to what they have done."

It is self-evident that if everyone, without exception, is judged according to their works, and a perfecting process in salvation exists, then this is a very high standard for attaining eternal life into God's Kingdom in heaven and this implies the reality of reincarnation. Reincarnation allows everyone, through good works, to "work their way up" through the afterlife realms immediately after death toward attaining eternal life in the highest heaven. The idea that God gives a person only one chance at salvation in one very short life has to be abandoned at this point. Otherwise, if God gives people only one chance to "believe in Christ or be damned for eternity" then this presents many problems. What happens to babies and children too young to understand the gospel? What happens to those who have never been given the chance to hear about Jesus? Are they eternally damned? So, at this point, it is time to abandon the "one chance only" salvation theory to the kindergarten box and learn from the mystery teachings of Jesus as adult Christians.

D. Working For Salvation Where the First are Last and the Last are First

Now let's consider a series of related parables by Jesus concerning working for entry into the Kingdom of Heaven on Earth supporting judgment according to works and reincarnation. The first is the incident with Jesus and the rich young man:

Matthew 19:16-30: "Just then a man came up to Jesus and asked, 'Teacher, what good thing must i do to get eternal life?' 'Why do you ask me about what is good?' Jesus replied. 'There is only One who is good. If you want to enter life, keep the commandments.' 'Which ones?' he inquired. Jesus replied, 'You shall not murder, you shall not commit adultery, you shall not steal, you shall not give false testimony, honor your father and mother, and love your neighbor as yourself.' 'All these i have kept,' the young man said. 'What do I still lack?' Jesus answered, 'If you want to be perfect, go, sell your possessions and give to the poor, and you will have treasure in heaven. Then come, follow me.' When the young man heard this, he went away sad, because he had great wealth. Then Jesus said to his disciples, 'Truly I tell you, it is hard for someone who is rich to enter the kingdom of heaven. Again I tell you, it is easier for a camel to go through the eye of a needle than for someone who is rich to enter the kingdom of God.' When the disciples heard this, they were greatly astonished and asked, 'Who then can be saved?' Jesus looked at them and said, 'With man this is impossible, but with God all things are possible.' Peter answered him, 'We have left everything to follow you! What then will there be for us?' Jesus said to them, 'Truly I tell you, at the renewal of all things, when the Son of Man sits on his glorious throne, you who have followed me will also sit on twelve thrones, judging the twelve tribes of Israel. And everyone who has left houses or brothers or sisters or father or mother or wife or children or fields for my sake will receive a hundred times as much and will inherit eternal life. But many who are first will be last, and many who are last will be first.'"

As previously mentioned in Part 1, the "renewal of all things" in verse 28 of the above verse in Matthew 19:16-30 is a Greek word "palingenesía" which is sometimes translated "regeneration" but is a word the Greeks used when referring to reincarnation. The above passage is also a reference to the "first resurrection" (reincarnation) at the beginning of the thousand year reign of Christ on Earth as described in Revelation 20:4-6. The "first resurrection" is the beginning of the souls of God's people in heaven reincarnating into the established Kingdom of Heaven on Earth. More about this will be described later in Part 6 this article. Jesus mentioned how the "first will be last" and the "last will be first" which is a reference to how the rich people of the world ("the first") will be considered "the last" in God's Kingdom on Earth. The followers of Jesus ("the last" of the world) - those Christians who left everything to follow Jesus - will be considered "the first" in God's Kingdom on Earth. Notice also how the followers of Jesus ("the first") will receive "a hundred times as much" in family during the thousand year Kingdom of Heaven on Earth. This implies karma and reincarnation. People receiving "a hundred times as much" of houses and family on Earth can only happen through reincarnation. Notice also both "the first" and "the last" receive the same reward - entrance into the God's Kingdom on Earth. But the rich man will only be allowed entrance into the Kingdom and not receive the reward of receiving "a hundred times as much" in houses and family because he only kept the Ten Commandments but refused to be perfect by selling his riches and giving it to the poor.

The next reference to "the last will be first" is Jesus' Parable of the Narrow Door where he warned people living in his day how they ("the first" given the opportunity for salvation) would become "the last" and be denied entry into the Kingdom of God on Earth if they practice evil. And "the last" people given the opportunity for salvation (the ancient people of the Hebrew Bible dwelling in Sheol) will be "the first" to enter the Kingdom of God on Earth:

Luke 13:22-30: "Then Jesus went through the towns and villages, teaching as he made his way to Jerusalem. Someone asked him, 'Lord, are only a few people going to be saved?' He said to them, 'Make every effort to enter through the narrow door, because many, I tell you, will try to enter and will not be able to. once the owner of the house gets up and closes the door, you will stand outside knocking and pleading, 'Sir, open the door for us.' But he will answer, 'I don't know you or where you come from.' Then you will say, 'We ate and drank with you, and you taught in our streets.' But he will reply, 'I don't know you or where you come from. Away from me, all you evildoers!' There will be weeping there, and gnashing of teeth, when you see Abraham, Isaac and Jacob and all the prophets in the kingdom of God, but you yourselves thrown out. People will come from east and west and north and south, and will take their places at the feast in the kingdom of God. Indeed there are those who are last who will be first, and first who will be last.'"

Matthew 20:1-16: "'For the kingdom of heaven is like a landowner who went out early in the morning to hire workers for his vineyard. He agreed to pay them a denarius for the day and sent them into his vineyard. About nine in the morning he went out and saw others standing in the marketplace doing nothing. He told them, 'You also go and work in my vineyard, and I will pay you whatever is right.' So they went. He went out again about noon and about three in the afternoon and did the same thing. About five in the afternoon he went out and found still others standing around. He asked them, 'Why have you been standing here all day long doing nothing?' 'Because no one has hired us,' they answered. He said to them, 'You also go and work in my vineyard.' When evening came, the owner of the vineyard said to his foreman, 'Call the workers and pay them their wages, beginning with the last ones hired and going on to the first.' The workers who were hired about five in the afternoon came and each received a denarius. So when those came who were hired first, they expected to receive more. But each one of them also received a denarius. When they received it, they began to grumble against the landowner. 'These who were hired last worked only one hour,' they said, 'and you have made them equal to us who have borne the burden of the work and the heat of the day.' But he answered one of them, 'I am not being unfair to you, friend. Didn't you agree to work for a denarius? Take your pay and go. I want to give the one who was hired last the same as I gave you. Don't I have the right to do what I want with my own money? Or are you envious because I am generous?' So the last will be first, and the first will be last."

In the above parable, Jesus teaches it's not important how long a person has been working for the Kingdom of Heaven on Earth regarding the wage for working for it. The wage is the same for all workers which is membership into the Kingdom. As long as the invitation to work is accepted before the time the Kingdom of

Heaven arrives, and the work is completed, everyone is paid the same wage. What is important is that people work meritoriously for their wage until the Kingdom does arrive. And we must be constantly at work and be ready because no one knows when their "day of reckoning" will come or when the Kingdom does arrive. When a person's "last day" on Earth occurs, they die and "resurrect" into the afterlife, and its "judgment day." What is important is their level of spiritual growth when it is time for the Kingdom to arrive on Earth and whether or not the person has attained the spiritual maturity and purity to receive more rewards for their work.

The following verse in the Book of Revelation describes the time immediately before the Second Coming of Christ and the establishment of the thousand year Kingdom of Heaven on Earth:

Revelations 7:13-14: "Then one of the elders asked me, 'These in white robes - who are they, and where did they come from?' I answered, 'Sir, you know.' And he said, 'These are they who have come out of the great tribulation; they have washed their robes and made them white in the blood of the Lamb.'"

Notice how the above verse clearly states the people of the Kingdom had washed their own robes and made them white. They themselves did the washing; the Lamb did not, although they certainly had his help. This verse supports the idea of working out our own salvation, taking up our own cross and following Jesus for our salvation and this implies reincarnation. We cannot sit back, rely only upon the cross of Christ, and assume he will do all the work for us. The Creator has placed in creation the mechanism for salvation and provided us the knowledge of how we may work toward our own salvation and given requisite strength to those who are willing to work for it. This knowledge of salvation (or "gnosis") came to the world at very great cost including the suffering and crucifixion of Jesus.

E. The Near-Death "Life Review" as Judgment Day

The "life review" undergone by those who have had a near-death experience (NDE) strongly resembles God's judgment "according to works" as mentioned in the Bible. The NDE life review and the biblical judgment "according to works" supports the idea that life is a "test" for which we are "graded" immediately after death for the purpose of determining our level of soul growth and the corresponding afterlife level or realm earned. As previously mentioned, people are reincarnated into an Earth life according to God's plan for souls, through good works, to "work their way up" through the afterlife realms immediately after death with the goal of attaining eternal life in God's Kingdom in heaven.

The following is how Bruce Horacek, Ph.D., and the International Association of Near-Death Studies (IANDS) describe the life review in his article entitled "Impact of the Near-Death Experience on Grief and Loss."

Bruce Horacek: "During a predominantly pleasurable NDE, usually while in the light, the neaqr-death experiencer (NDEr) may experience a life review. In this review, the NDEr typically re-views (sees again) and re-experiences every moment of his/her life. At the same time, the NDEr fully experiences being every other person with whom the NDEr interacted. The NDEr knows what it was to be on the receiving end of his/her own actions including those causing other people harm. At this time, the NDEr usually reports feeling profound remorse, along with extreme regret of harm not being able to be undone. At the same time, the NDEr typically reports feelings consistent with unconditional love from the light, which communicates forgiveness because the NDEr was still learning how to become a more loving person. NDErs tend to say 'learning how to love' is the purpose of life.

The revealing of a person's every moment of their life during their life review is supported by Jesus' words in the Bible:

Luke 12:2-3: "There is nothing concealed that will not be disclosed, or hidden that will not be made known. What you have said in the dark will be heard in the daylight, and what you have whispered in the ear in the inner rooms will be proclaimed from the roofs."

The following are a few NDE examples of the "judgment" aspect of the life review:

Dannion Brinkley: "You literally re-live it. Next you watch your life from a second person's point of view. In this life we're taught to be sympathetic toward others. But from the second person's point of view, you'll feel empathy, not sympathy. After that, you literally will become every person that you've ever encountered. You will feel what it feels like to be that person and you will feel the direct results of your interaction between you and that person. You know the story of the Book of Judgment? Guess what? When you have your panoramic life review, you are the judger ... You do the judging. If you doubt me, believe this: you are the toughest judge you will ever have."

P.M.H. Atwater: "And into this great peace that I had become there came the life of Phyllis parading past my view. Not as in a movie theatre, but rather as a reliving. Had it been a reliving of just deeds done, it would have been as expected because I had heard of that before. But for me it was far more involved. The reliving included not only the deeds committed by Phyllis since her birth in 1937 in Twin Falls, Idaho, but also a reliving of every thought ever thought and every word ever spoken PLUS the effect of every thought, word and deed upon everyone and anyone who had ever come within her sphere of influence whether she actually knew them or not PLUS the effect of her every thought, word and deed upon the weather, the air, the soil, plants and animals, the waters, everything else within the creation we call Earth and the space Phyllis once occupied. It was a gestalt experience, meaning complete and whole on all levels, a total viewing and reliving of the totality of one woman's life complete with all the ripples and consequences of her ever having lived. I had no idea a past-life review could be like this. I never before realized that we were responsible and accountable for EVERY SINGLE THING WE DID. That was overwhelming. It was me judging me, not some heavenly St. Peter. And my judgment was critical and stern. I was not satisfied with many, many things Phyllis had done, said or thought. There was a feeling of sadness and failure, yet a growing feeling of joy when the realization came that Phyllis had always done SOMETHING. She did many things unworthy and negative, but she did something. She tried. Much of what she did was constructive and positive. She learned and grew in her learning. This was satisfying. Phyllis was okay."

Laurelynn Martin: During her life review, Laurelynn Martin relived an event when she was five years old and teased another girl to the point of tears. Laurelynn then felt exactly what the other girl was feeling. Laurelynn realized how the girl needed love, nurturing and forgiveness. Laurelynn then felt a love for this child that was so deep and tender, it was like the love between a mother and child. She realized that by hurting another person, she was only hurting herself.

109

It was an experience oneness with everyone.

Some NDErs are shown - not only a review of their life just lived - but a review of many of their past lives as well:

Christian Andreason: "I saw four translucent screens appear (and form a kind of gigantic box around me). It was through this method that I was shown my life review. (Or rather I should say my LIVES IN REVIEW!) Without ever having to turn my head, I saw my past, my present, my future and there was even a screen that displayed a tremendous amount of scientific data, numbers and universal codes. I saw the beginning of my known existence as a Soul and saw that I had existed Spiritually long before this incarnation - where I am now a male human known as Christian Andreason! In Heaven, I undeniably saw that I had lived an innumerable amount of lives. Yet, what I saw went way beyond our comprehension of what we think reincarnation is. So, I am not exactly speaking of being born again and again on this planet alone. I saw that it is a big Universe out there and God has it all organized perfectly. Each of us is sent where we can obtain the best growth according to our Divine purpose."

Two of Dr. Kenneth Ring's NDE study subjects mentioned learning of his past lives, one of them during his life review: "My whole life went before me of things I have done and haven't done, but not just of this one lifetime, but of all the lifetimes. I know for a fact there is reincarnation. This is an absolute. I was shown all those lives and how I had overcome some of the things I had done in other lives. There was still some things to be corrected."

Another NDEr whose testimony is included in Ring's audiotape archives gave this account:

"I had a lot of questions, and I wanted to know what they [the light beings she encountered in her NDE] were doing - why are you just kind of milling around here? And someone stepped forward ... it wasn't just one ... I got information from a number of them ... that they were all waiting for reincarnation." (Amber Wells, Reincarnation Belief Among Near-Death Experiencers, JNDS Vol. 12, No. 1, Fall 1993.)

According to NDE testimonies from the life review, "God's judgment" after death is really self-judgment at which time we enter the light of God where all is made known. Having your true inner self revealed in the light can be "hell" for those who have been motivated mostly by negative forces and bad karma in life. Having your true inner self revealed can be "heaven" for those who have been motivated mostly by positive forces and good karma in life. Everyone's true inner nature, their spirit, is a part of God - a "spark of the divine." Everyone who enters the afterlife after death begins to realize their true inner nature. Those who lived a life against their inner self will find difficulties when entering into the light. This is the self-realization and self-judgment as revealed by Jesus:

John 3:19-21: "This is the verdict: Light has come into the world, but men loved darkness instead of light because their deeds were evil. Everyone who does evil hates the light, and will not come into the light for fear that his deeds will be exposed. But whoever lives by the truth comes into the light, so that it may be seen plainly that what he has done has been done through God."

F. Salvation Is Not By Faith Alone

Contrary to what many Christians believe today, people do not attain eternal life by merely giving verbal and/or mental assent to the idea of "Jesus is Lord" or "Jesus is God" or "Jesus is Savior." And because salvation is through "good works of faith" toward perfection and sanctification into Christ's image, this implies the salvation process takes more than a single lifetime and implies reincarnation. The following Bible verses support this:

1 John 2:6: "Whoever claims to live in him must live as Jesus did."

Matthew 7:21-23: "Not everyone who says to me, 'Lord, Lord,' will enter the kingdom of heaven, but only the one who does the will of my Father who is in heaven. Many will say to me on that day, 'Lord, Lord, did we not prophesy in your name and in your name drive out demons and in your name perform many miracles?' Then I will tell them plainly, 'I never knew you. Away from me, you evildoers!'"

The brother of Jesus, James the Just, knew Jesus perhaps better than anyone else. James had this to say about "faith only" salvation versus "good works" salvation:

"What good is it, my brothers and sisters, if someone claims to have faith but has no deeds? Can such faith save them? Suppose a brother or a sister is without clothes and daily food. If one of you says to them, 'Go in peace; keep warm and well fed,' but does nothing about their physical needs, what good is it? In the same way, faith by itself, if it is not accompanied by action, is dead.

James 2:14-26: "But someone will say, 'You have faith; I have deeds.' Show me your faith without deeds, and I will show you my faith by my deeds. You believe that there is one God. Good! Even the demons believe that - and shudder. You foolish person, do you want evidence that faith without deeds is useless? Was not our father Abraham considered righteous for what he did when he offered his son Isaac on the altar? You see that his faith and his actions were working together, and his faith was made complete by what he did. And the scripture was fulfilled that says, 'Abraham believed God, and it was credited to him as righteousness,' and he was called God's friend. You see that a person is considered righteous by what they do and not by faith alone. In the same way, was not even Rahab the prostitute considered righteous for what she did when she gave lodging to the spies and sent them off in a different direction? As the body without the spirit is dead, so faith without deeds is dead."

There are many other Bible verses proving salvation is by performing good works of faith and not by faith alone. Salvation by performing good works implies a perfecting process involving reincarnation. Here are some Bible verses supporting this:

Proverbs 21:3: "To do what is right and just is more acceptable to the Lord than sacrifice."

1 Corinthians 7:19: "Circumcision is nothing and uncircumcision is nothing. Keeping God's commands is what counts."

1 Corinthians 13:2-3: "If I have the gift of prophecy and can fathom all mysteries and all knowledge, and if I have a faith that can move mountains, but do not have love, I am nothing. If I give all I possess to the poor and give over my body to hardship that I may boast, but do not have love, I gain nothing."

Philippians 2:12-13: "Continue to work out your salvation with fear and trembling, for it is God who works in you to will and to act in order to fulfill his good purpose."

1 John 2:3-6: "We know that we have come to know him if we keep his commands. Whoever says, 'I know him,' but does not do what he commands is a liar, and the truth is not in that person. But if anyone obeys his word, love for God is truly made complete in them. This is how we know we are in him: Whoever claims to live in him must live as Jesus did."

Revelation 20:13: "Each person was judged according to what

they had done."

Titus 2:11-12: "For the grace of God has appeared that offers salvation to all people. It teaches us to say 'No' to ungodliness and worldly passions, and to live self-controlled, upright and godly lives in this present age."

G. Salvation Begins By Working To No Longer Practice Sin

To be acceptable to God, one must be more righteous than the Pharisees, fear God, do what is right, stop practicing sin, and forgive others. To attain such a life - a life of sinlessness - is obviously not an easy achievement. Considering how too often life is so short for many people, it is also obvious how such an achievement is much more than a single lifetime process:

Matthew 5:20: "For I tell you that unless your righteousness surpasses that of the Pharisees and the teachers of the law, you will certainly not enter the kingdom of heaven."

Hebrews 10:26-31: "If we deliberately keep on sinning after we have received the knowledge of the truth, no sacrifice for sins is left, but only a fearful expectation of judgment and of raging fire that will consume the enemies of God. Anyone who rejected the law of Moses died without mercy on the testimony of two or three witnesses. How much more severely do you think someone deserves to be punished who has trampled the Son of God underfoot, who has treated as an unholy thing the blood of the covenant that sanctified them, and who has insulted the Spirit of grace? For we know him who said, 'It is mine to avenge; I will repay,' and again, 'The Lord will judge his people.' It is a dreadful thing to fall into the hands of the living God."

Acts 10:34-35: "Then Peter began to speak: 'I now realize how true it is that God does not show favoritism but accepts from every nation the one who fears him and does what is right."

Matthew 6:14-15: "For if you forgive other people when they sin against you, your heavenly Father will also forgive you. But if you do not forgive others their sins, your Father will not forgive your sins."

H. Summary

God's law of divine justice, karma, universal salvation, preexistence, Christian perfection, a "correcting judgment" process and reincarnation are mentioned many times throughout the Bible. People who are not perfected must be reincarnated until they become perfected. The Bible mentions that Jesus needed to be perfected by suffering on the cross implying he had a human nature subjected to reincarnation. The process of sanctification obviously takes more than one lifetime because the goal for everyone is to become like Christ - the perfect image of God within man. Only reincarnation offers continued personal identity and further spiritual growth after death. People are judged according to God's law based upon their good and bad works. People who have not overcome their bad works must reincarnate until they do. The Bible repeatedly states that God's law (the Ten Commandments) has never been abrogated and Jesus affirmed this fact. Paul apparently dismissed "the law"; but careful scholarship shows Paul rejecting the Jewish Mosaic law of mitzvot, which Jesus himself did, and not the Ten Commandments. There are abundant Bible verses teaching salvation by soul growth through performing "good works of faith" according to God's law - especially in the teachings of Jesus - and perfecting through the Holy Spirit. Salvation begins with repentance and the continual non-practice of sin. Those sinners who refuse to do so will not attain eternal life and will instead continue the cycle of reincarnation until they do. Everyone is working toward the goal of permanent citizenship in God's highest heaven - eternal life - whether they are aware of it or not; and the method is through reincarnation. Jesus has shown us the way - the pattern to follow. Jesus is the way-shower. We must take up our own crosses and follow his example if we want to attain the highest heaven. The NDE life review experienced by millions of people proves how people are judged by their deeds after death and that past lives are also reviewed after death. For all these reasons and more, reincarnation must now become a doctrine of Christianity as it was widely believed during the first hundred years of Christian history.

CHAPTER 5:
REINCARNATION IN THE BIBLE (PART 5)

1. Preexistence of the Soul and Election Implies Reincarnation

A. Preexistence of the Soul In Biblical Times

As previously mentioned, preexistence is the doctrine of the soul/spirit not being created at birth; but rather having existed before birth in heaven and/or in past lives on Earth. All Bible verses referring to reincarnation assumes the reality of the preexistence of the soul. All Bible verses referring to preexistence of the soul implies the reality of reincarnation. Both concepts of reincarnation and preexistence are inseparable and both concepts were common knowledge in Jesus' day. The preexistence of the soul was an accepted teaching held by early Christians until it was officially condemned by the Church in 553 A.D. along with reincarnation and other teachings associated with the early Church Father Origen. But although the Church did its best to destroy all Christian writings and gospels mentioning preexistence and reincarnation, the Church could not destroy the references already in the Bible.

Skeptics who assume preexistence and reincarnation are false doctrines must explain why there is such an incredible amount of inequities and apparent injustices in life. All over the world we see how some people are born into families with many resources, with excellent health, provided the best education, live in large estates, and many other favorable conditions. While, on the other hand, an even larger percentage of people on Earth are born in extreme poverty, with severe handicaps, uneducated, destitute, or many other unfavorable conditions. Without preexistence and reincarnation this inequity and apparent injustice between people might make a person conclude God to be extremely unjust. In fact, this is one of the main arguments skeptics use against the existence of God. So without preexistence and reincarnation how are we to explain this? This very question was asked of Jesus by his disciples in the following Bible verse:

"As he went along, he saw a man blind from birth. His disciples asked him, 'Rabbi, who sinned, this man or his parents, that he was born blind?' 'Neither this man nor his parents sinned,' said Jesus, 'but this happened so that the works of God might be displayed in him.'" (John 9:1-3)

The disciples asked Jesus if the man committed a sin causing him to be born blind. Given the fact the man was blind since birth, this is an unusual question to ask unless they believed in preexistence and reincarnation. How can a man sin before he is even born? An obvious answer to such a reincarnation question is he committed a sin in a past life causing his current blind condition. And although Jesus stated the reason the man was born blind was to manifest the works of God, and not because of sin, this does not mean everyone who is born in unfavorable circumstances are born this way to manifest the work of God. The fact that this blind man and his circumstances are described in the Bible may be exactly what Jesus was referring to concerning him manifesting the works of God. When the blind man was brought before the Pharisees, they rejected his testimony because they believed he sinned before he was even born:

"They answered and said to him, 'You were completely born in sins, and are you teaching us?' And they cast him out" (John 9:34)

Notice how Jesus did nothing to dispel or correct the idea of the disciples believing in the possibility of sinning before birth or believing in reincarnation. If reincarnation is a false doctrine, this would have been an excellent opportunity for Jesus to say so. But the fact is, nowhere in the Bible does Jesus teach against reincarnation. He does, in fact, teach reincarnation throughout the Bible. And because of this, we can assume Jesus believed preexistence was certainly a possibility as well.

The idea of a person sinning before birth can also be found in the Old Testament:

Psalm 51:5: "Surely I was sinful at birth, sinful from the time my mother conceived me."

Unless preexistence and reincarnation are true, the above Bible verse is nonsense.

B. The Preexistent Jesus

The Bible affirms the preexistence of Jesus. Here are some examples:

John 1:1-2: "In the beginning was the Word, and the Word was with God, and the Word was God. He was with God in the beginning."

John 3:13: "No one has ever gone into heaven except the one who came from heaven - the Son of Man."

John 8:23: "I am not of this world."

John 8:56-58: "'Your father Abraham rejoiced at the thought of seeing my day; he saw it and was glad.' 'You are not yet fifty years old,' they said to him, 'and you have seen Abraham!' 'Very truly I tell you,' Jesus answered, 'before Abraham was born, I am!'"

John 16:28: "I came from the Father and entered the world; now I am leaving the world and going back to the Father."

John 17:5: "And now, Father, glorify me in your presence with the glory I had with you before the world began."

1 John 4:2-3: "This is how you can recognize the Spirit of God: Every spirit that acknowledges that Jesus Christ has come in the flesh is from God, but every spirit that does not acknowledge Jesus is not from God. This is the spirit of the antichrist, which you have heard is coming and even now is already in the world."

Micah 5:2: "But you, Bethlehem Ephrathah, though you are small among the clans of Judah, out of you will come for me one who will be ruler over Israel, whose origins are from of old, from ancient times."

1 Peter 1:20: "He was chosen before the creation of the world, but was revealed in these last times for your sake."

C. The Preexistent Human Being

Jesus referred to the people around him to be the same people who were alive in the days of Moses:

John 6:30-32: "So they asked him, 'What sign then will you give that we may see it and believe you? What will you do? Our ancestors ate the manna in the wilderness; as it is written: 'He gave them bread from heaven to eat.' Jesus said to them, 'Very truly I tell you, it is not Moses who has given you the bread from heaven, but it is my Father who gives you the true bread from heaven.'"

Consider the following Bible verse which suggests human preexistence:

Ephesians 1:4: "For he chose us in him before the creation of the world to be holy and blameless in his sight."

The above verse declares how God chose people before the world was created to be holy implying they existed before Creation. A skeptic may object to this interpretation by claiming the chosen people existed only as a thought in the Mind of God. But even if we assume this was true, it would not negate preexistence. After all, there may be no difference between existing as a thought in the Mind of God and existing as a spirit. And because Jesus himself had a human nature and spirit, it is not a leap of faith to believe other human beings preexisted as Jesus did. In fact, this is exactly what the Bible says:

Ecclesiastes 12:7: "The dust returns to the ground it came from, and the spirit returns to God who gave it."

John 17:14-16: "I (Jesus) have given them your word and the world has hated them, for they are not of the world any more than I am of the world. My prayer is not that you take them out of the world but that you protect them from the evil one. They are not of the world, even as I am not of it."

These words of Jesus are astonishing when you think of them. Jesus revealed that his disciples were "not of the world" any more than he was of the world. So if the disciples preexisted, we can assume other people preexisted as well. And preexistence implies reincarnation. They go together.

The Book of Genesis implies all human beings preexisted:

Genesis 2:7: "And the Lord God formed man of the dust of the ground, and breathed into his nostrils the breath of life; and man became a living soul."

Although we must assume the creation account of Genesis to be a metaphor for evolution, it doesn't say man "became a soul" - it says man "became a LIVING soul" resulting from God's breath of life. This implies Adam preexisted as a soul, without a body, before becoming a living human being. Verses in the Book of Ecclesiastes agree with Genesis in suggesting the soul is preexistent:

Ecclesiastes 6:10: "Whatever man is, he has been named that long ago, and it is known that it is Adam; nor can he contend with Him who is mightier than he whether God or death."

Ecclesiastes 1:9: "What has been will be again, what has been done will be done again; there is nothing new under the sun."

As previously mentioned, we have the case of Jacob and Esau, who, before they were even born, God assigned them their karmic lots in life:

Romans 9:10-13: "Not only that, but Rebekah's children were conceived at the same time by our father Isaac. Yet, before the twins were born or had done anything good or bad - in order that God's purpose in election might stand: not by works but by him who calls - she was told, 'The older will serve the younger.' Just as it is written: 'Jacob I loved, but Esau I hated.'"

Of course, as a Pharisee, Paul could have explained this apparent divine injustice according to bad karma from a previous lifetime. Instead, he leaves it at the feet of God:

Romans 9:21: "Does not the potter have power over the clay, from the same lump to make one vessel for honor and another for dishonor?"

But Paul also states in his Second Epistle to Timothy of people making themselves into vessels of honor prepared for good work:

2 Timothy 2:20-21: "But in a great house there are not only vessels of gold and silver, but also of wood and clay, some for honor and some for dishonor. Therefore if anyone cleanses himself from the latter, he will be a vessel for honor, sanctified and useful for the Master, prepared for every good work."

In the Book of Jeremiah, God told the following to the prophet Jeremiah:

Jeremiah 1:5: "Before I formed you in the womb I knew you, before you were born I set you apart; I appointed you as a prophet to the nations."

If God foreknew the prophet Jeremiah, it is no leap of faith to assume God foreknew everyone else. And foreknowledge by God has further implications including preexistence and reincarnation. Also, in Part 1 of this article, Jesus taught John the Baptist preexisted as Elijah the Prophet. And because James (the brother of Jesus) declared Elijah to be "a human being, even as we are," (James 5:17) we can safely conclude all human beings preexisted as Elijah did.

D. Foreknowledge By God Implies Preexistence of the Soul

As was the case with Jacob and Esau, the Bible states that people have been predestined, elected, foreknown, called, and chosen by God before the beginning of time. As applied to reincarnation and universal salvation, predestination means that God has ultimately chosen everyone for salvation according to His own timetable. In fact, Paul states in his Epistle to the Ephesians that everything - and by extension - everyone has been predestined by God:

Ephesians 1:11: "In him we were also chosen, having been predestined according to the plan of him who works out everything in conformity with the purpose of his will."

The following list of Bible verses are proof of the predestination and preexistence of the soul implying the reality of reincarnation:

Titus 1:1-2: "Paul, a servant of God and an apostle of Jesus Christ to further the faith of God's elect and their knowledge of the truth that leads to godliness - in the hope of eternal life, which God, who does not lie, promised before the beginning of time."

Ephesians 1:4: "For he chose us in him before the creation of the world to be holy and blameless in his sight."

Isaiah 49:1: "Before I was born the Lord called me; from my mother's womb he has spoken my name."

Galatians 1:15-16: "But when God, who set me apart from my mother's womb and called me by his grace, was pleased to reveal his Son in me so that I might preach him among the Gentiles."

1 Peter 1:1-2: To God's elect... who have been chosen according to the foreknowledge of God the Father, through the sanctifying work of the Spirit, to be obedient to Jesus Christ and sprinkled with his blood: Grace and peace be yours in abundance."

2 Timothy 2:10: "Therefore I endure everything for the sake of the elect, that they too may obtain the salvation that is in Christ Jesus, with eternal glory."

2 Peter 1:10: "Therefore, my brothers and sisters, make every

effort to confirm your calling and election. For if you do these things, you will never stumble."

James 2:5: "Listen, my dear brothers and sisters: Has not God chosen those who are poor in the eyes of the world to be rich in faith and to inherit the kingdom he promised those who love him?"

1 Corinthians 1:27-28: "But God chose the foolish things of the world to shame the wise; God chose the weak things of the world to shame the strong. God chose the lowly things of this world and the despised things - and the things that are not - to nullify the things that are."

1 Peter 2:9: "But you are a chosen people, a royal priesthood, a holy nation, God's special possession, that you may declare the praises of him who called you out of darkness into his wonderful light."

Revelation 17:14: "They will wage war against the Lamb, but the Lamb will triumph over them because he is Lord of lords and King of kings - and with him will be his called, chosen and faithful followers."

Romans 8:33: "Who will bring any charge against those whom God has chosen? It is God who justifies."

E. The Church's Condemnations of Preexistence and Reincarnation

The history of the Church's official stance on preexistence and reincarnation is actually a very complex one. The Second Council of Constantinople (553 AD) was initiated and headed by Emperor Justinian (527-565 AD) at a time when the Emperor was engaged in a bitter conflict with Pope Vigilius (died 555 AD). Although the main objective was to reconcile differences between the churches of the East and West, the Council's preparations heavily favored the East. For this reason, Justinian ordered the Council to consider the condemnation of the teachings of Origen (185-254 AD) which was not an item on the previously announced agenda. In the process, fifteen condemnations (anathemas) proposed by the Emperor against Origen were ratified.

The first of the "Anathemas Against Origen" states: "If anyone asserts the fabulous preexistence of souls, and shall assert the monstrous restoration which follows from it: let him be anathema." (Decree of the Fifth Ecumenical Council in A.D. 545, officially ratified in 553 AD at Second Council of Constantinople)

The heretical condemnations against Origen's teachings were not the only unbiblical and unjust condemnations by the Church. Of note were also the unbiblical and unjust heretical condemnations against Arius (256-336 AD) and his teachings; and Nestorius (386-450 AD) and his teachings:

The fifteenth anathema stated in part: "If anyone does not anathematize Arius, Eunomius, Macedonius, Apollinaris, Nestorius, Eutyches, and Origen as well as their impious writings ... let him be anathema." (Decree of the Second Council of Constantinople in 553 AD)

Arius was a priest in in Alexandria, Egypt, whose teachings about the nature of the Godhead in Christianity emphasized the Father's divinity over the Son, and his opposition to what would become the dominant Christology: "Jesus as God in the flesh." This made Arius' teachings a heresy, the Arian Controversy, at the First Council of Nicaea convened by Emperor Constantine in 325 AD. The other notable "heretic" was Nestorius who was the Patriarch of Constantinople whose Christological teachings (Nestorianism) emphasized a distinction between the human and divine persons of Jesus. Nestorianism led to the Nestorian Schism when churches supporting Nestorius broke with the rest of the Christian Church from 431-544 AD.

The condemnation of Origen's teachings in 553 AD led to the rejection of preexistence and reincarnation by the entire Church. Of the 165 bishops who signed the condemnations against Origen, not more than six could have been from the West. Pope Vigilius' appeal for equal representation of bishops from East and West were denied. In protest, the Pope boycotted the Council. So there are no records documenting Pope Vigilius approval of the condemnations issued by Eastern bishops. For this reason scholars today question the Council's legitimacy and separate the Roman Church from the condemnations of the teachings of Origen. Therefore, they argue the Roman Catholic Church has never really declared the teaching of reincarnation to be heresy. Nevertheless, at Justinian's instigation the Council's condemnation of Origen's teaching resulted in Origenist monks being expelled and much of Origen's writings destroyed. The Council's action was accepted in practice by the Church making reincarnation incompatible with Christianity and the Christian "heretics" who believed in reincarnation persecuted and killed. But today we have the freedom to reexamine Christian theology and discover how Origen's teachings were more in synch with the teachings of Christ than the later teachings of the later orthodox Church Fathers.

Origen was acknowledged to be the most educated and most original thinker of the early Christian Fathers. In his book, entitled "On First Principles," Origen explained how souls are assigned to their "place or region or condition" based upon their actions "before the present life." God has:

Origen: "...arranged the universe on the principle of a most impartial retribution." (Origen, On First Principles, trans. Butterworth,, pp. 136-137)

Origen wrote how God did not create on the basis of favoritism but gave souls bodies "according to the sin of each." Origen asked:

Origen: "If souls did not preexist, why is it that we find some blind from birth, having done no sin, while others are born having nothing wrong with them?" (Origen, On First Principles, trans. Butterworth)

Answering his own question, Origen wrote: "It is clear that certain sins existed (were committed) before the souls came into the bodies and as a result of these sins each soul receives recompense in proportion to its deserts." (Origen, On First Principles, trans. Butterworth, p. 67)

In other words, people's current conditions are based upon their past actions in past lives.

F. More on Origen's Teaching of Preexistence and Reincarnation

Reincarnation is closely linked with two of Origen's favorite themes: God is just, and human beings have free will. God's justice can be defended, Origen argued, only if each person:

Origen: "...contains within himself the reasons why he has been placed in this or in that rank of life." (Origen, On First Principles, trans. Butterworth, p. 241)

Therefore, we can believe God is just only if we believe our actions in some previous existence are the cause of our present fate. If we are unfortunate, we can either blame God or see our misfortune as the result of our own past actions - and then do something to change it. The idea of people being responsible for their destiny leads directly to the other key concept in Origen's thought - free will. It was for this idea, as much as any other, the reason his writings came under fire by the Church. The concept of free will made the orthodox uncomfortable because it implied Christians could fall away. It also implied a prostitute could rise to the level of the angels without help from the Catholic priesthood.

Origen believed God created the world as a place for human beings to exercise free will. Along with reincarnation and God's help, the soul is responsible for attaining salvation. God provides the repeated opportunity, lifetime after lifetime, for the soul to "work out" its own salvation (Philippians 2:12). Origen believed free will is implied throughout scripture and free will implies reincarnation. He saw every Bible verse affirming moral responsibility and also affirming free will. And because God has given us this freedom, we advance or decline our soul's status based upon our own merits. And because this is true; and we are destined to return to God, then logically, God must give us more than one chance or lifetime to do it. For Origen, freedom equals opportunity. If there is only one opportunity and lifetime - and it is often cut short - then there is no freedom. And Origen believed freedom to be an important part of God's plan. After all, Paul wrote:

2 Corinthians 3:17: "Where the Spirit of the Lord is, there is freedom."

Origen's interpretation of the Fall of man in the Garden of Eden also implies both free will and reincarnation. He taught how the story of the Fall represents the experience of every soul. Each of us once existed in a primordial state of divine union as an angel in heaven. Then came the Fall of souls from heaven, after which our souls were imprisoned in matter, bound to return to Earth again and again, each time acting and experiencing the corresponding reaction. Therefore, the differences in our circumstances are not based upon God's whim but upon our own actions. God's creation was equal and just in the beginning. Interesting enough, this was the exact interpretation of human origins according to the 20th century near-death experiencer and Christian psychic Edgar Cayce. Origen wrote of God creating:

Origen: "...all those whom he did create equal and alike." (Origen, On First Principles, trans. Butterworth)

In other words, God gave all of us the same opportunities and potential; but it is our own actions which causes our differences.

G. Summary

The Bible describes human beings preexisting as souls before the world began and having previous lifetimes. The preexistence of Jesus and human beings means souls are not created at the time of conception. The Bible also mentions preexisting sin implying preexistence, previous lifetimes, and reincarnation. God's foreknowledge, election of all people before birth, and universal salvation also implies preexistence and reincarnation. The Church's 6th century condemnation of the 2nd century Church Father Origen's teachings of preexistence and reincarnation were not officially sanctioned by the Pope at the time. This means the Church has not technically condemned preexistence or reincarnation. For all these reasons and more, preexistence and reincarnation must now become an official doctrine of Christianity.

2. The Mystery of God In Man Implies Reincarnation

A. Introduction to the Mystery of God in Man and Reincarnation

In this section, a biblical case will be made supporting the nature of the eternal, immortal, and indestructible human soul or spirit. Jesus taught "the Kingdom of God is within you" (Luke 17:20-21). You will see that because all humans partake in the divine spirit as Jesus did, the idea of reincarnation becomes a necessity. It is the spirit - the "spark" of the divine - within human beings that is reincarnated. Because the human spirit is a part of God, it cannot be destroyed nor can it suffer eternally in hell. It is the flesh which must be overcome, and through reincarnation this becomes possible. As co-heirs with Christ, humans can attain at-onement with God as Jesus did. It is self-evident that attaining perfection and at-onement with God requires more than one lifetime and this implies the necessity of reincarnation.

B. The Mystery of God in Jesus

Central to Christology in Christianity is the divine nature of Jesus

Christ. As previously mentioned, beginning in the fourth century AD, the Arian Controversy occurred within the Church specifically over the nature of Christ and his relationship to God the Father. The following is a list of the various Christian groups based upon the different beliefs of Christology:

Early Christian Christology

(1) The "Homoousian" group believed the Son was of the "same substance" as the Father (i.e. both uncreated). This form of Christology, "Jesus is God," was declared orthodox at the First Council of Constantinople in 381 AD and became the basis of modern trinitarianism.

(2) The "Homoiousian" group believed the Son was of a "similar substance" to the Father but not the same as the Father. This position was held by the Semi-Arians in the 4th century.

(3) The "Homoian" group believed the Son was "similar" to the Father, either "in all things" or "according to the scriptures," without speaking of substance. This position was held by the Acacians, a sect of the Arians, who separated themselves from the Niceans because they rejected the word "homoousios"; and from the Semi-Arians because of their surrender of the homoiousios; and from the Anomoeans by their insistence upon the term homoios.

(4) The "Heteroousian" group believed the Son was of a "different substance" from the Father (i.e., created) which was the position of Arianism.

(5) The Jews believed their Messiah was a coming human king - not "God" - which otherwise would be blasphemy to monotheistic Judaism. Then there were Jewish Christians who believed Jesus was their Messiah and prophet who was born with the fullness of the Holy Spirit (as was John the Baptist). This position was held by the early Jewish Christians in Jerusalem who were called Nazarenes and "Ebionites" ("the poor").

The fact of God dwelling within Jesus cannot be denied because it is clearly stated in the Bible:

Colossians 1:19: "For God was pleased to have all his fullness dwell in him."

The Bible also gives Jesus the title of the "Logos" - the Christian Gnostic concept of the incarnation of God in word, revelation and redemption:

John 1:1-3: "In the beginning was the Word, and the Word was with God, and the Word was God. He was with God in the beginning. Through him all things were made; without him nothing was made that has been made."

John 1:14: "The Word became flesh and made his dwelling among us. We have seen his glory, the glory of the one and only Son, who came from the Father, full of grace and truth."

The Bible also gives Jesus the title of "Son of Man" - the anointed one and the firstborn of all creation:

Colossians 1:15: "The Son is the image of the invisible God, the firstborn over all creation."

Hebrews 1:6: "And again, when God brings his firstborn into the world, he says, 'Let all God's angels worship him'."

The Hebrew word most often translated "worship" is "shachah", and it is usually rendered as "proskuneo" in the Greek Septuagint version of the Old Testament. The Greek word "proskuneo" is translated as "the act of bowing down in homage done before a superior in rank or a ruler. Thus David "bowed himself" (shachah) before Saul in 1 Samuel 24:8.

The following is another Bible verse referring to Jesus as the "firstborn":

Hebrews 12:22-23: "But you have come to Mount Zion, to the city of the living God, the heavenly Jerusalem. You have come to thousands upon thousands of angels in joyful assembly, to the church of the firstborn, whose names are written in heaven. You have come to God, the Judge of all, to the spirits of the righteous made perfect."

Then there is the mystery of Christ in humans:

Colossians 1:25-27: "I have become its servant by the commission God gave me to present to you the word of God in its fullness - the mystery that has been kept hidden for ages and generations, but is now disclosed to the Lord's people. To them God has chosen to make known among the Gentiles the glorious riches of this mystery, which is Christ in you, the hope of glory."

C. The Mystery of the Trinity

Whether or not a Christian believes in a "Trinity" (the Father, Son, and Holy Spirit), the Bible describes three parts of Christ (the Mind of Christ, the Body of Christ, and the Spirit of Christ), and three dimensions of God (light, life, and love) which the three-dimensional enlightened Christian shares (mind, body, and spirit):

The Mystery of the "Trinity" in Man (of Mind, Body, and Spirit)

The Mind of Christ: "Who has known the mind of the Lord so as to instruct him?' But we have the Mind of Christ" (1 Corinthians 2:16).

The LIGHT of God: "God is light" (1 John 1:5).

Claim: The enlightened mind is one with God.

Proof in Man: "May the God who gives endurance and encouragement give you the same attitude of mind toward each other that Christ Jesus had, so that with one mind and one voice you may glorify the God and Father of our Lord Jesus Christ." (Romans 15:5-6)

Proof in Christ: "I (Jesus) and the Father are one" (John 10:30).

Conclusion: The "Mind of Christ" is the Father (light) of whom our minds are one with as well.

The Body of Christ: "Now you are the Body of Christ, and each one of you is a part of it" (1 Corinthians 12:27).

The LIFE of God: God is "eternal life" (1 John 5:20)

Claim: The body in which Christ dwells has eternal life and we are a part of Christ.

Proof in Man: "I (Paul) have been crucified with Christ and I no longer live, but Christ lives in me. The life I now live in the body, I live by faith in the Son of God, who loved me and gave himself for me." (Galatians 2:20)

Proof in Christ: "I (Jesus) am the resurrection and the life" (John 11:25).

Conclusion: The "Body of Christ" is the Son (life) of whom our bodies are a part.

The Spirit of Christ: "You, however, are not in the realm of the flesh but are in the realm of the Spirit, if indeed the Spirit of God lives in you. And if anyone does not have the Spirit of Christ, they do not belong to Christ" (Romans 8:9).

The LOVE of God: "God is love" (1 John 4:8).

Claim: The Spirit of God dwells in everyone who loves others.

Proof in Man: "God is love. Whoever lives in love lives in God, and God in them." (1 John 4:16)

Proof in Man: "This is my (Jesus') command: Love each other." (John 15:17)

Proof in Man & Christ: "If you keep my commands, you will remain in my love, just as I have kept my Father's commands and remain in his love." (John 15:10)

Conclusion: The "Spirit of Christ" is the Holy Spirit (love) who lived in Jesus and lives within us as well.

So now we understand the mystery of God within humanity, the so-called "Trinity," to be the three-dimensional image of God (light, life, love) within the mind, body and spirit of a human being. The Christ spirit, the metaphysical divine "Logos" of God indwelling in flesh, is the perfected image of God in humanity and the fulfillment of God's Word spoken in the Book of Genesis at creation.

Genesis 1:26: "Then God said, 'Let us make mankind in our image, in our likeness.'"

The mystery of God in humanity defines all of humanity created with a spirit in the image and likeness of God's Spirit. The human spirit is a "spark of the divine" and is immortal and indestructible. Because of the nature of the spirit, the human spirit is preexistent before the creation of the world. Because of the nature of the Fall of spirits from heaven, the human spirit is "unawakened" ("spiritually dead" in biblical terms - see Romans 5:12-21, 1 Corinthians 15:21-22, 1 Corinthians 2:14), "trapped in flesh" and therefore, subject to the cycle of birth, death and rebirth (John 3:3). This is why God sent Jesus (John 3:16). God's plan is to rescue all souls through the ministry of Jesus by allowing them return to their original home in heaven through a new form of resurrection - spiritual regeneration by the Holy Spirit (John 3:3-6)

D. God In Jesus Does Not Mean God Is Jesus

Although the Bible declares Jesus to be "one with God," having God as his "Father", being the "Logos" (the human creative power of God), being a literal "mouthpiece" of God (the Word), being the "Son" of God; having the "fullness" of God (Spirit) within him; and having the perfect human-divine unity. But it would be incorrect to say "Jesus is God." We can only say "Jesus is Lord" (Romans 10:9). This is because there is only one God (the Father) and one Lord (Jesus) as perfectly explained in the Book of Ephesians:

Ephesians 4:4-6: "There is one body (Christ, the Church) and one Spirit, just as you were called in one hope of your calling; one Lord, one faith, one baptism; one God and Father of all, who is above all, and through all, and in you all."

So there is one God, the Father, and one Lord, Christ the Son. In the Christian phrase "Jesus is Lord," the general use of the term "lord" in antiquity was a courtesy title for social superiors, but its root meaning was "ruler". Kings everywhere were titled "Lord" and often considered divine beings so the word acquired a religious significance. Here is another verse supporting Jesus being subject to God:

1 Corinthians 15:27-28: "For he (God) 'has put everything under his (Christ's) feet.' Now when it says that 'everything' has been put under him, it is clear that this does not include God himself, who put everything under Christ. When he has done this, then the Son himself will be made subject to him who put everything under him, so that God may be all in all."

The above verse says the Son "will be made subject" to God. Notice also the same sentence says Jesus will be subject to God so that "God may be all in all" - a reference to universal reconciliation and salvation as mentioned in Acts 3:19-21 and Part 3 of this article.

Here are a few Bible verses to support the idea that God is not Jesus:

Numbers 23:19: "God is not human, that he should lie, not a human being, that he should change his mind."

John 14:28: "The Father is greater than I (Jesus)."

1 Corinthians 8:6: "For us there is but one God, the Father, from whom all things came and for whom we live; and there is but one Lord, Jesus Christ, through whom all things came and through whom we live."

Revelation 3:14: "And to the angel of the church of the

Laodiceans write, 'These things says the Amen, the Faithful and True Witness, the Beginning of the creation of God."

John 1:18: "No one has ever seen God; the only Son, who is in the bosom of the Father, he has made him known."

Mark 13:32: "But about that day or hour no one knows, not even the angels in heaven, nor the Son, but only the Father."

Matthew 19:16-17: "Just then a man came up to Jesus and asked, 'Teacher, what good thing must I do to get eternal life?' 'Why do you ask me about what is good?' Jesus replied. 'There is only One who is good. If you want to enter life, keep the commandments.'"

Nontrinitarianism refers to belief systems within Christianity rejecting the mainstream Christian doctrine of the Trinity - of three manifestations of God: the Father, the Son, and the Holy Spirit. Trinitarianism was declared to be Christian doctrine at the 4th-century First Council of Nicaea (325 AD) which declared the full divinity of the Son. The First Council of Constantinople (381 AD) declared the divinity of the Holy Spirit. Nontrinitarian denominations today are a minority of modern Christians which include the Church of Jesus Christ of Latter-day Saints ("Mormons"), Jehovah's Witnesses, Christian Scientists, Unitarian Universalists, and the United Church of God; although nontrinitarian views differ widely on the nature of God, Jesus, and the Holy Spirit. Biblical and historical evidence indicate that first-century Christians did not worship Jesus as equal to God. The doctrine of the Trinity is not a part of the other major Abrahamic religions, Judaism and Islam, which views the doctrine as blasphemy to monotheism.

If you think of God as "light" (1 John 1:5), then you will find "God" is the Ultimate Reality in all the major religions: Buddhism (Clear Light, Luminous Mind, Buddhahood), Hinduism (Brahman), Judaism, Christianity, and Islam. In NDE studies, God is viewed as "the Light" and the "life review" as enlightenment. Even atheists must admit that light (electromagnetic radiation) has many ":god-like" properties to it according to quantum mechanics. Eminent physicist, David Bohm, viewed all matter as "condensed" or "frozen light." Physicist Stephen Hawking once stated ,"When you break subatomic particles down to their most elemental level, you are left with nothing but pure light." Science discovered light was pervasive at the beginning of the universe. Scientists recently discovered the so-called "God Particle" - the particle which bestows mass upon all other particles. This particle is very crucial to physics because it is a critical understanding of the structure of all matter. Albert Einstein's great equation E=mc2 (where E is for energy, m for mass and c is the speed of light) describes the awesome power and energy holding all atoms together. Surprisingly, the Bible supports Einstein's equation when it declares: God is the invisible power "holding all things together" (Colossians 1:17). If a person could travel at the speed of light, they would be able to live forever because time would cease to exist. The transcendent view of consciousness as "light" is the basis for major world religions. So it shouldn't be surprising why the original top quantum physicists where influenced by religion. Erwin Schrodinger, for example, studied Hinduism; Werner Heisenberg looked into Plato's theory of the ancient Greeks; Niels Bohr was drawn to Taoism; and Wolfgang Pauli to the Kabbalah - all of which hold to the doctrine of reincarnation.

E. The Mystery of God In Humans

Jesus proclaimed his oneness with God (the Father) before his religious enemies who thought it was blasphemy. In Judaism, a father's son was equal in status to his father. Therefore, when Jesus was claiming God was his father, he was also claiming equal status with God. Of course, Jesus was merely stating his human-divine unity due to unique relationship with God which his enemies didn't understand. Jesus answered his religious enemies by quoting Psalm 82:6 where God refers to all "sons of God" as "gods" - an obvious reference to God's Spirit in humanity:

John 10:30-36: "'I and the Father are one.' Again his Jewish opponents picked up stones to stone him, but Jesus said to them, 'I have shown you many good works from the Father. For which of these do you stone me?' 'We are not stoning you for any good work,' they replied, 'but for blasphemy, because you, a mere man, claim to be God.' Jesus answered them, 'Is it not written in your Law, 'I have said you are gods?' If he called them gods, to whom the word of God came - and Scripture cannot be set aside - what about the one whom the Father set apart as his very own and sent into the world? Why then do you accuse me of blasphemy because I said, 'I am God's Son?'"

Psalm 82:6: "I (God) said, 'You are gods; you are all sons of the

Most High.'"

The mystery of God in Christ and humans is the revelation of God's Spirit residing within human beings. Of course, Jesus was born with the "fullness" of the Holy Spirit as the "Logos". But all God's "sons" or "children" can be said to have God's Holy Spirit:

1 Corinthians 2:7: "We declare God's wisdom, a mystery that has been hidden and that God destined for our glory before time began."

Romans 8:14: "For as many as are led by the Spirit of God, they are the sons of God."

John 1:12-13: "But as many as received him, to them gave he power to become the sons of God, even to them that believe on his name: Which were born, not of blood, nor of the will of the flesh, nor of the will of man, but of God."

1 John 3:1: "Behold, what manner of love the Father hath bestowed upon us, that we should be called the sons of God: therefore the world knoweth us not, because it knew him not."

And there are many Bible verses stating flat out of God residing within His "children":

1 John 4:12-16): "No one has ever seen God; but if we love one another, God lives in us and his love is made complete in us. This is how we know that we live in him and he in us: He has given us of his Spirit. And we have seen and testify that the Father has sent his Son to be the Savior of the world. If anyone acknowledges that Jesus is the Son of God, God lives in them and they in God. And so we know and rely on the love God has for us. God is love. Whoever lives in love lives in God, and God in them."

"On that day you will realize that I am in my Father, and you are in me, and I am in you." (John 14:20)

John 14:23: "Jesus replied, 'Anyone who loves me will obey my teaching. My Father will love them, and we will come to them and make our home with them.'"

Just as Jesus proclaimed, "I and the Father are one" (John 10:30), Jesus proclaims God's children are also "one" with the Father:

John 17:11: "Holy Father, protect them by the power of your name, the name you gave me, so that they may be one as we are one."

John 17:20-22: "My prayer is not for them alone. I pray also for those who will believe in me through their message, that all of them may be one, Father, just as you are in me and I am in you. May they also be in us so that the world may believe that you have sent me. I have given them the glory that you gave me, that they may be one as we are one."

F. The Mystery of Christ in Humans

As children of the Father, we are part of the "body of Christ" (1 Corinthians 12:27), having the "Spirit of Christ" (Romans 8:9), with the "mind of Christ" (1 Corinthians 2:16). In other words, we share the same nature as Christ:

1 Corinthians 6:17: "But whoever is united with the Lord is one with him in spirit."

Galatians 2:20: "I have been crucified with Christ and I no longer live, but Christ lives in me."

2 Corinthians 4:10-11: "We always carry around in our body the death of Jesus, so that the life of Jesus may also be revealed in our body. For we who are alive are always being given over to death for Jesus' sake, so that his life may also be revealed in our mortal body."

2 Corinthians 13:5: "Examine yourselves to see whether you are in the faith; test yourselves. Do you not realize that Christ Jesus is in you - unless, of course, you fail the test?"

The mystery of Christ in humans is the mystery of God in humans - as God's children, we are growing more and more into the image of His Son, the Logos:

2 Corinthians 3:18: "And we all, who with unveiled faces contemplate the Lord's glory, are being transformed into his image with ever-increasing glory, which comes from the Lord, who is the Spirit."

1 Corinthians 15:49: "And just as we have borne the image of the earthly man, so shall we bear the image of the heavenly man."

Romans 8:29-30: "For those God foreknew he also predestined to be conformed to the image of his Son, that he might be the firstborn among many brothers and sisters. And those he predestined, he also called; those he called, he also justified; those he justified, he also glorified." Also, see Genesis 1:26-27

Romans 8:17: "Now if we are children, then we are heirs - heirs of God and co-heirs with Christ, if indeed we share in his sufferings in order that we may also share in his glory."

Revelation 3:21: "To the one who is victorious, I will give the right to sit with me on my throne, just as I was victorious and sat down with my Father on his throne."

G. The Mystery of Humans Evolving Into the Image of Christ

Christian theology, the Greek word "theosis" is translated divinization (deification, making divine) and is the perfecting effect of divine grace by the atonement of Christ and spiritual regeneration by the Holy Spirit. It literally means to become more divine, or to become God. In the Bible it is also referred to as "glorification" which is the process of sanctification or perfection of the Christian. It is self-evident that divinization is a very long and arduous process; and because it is the goal of every human being to attain divinization through good works, then reincarnation becomes a necessity. The teaching of deification or "theosis" in Eastern Orthodox Christianity refers to the attainment of the likeness of God, the Christian's union with God or reconciliation with God.

There are several Bible verses stating how, through Christ, people realize their divine nature and become "heirs of God and joint heirs with Christ" and "inherit all things" just as Christ inherits all things:

2 Peter 1:4: "Through these he has given us his very great and precious promises, so that through them you may participate in the divine nature, having escaped the corruption in the world caused by evil desires."

Galatians 4:7: "So you are no longer a slave, but God's child; and since you are his child, God has made you also an heir."

1 Corinthians 3:21-23: "So then, no more boasting about human leaders! All things are yours, whether Paul or Apollos or Cephas or the world or life or death or the present or the future - all are yours, and you are of Christ, and Christ is of God."

Revelation 21:1-7: "Then I saw a new heaven and a new Earth, for the first heaven and the first Earth had passed away, and there was no longer any sea. I saw the Holy City, the new Jerusalem, coming down out of heaven from God, prepared as a bride beautifully dressed for her husband... 'Those who are victorious will inherit all this, and I will be their God and they will be my children.'"

There were many references to divinization in the writings of the orthodox Catholic Church Fathers.

Irenaeus, bishop of Lyons (130-202 AD) and one of the first great Christian theologians, wrote how:

Irenaeus: "God became what we are in order to make us what he is himself." (Irenaeus, Against Heresies 5)

Irenaeus: "If the Word became a man, It was so men may become gods." He added: "Do we cast blame on him [God] because we were not made gods from the beginning, but were at first created merely as men, and then later as gods? Although God has adopted this course out of his pure benevolence, that no one may charge him with discrimination or stinginess, he declares, 'I have said, Ye are gods; and all of you are sons of the Most High.'... For it was necessary at first that nature be exhibited, then after that what was mortal would be conquered and swallowed up in immortality." (Irenaeus, Against Heresies 4.38)

Justin Martyr (100-165 AD), regarded as the foremost interpreter of the theory of the Logos in the 2nd century, insisted how in the beginning:

Justin Martyr: "Men were made like God, free from suffering and death," and how they are thus "deemed worthy of becoming gods and of having power to become sons of the highest." (Justin Martyr, Dialogue with Trypho, 124)

Augustine of Hippo (354-430 AD), viewed as one of the most important Church Fathers in Western Christianity, wrote:

Augustine: "But he himself that justifies also deifies, for by justifying he makes sons of God. 'For he has given them power to become the sons of God' [referring to John 1:12]. If then we have been made sons of God, we have also been made gods."[On the Psalms, 50.2] "To make human beings gods," Augustine said, "He was made man who was God" (sermon 192.1.1). Augustine goes on to write that "[they] are not born of His Substance, that they should be the same as He, but that by favor they should come to Him... (Ibid)." (Augustine, "Psalm 50", Exposition on the Book of Psalms)

Theophilus of Antioch (120-190 AD), whose writings are most notable for being the earliest extant Christian work to use the word "Trinity" except as "God, his Word (Logos) and his Wisdom (Sophia), wrote:

Theophilus: "For if He had made him immortal from the beginning, He would have made him God. Again, if He had made him mortal, God would seem to be the cause of his death. Neither, then, immortal nor yet mortal did He make him, but, as we have said above, capable of both; so that if he should incline to the things of immortality, keeping the commandment of God, he should receive as reward from Him immortality, and should become God." (Theophilus, "Book II, Chapter 27", To Autolycus)

Hippolytus of Rome (170-235 AD), the most important 3rd-century theologian in the Church in Rome wrote:

Hippolytus: "And you shall be a companion of the Deity, and a co-heir with Christ, no longer enslaved by lusts or passions, and never again wasted by disease. For you have become God: for whatever sufferings you underwent while being a man, these He gave to you, because you were of mortal mold, but whatever it is consistent with God to impart, these God has promised to bestow upon you, because you have been deified, and begotten unto immortality." (Hippolytus, "Book X, Chapter 30", Refutation of all Heresies, and The Discourse on the Holy Theophany)

Gregory of Nyssa (335-395 AD), a Catholic saint and believer in reincarnation who was greatly influenced by Origen, wrote:

Gregory of Nyssa: "For just as He in Himself assimilated His own human nature to the power of the Godhead, being a part of the common nature, but not being subject to the inclination to sin which is in that nature (for it says: 'He did no sin, nor was deceit found in his mouth'), so, also, will He lead each person to union with the Godhead if they do nothing unworthy of union with the Divine." (Gregory of Nyssa, On Christian Perfection, p. 116)

Of course, there is only one God - the one Holy Spirit (Ephesians 4:4-6). Divinization mean exactly what Jesus and the Bible says, humans can become "gods" or "godlings" - not "Gods" - but "sons" of God, "children" of God, an "image" of God, like "the Logos," like Christ, a "part" of God, a "thought" within the Mind of God. A better definition of "gods" is a mathematical definition - "fractals" of God. A fractal is a part of the Whole (like a "chip" off the "old block") which is identical in image to the Whole.

So because all human beings have a spirit which is a "fractal" of God, whether they are spiritually "awakened" to the fact or not - an eternal spirit which cannot be destroyed - the idea of reincarnation becomes a necessity. Because all humans are undergoing a process of perfection, then it is self-evident that this process takes a number of successive lifetimes to accomplish it. According to NDE studies, everyone is born into this world with a "mission" from God - lessons in life to learn toward spiritual growth and perfection. After people die, they have a "life review" during which their entire life is evaluated. The life review implies life is a "test" after which we are graded for educational purposes. The life review also reveals one lifetime is not enough to accomplish all a person must accomplish on Earth including the process of spiritual growth. During a life review, some people have been shown past lives. NDE studies also support and incorporate reincarnation studies.

H. Summary

God's law of divine justice, karma, universal salvation, Christian perfection, preexistence, indwelling Spirit, divinization, and reincarnation are mentioned many times throughout the Bible. The process of perfection obviously takes more than one lifetime because the goal for everyone is to become like Christ - the image of God within humanity. Only reincarnation offers continued personal identity and further spiritual growth after death. The mystery of God within human beings means everyone can partake in the divine nature through the spirit within flesh. The human spirit must first be "awakened" (regenerated) from a state of "spiritual death" to a new life through the Holy Spirit. Sanctification means the flesh must then be completely overcome through reincarnation. The mystery of the "Trinity" is God within humanity: the "Mind of Christ" (the Father, God is light, 1 John 1:5), the "Body of Christ" (the Son, God is life, 1 John 5:20), and the "Spirit of Christ" (the Holy Spirit, God is love, 1 John 4:8). As co-heirs with Christ, humans can also attain at-onement with God through the mind, body, and spirit of Christ (the light, life, and love of God) - the "Logos", the human "image" of God in three-dimensions. Attaining perfection and at-onement with God obviously requires more than one lifetime. Evidence in the Bible and NDE studies have shown humans living many lifetimes on the path toward at-onement with God. For all these reasons and more, reincarnation must now become an official doctrine of Christianity.

CHAPTER 6:
REINCARNATION IN THE BIBLE (PART 6)

1. More Reincarnating Biblical Personalities

A. Fallen Angels as Reincarnating Human Beings

In Genesis 28, the concept of reincarnation appears through the continued coming and going of spirits (described as "angels" of God) from the Earth to the spiritual realm. Jacob, son of Isaac and grandson of Abraham, had a dream in which he saw a "stairway" on the Earth reaching to heaven:

Genesis 28:12: "He (Jacob) had a dream in which he saw a stairway resting on the Earth, with its top reaching to heaven, and the angels of God were ascending and descending on it."

This story of "Jacob's Ladder" describes "angels" ascending and "angels" descending a heavenly "stairway." Ascending this stairway implies death and going to heaven. Descending this stairway implies returning to Earth and reincarnation. The clue is in the phrase "resting on the Earth" meaning the "stairway" is positioned upon Earth where the body is located. In other parts of the Bible where angels are mentioned, such as Gabriel who appeared before Mary in Luke 1:26, there is no mention of a stairway as a means of travel. This verse in Genesis and the concept of spirit beings entering and leaving the Earth realm through divine means is supported by other Bible verses dealing with reincarnation such as the following:

Amos 9:2: "Though they dig into Sheol, from there shall my hand take them; though they climb up to heaven, from there I will bring them down."

The idea of a "stairway to heaven" is also a useful metaphor for the near-death experience (NDE) tunnel which so many NDE experiencers travel through during their NDEs. One particular experiencer, David Oakford, has provided an excellent description of the NDE tunnel resembling the description of "Jacob's Ladder":

David Oakford: "We started to head back toward Gaia (the personal name for Earth). We went to a place in the shadow of Gaia. It was a great city in the clouds. The city had these beautiful white buildings as far as I could see. I saw spirits living there all of which had vibration but no real physical body. These inhabitants went to and from the buildings - going to work and play too. I saw a place where spirits went to get what I thought was water. There were no vehicles there. Spirits seemed to get around the same way my being and I got around, by flying. The city had no boundaries that I could see. This was a place full of life of all kinds. There was nature there, many pure plants, trees, and water just like on Gaia but more pure. Nature there was absolutely perfect. It was untainted by human manipulation. This place was just like Gaia only without the problems and negativity. I felt that this was what is called heaven in Earth terms. I saw spirits going to and from Gaia and the city. I could tell the development of the spirits going to and from by the energy they emanated. I could see that animals came to and from Gaia just like humans do. I could see many spirits leave Gaia with guides and could see spirits returning to Gaia without guides. The being told me that some of the spirits passing were the ones that were doing the work with humans on Gaia. I could make out the type of spirits that were doing the work and the spirits that were coming to the great city to become replenished to eventually go back to Gaia to experience and further evolve. I could feel the emotions of the ones coming back for replenishment. I could feel that some of them were sad, beaten and scared, much like I felt before my being came to me."

One very interesting proof in the Bible of angels reincarnating as humans can be found in the story of the Nephilim:

Genesis 6:1-4: "When human beings began to increase in number on the Earth and daughters were born to them, the sons of God saw that the daughters of humans were beautiful, and they married any of them they chose... The Nephilim were on the Earth in those days -

and also afterward - when the sons of God went to the daughters of humans and had children by them. They were the heroes of old, men of renown."

We know this story in the Bible is a metaphor for an event having a deeper spiritual meaning for a number of reasons:

Why the Story of the Nephilim (Fallen Angels) is a Metaphor For Fallen Souls

(1) Angels don't have genitals and cannot have sex. So the "children" of the union between "daughters of humans" and the "sons of God" is a metaphor for something else. NDE studies reveal that spiritual bodies don't have genitals.

(2) Angels neither marry nor are given in marriage as Jesus indicated in Matthew 22:23-30. So the "marriage" of the "sons of God" and the "daughters of humans" is a metaphor for something else.

(3) The Hebrew word for "Nephilim" has been mistranslated as "giants" when the actual translation is "those who fell" (another reference appears in Ezekiel 32:27 translated as "the fallen warriors of old").

(4) The famous Christian psychic and near-death experiencer, Edgar Cayce (1877-1945), gave the correct interpretation of the Nephilim story to mean when souls fell from heaven and began possessing the bodies of homo erectus "ape-men" during the process of evolution thereby creating the human race.

(5) Early Christian writers such as Justin Martyr, Eusebius, Clement of Alexandria, Origen, and Commodianus believed the "sons of God" in Genesis 6:1-4 were "fallen angels" - fallen souls from heaven.

(6) In the Book of Job, the "sons of God" are described existing in heaven before the Earth was created. The "morning stars" are another name for "sons of God" as in Jesus (Revelation 22:16), Lucifer (Isaiah 14:12), John the Baptist, Mary (mother of Jesus), and other human beings (2 Peter 1:19),

Job 38:4-7: "Where were you when I began building the Earth? Tell Me, if you have understanding. Who decided how big it was to be, since you know? Who looked to see if it was as big as it should be? What was it built upon? Who laid its first stone, when the morning stars sang together and all the sons of God called out for joy?"

Job 1:6: "Now there was a day when the sons of God came to present themselves before the Lord, and Satan came also among them."

Job 2:1: "Again there was a day when the sons of God came to present themselves before the Lord, and Satan came also among them to present himself before the Lord."

So the evidence shows that all of humanity, as preexistent souls, had fallen from God's grace from the highest spiritual heaven before the creation of the physical realm (a lower spiritual realm). The Bible allegorically refers to this event as the Fall in the Garden of Eden in the Book of Genesis and the revolt of the angels in the Book of Revelation. This event is also the basis for the cosmology of Christian Gnosticism and Jewish mystery teachings. According to this cosmology, God's plan for fallen human souls is a limited series of reincarnations with periods in between of dwelling in other heavenly dimensions (afterlife realms) with increasingly righteous souls dwelling in higher afterlife realms while increasingly unrighteous souls dwelling in lower afterlife realms. Reincarnation would continue until a soul's every thought and action of the physical body was in accord with the plan originally laid out for the soul (i.e., toward a human-divine unity, Christ consciousness). This plan of the conquest of the physical body that had trapped souls was fostered by a soul who had completed his experience of creation, attained Christhood, returned to God, and became a companion to God and a co-creator. This is the soul known as Jesus (4 BC-30 AD). The soul of Jesus was deeply concerned about the plight of his fellow souls trapped in Earth. Jesus realized it was necessary to give humanity a pattern by which they could follow in order to return to God. Jesus achieved this goal by incarnating and becoming victorious over the death of the physical body by laying aside the ego, and accepting the crucifixion of the body in order to return to God. Through the acts of leading a perfect life and becoming unjustly killed, Jesus reversed the negative karma which originated from Adam. When a person has successfully followed the pattern set by Christ and attained complete human-divine unity, its cycle of reincarnations finished. The person's soul is then liberated and merges with God in the highest heaven becoming a permanent citizen.

B. Satan as a Reincarnating Human Being

There are two specific instances in the Book of Ezekiel where Satan is referred to as a man. One of them is in Ezekiel 28 where the King of Tyre is referred to as an incarnation of Satan. In Ezekiel 27, God condemns the city of Tyre because of its many sins and its dishonest trade. Then in Ezekiel 28, God condemns the King of Tyre himself:

Ezekiel 28:11-19: "The word of the Lord came to me: 'Son of man, take up a lament concerning the king of Tyre and say to him: 'This is what the Sovereign Lord says: 'You were the seal of perfection, full of wisdom and perfect in beauty. You were in Eden, the garden of God; every precious stone adorned you: carnelian, chrysolite and emerald, topaz, onyx and jasper, lapis lazuli, turquoise and beryl. Your settings and mountings were made of gold; on the day you were created they were prepared. You were anointed as a guardian cherub, for so I ordained you. You were on the holy mount of God; you walked among the fiery stones. You were blameless in your ways from the day you were created till wickedness was found in you. Through your widespread trade you were filled with violence, and you sinned. So I drove you in disgrace from the mount of God, and I expelled you, guardian cherub, from among the fiery stones. Your heart became proud on account of your beauty, and you corrupted your wisdom because of your splendor. So I threw you to the Earth; I made a spectacle of you before kings. By your many sins and dishonest trade you have desecrated your sanctuaries. So I made a fire come out from you, and it consumed you, and I reduced you to ashes on the ground in the sight of all who were watching. All the nations who knew you are appalled at you; you have come to a horrible end and will be no more.'"

The second instance is in Isaiah 14 where the King of Babylon is referred to as an incarnation of Lucifer (the "morning star", son of the dawn):

Isaiah 14:3-17: "On the day the Lord gives you relief from your suffering and turmoil and from the harsh labor forced on you, you will take up this taunt against the king of Babylon... "How you have fallen from heaven, morning star, son of the dawn! You have been cast down to the Earth, you who once laid low the nations! You said in your heart, 'I will ascend to the heavens; I will raise my throne above the stars of God; I will sit enthroned on the mount of assembly, on the utmost heights of Mount Zaphon. I will ascend above the tops of the clouds; I will make myself like the Most High.' But you are brought down to the realm of the dead, to the depths of the pit. Those who see you stare at you, they ponder your fate: 'Is this the man who shook the Earth and made kingdoms tremble, the man who made the world a wilderness, who overthrew its cities and would not let his captives go home?'"

There are also two instances in the gospels where Satan momentarily "possesses" the bodies of two of the apostles of Jesus in an attempt to thwart Jesus' mission. This type of possession of a body by a discarnate spirit is the same kind of reincarnation called a "walk-in" only it is temporary. Here are the two instances:

Matthew 16:21-23: "From that time on Jesus began to explain to his disciples that he must go to Jerusalem and suffer many things at the hands of the elders, the chief priests and the teachers of the law, and that he must be killed and on the third day be raised to life. Peter took him aside and began to rebuke him. 'Never, Lord!' he said. 'This shall never happen to you!' Jesus turned and said to Peter, 'Get behind me, Satan! You are a stumbling block to me; you do not have in mind the concerns of God, but merely human concerns.'"

Luke 22:3-4: "Then Satan entered Judas, called Iscariot, one of the Twelve. And Judas went to the chief priests and the officers of the temple guard and discussed with them how he might betray Jesus."

Then there are the historical cases of "evil incarnate" individuals such as Adolf Hitler, Genghis Khan and Nero. The Bible also refers to the Antichrist and the "man of sin" who are described in terms of the "son of Satan" in the same manner Christians are described as "sons of God." So if the leader of the earthly rebellion of fallen angels incarnates and reincarnates as a human being, then it is no great leap of faith to believe all fallen angels on Earth incarnate and reincarnate as human beings as well.

C. Human Beings as Angels and Vice Versa

In the Epistle of Jude, the author (Jude, the brother of Jesus) used heavy Christian Gnostic terminology when referring to "some sinful men" who crept into the church who were actually Nephilim fallen "angels" of Genesis 6:1-4 who "left" heaven of whom "long ago it was written":

Jude 1:4-6: "Some sinful men have come into your church without anyone knowing it. They are living in sin and they speak of the loving-favor of God to cover up their sins. They have turned against our only Leader and Lord, Jesus Christ. Long ago it was written that these people would die in their sins. You already know all this, but think about it again. The Lord saved His people out of the land of Egypt. Later He destroyed all those who did not put their trust in Him. Angels who did not stay in their place of power, but left the place where they were given to stay, are chained in a dark place. They will be there until the day they stand before God to be judged."

In the above verse, Jude demonstrated he was familiar with the Christian Gnostic mystery teachings including the Hebrew mystery writings of the Book of Enoch. These mystery teachings viewed the human soul as preexistent, incarnating into a "prison" of flesh and being subject to reincarnation. The metaphor of a "prison" appears in many of the parables of Jesus such as Matthew 5:25-26 (and Luke 12:58-59) and Matthew 18:34-35. The metaphor of "souls" being freed from "prison" also appears in the New Testament implying reincarnation. The Gnostics believed humans were identical to the fallen angels whose origin was heaven. Jude quoted directly from the Book of Enoch - a remarkable fact considering the Epistle of Jude is part of the Bible and the Book of Enoch is not:

Jude 1:14-15: "Enoch, the seventh from Adam, prophesied about them: 'See, the Lord is coming with thousands upon thousands of his holy ones to judge everyone, and to convict all of them of all the ungodly acts they have committed in their ungodliness, and of all the defiant words ungodly sinners have spoken against him.'"

Jude had harsh words for these "ungodly men" whom he refers to as "stars" - a Biblical metaphorical reference to angels - "morning stars." Jude also referred to them as "twice dead" - another reference to reincarnation:

Jude 1:12-13: "These people are blemishes at your love feasts, eating with you without the slightest qualm - shepherds who feed only themselves. They are clouds without rain, blown along by the wind; autumn trees, without fruit and uprooted - twice dead. They are wild waves of the sea, foaming up their shame; wandering stars, for whom blackest darkness has been reserved forever."

The Book of Enoch was cherished by the Essenes, ancient Jews and early Christians. The Book of Enoch was considered as scripture by many of the early Church Fathers, such as Clement of Alexandria, Irenaeus and Tertullian, who wrote in 200 AD that the Book of Enoch had been rejected by Rabbinical Jews because it contained prophecies pertaining to Christ. However, later Fathers denied the canonicity of the Book of Enoch, and some later Church Fathers even considered the Epistle of Jude uncanonical because it refers to an "apocryphal" work. Thus, the Book of Enoch was denounced, banned and "lost" for over a thousand years until, in 1773, a Scottish explorer discovered three copies in Ethiopia. Nevertheless, in the Bible, the Book of Genesis says:

Genesis 5:24: "Enoch walked faithfully with God; then he was no more, because God took him away."

The Book of Enoch reveals God allowed Enoch to be taken into heaven and return to Earth to give his children certain secrets. The premise of the Book of Enoch is angels left their positions in heaven and incarnated into human bodies (the "Nephilim"). Yahweh saw the lawlessness which resulted and sent a flood to destroy them. Then the archangels Michael, Raphael, Gabriel and Uriel bound the fallen souls "under the Earth" for "Judgment Day."

Another extra-Biblical text, the Book of Jubilees, describes how the archangels bound the "ancestors" of the Nephilim, the fallen "angels" (souls) referred to as "the Watchers," in the "depths of the Earth" and imprisoned them in great darkness in a mysterious "second heaven." This "outer darkness" realm appears in many NDEs as a transitory realm known as The Void. The Book of Jubilees was considered canonical by Beta Israel (Ethiopian Jews) as well as the Ethiopian Orthodox Church. This is important because the Ethiopian Orthodox Bible is the largest and most diverse biblical canon in traditional Christendom having escaped the political purges of the Roman Church. So the Book of Jubilees is considered part of the Pseudepigrapha by Protestant, Roman Catholic, and Eastern Orthodox Churches. The Book of Jubilees was well known to early Christians, as evidenced by the writings of Origen, Epiphanius, Justin Martyr and others. The text was also utilized by the Essene community of the Dead Sea Scrolls.

Throughout the gospels, Jesus taught of the spiritual "resurrection" (spiritual rebirth, spiritual regeneration) of the Holy Spirit of the living, and the bodily "resurrection" (physical rebirth, reincarnation) of the dead. In Luke 20:27-38, the Sadducees, who did not believe in either resurrection, tested Jesus by posing a hypothetical they believed disproved the concept of an afterlife. Jesus answered their hypothetical by refuting their assumption of resurrection to mean "resting in peace" in "Abraham's bosom" until corpses come out of their graves at the end times. He did this by defining the true nature of bodily resurrection as not "of the dead," but as a reincarnation "of the living." In doing so, Jesus equated the souls of human beings to angels, then as children "of the resurrection" (i.e., reincarnation). The passage is as follows:

Luke 20:27-38: "Some of the Sadducees, who say there is no resurrection, came to Jesus with a question. 'Teacher,' they said, 'Moses wrote for us that if a man's brother dies and leaves a wife but no children, the man must marry the widow and have children for his brother. Now there were seven brothers. The first one married a woman and died childless. The second and then the third married her, and in the same way the seven died, leaving no children. Finally, the woman died too. Now then, at the resurrection whose wife will she be, since the seven were married to her?' Jesus replied, 'The people of this age marry and are given in marriage. But those who are considered worthy of taking part in that age and in the resurrection from the dead will neither marry nor be given in marriage, and they can no longer die; for they are like the angels. They are God's children, since they are children of the resurrection. But in the account of the bush, even Moses showed that the dead rise, for he calls the Lord 'the God of Abraham, and the God of Isaac, and the God of Jacob.' He is not the God of the dead, but of the living, for to him all are alive.'"

The Sadducees wanted to know which brother would be married to the woman when their corpses would be resurrected at the end times assuming the Persian form of resurrection. Jesus corrected the Sadducees by teaching them how, at death, people become like angels. They do not rest in Abraham's bosom until the end times as the Sadducees assumed Jesus believed. Jesus' metaphor of death as people becoming "like the angels" is a good way to refute the Sadducees who didn't even believe in angels. Death means the soul leaves the corpse and returns to heaven with the possibility of returning to Earth. Jesus said becoming like the angels after death is to become "children of the resurrection" which is a good description of how the soul returns to heaven after death with the possibility of reincarnating and becoming a child again. Jesus corrected the Sadducees' misunderstanding of life after death by telling them God is not the God of the dead, but of the living. These words of Jesus are the key to his teachings. People do not wait until the end times for the "resurrection." It can be attained during life. People are physically reborn until they become spiritually reborn through the Holy Spirit to attain eternal life and escape the cycle of birth-death and rebirth (John 3:3).

Throughout the gospels, Jesus expressed a special concern for children. Jesus' reference to the "children of the resurrection" can be better understood when comparing it with the following Bible verses:

Matthew 18:3-5: "And he said: 'Truly I tell you, unless you change and become like little children, you will never enter the kingdom of heaven. Therefore, whoever takes the lowly position of this child is the greatest in the kingdom of heaven. And whoever welcomes one such child in my name welcomes me.'"

Matthew 18:10: "See that you do not despise one of these little ones. For I tell you that their angels in heaven always see the face of my Father in heaven."

As for children having "angels in heaven," the word "angels" is a great metaphor for "souls" in general and how children are "closer to the Source" than are adults. When Jesus taught of human beings having "angels in heaven" he may have been expressing the concept well-known in his day - the concept found in the Book of Enoch of fallen angels becoming human beings.

There are also Bible verses which specifically refers to human beings as angels and vice versa:

Acts 12:13-15: "Peter knocked at the outer entrance, and a servant girl named Rhoda came to answer the door. When she recognized Peter's voice, she was so overjoyed she ran back without opening it and exclaimed, 'Peter is at the door!' 'You're out of your mind,' they told her. When she kept insisting that it was so, they said, 'It must be his angel.'"

Hebrews 13:2: "Do not forget to show hospitality to strangers, for by so doing some people have shown hospitality to angels without knowing it."

Genesis 18:1-8: "The Lord appeared to Abraham near the great trees of Mamre while he was sitting at the entrance to his tent in the heat of the day. Abraham looked up and saw three men standing nearby. When he saw them, he hurried from the entrance of his tent to meet them and bowed low to the ground... He then brought some curds and milk and the calf that had been prepared, and set these before them. While they ate..."

Genesis 19:1-5: "The two angels arrived at Sodom in the evening, and Lot was sitting in the gateway of the city. When he saw them, he got up to meet them and bowed down with his face to the ground. 'My lords,' he said, 'please turn aside to your servant's house. You can wash your feet and spend the night and then go on your way early in the morning.' 'No,' they answered, 'we will spend the night in the square.' But he insisted so strongly that they did go with him and entered his house. He prepared a meal for them, baking bread without yeast, and they ate. Before they had gone to bed, all the men from every part of the city of Sodom - both young and old - surrounded the house. They called to Lot, 'Where are the men who came to you tonight? Bring them out to us so that we can have sex with them.'"

1 Corinthians 6:1-3: "If any of you has a dispute with another, do you dare to take it before the ungodly for judgment instead of before the Lord's people? Or do you not know that the Lord's people will judge the world? And if you are to judge the world, are you not competent to judge trivial cases? Do you not know that we will judge angels? How much more the things of this life!"

In the above verse, Paul mentions humans judging angels. Because the NDE "life review" reveals people judge themselves, rather than God or Jesus judging people (John 5:22-27, John 8:15-16, John 12:47-48), Paul's reference of people judging themselves as "angels" is true. This supports the early Christian Gnostic cosmology of humans as spirit beings who fell from heaven as angels before the creation of the physical world who are imprisoned in flesh and in lower afterlife realms who are subjected to reincarnation with the goal of attaining the highest heaven and oneness with God as it was in the beginning.

D. Angels and Humans Who Are Rescued From Hell

In the Second Epistle of Peter, the Apostle Peter referred to imprisoned spirits in hell held for judgment:

2 Peter 2:4-9: "For if God did not spare angels when they sinned,

but sent them to hell, putting them in chains of darkness to be held for judgment; if he did not spare the ancient world when he brought the flood on its ungodly people, but protected Noah, a preacher of righteousness, and seven others; if he condemned the cities of Sodom and Gomorrah by burning them to ashes, and made them an example of what is going to happen to the ungodly; and if he rescued Lot, a righteous man, who was distressed by the depraved conduct of the lawless (for that righteous man, living among them day after day, was tormented in his righteous soul by the lawless deeds he saw and heard) - if this is so, then the Lord knows how to rescue the godly from trials and to hold the unrighteous for punishment on the day of judgment."

In the First Epistle of Peter, the Apostle Peter referred to Jesus descending into hell to rescue these same imprisoned spirits including the Nephilim. This is an event known in Christianity as the "Harrowing of Hell":

1 Peter 3:18-20: "For Christ also suffered once for sins, the righteous for the unrighteous, to bring you to God. He was put to death in the body but made alive in the Spirit. After being made alive, he went and made proclamation to the imprisoned spirits - to those who were disobedient long ago when God waited patiently in the days of Noah while the ark was being built. In it only a few people, eight in all, were saved through water."

1 Peter 4:6: "For this is the reason the gospel was preached even to those who are now dead, so that they might be judged according to human standards in regard to the body, but live according to God in regard to the spirit."

The above references to imprisoned souls/angels whom Jesus freed from hell is incompatible with a corpse resurrection at the end times; but is a good reference to reincarnation. As Jesus mentioned about the God of Abraham, Isaac and Jacob, it should be self-evident by now that such liberated spirits were "resurrected" to life through reincarnation. This liberation of spirits is mentioned several times in the Bible:

Ephesians 4:8-10: "When he ascended on high, he took many captives and gave gifts to his people. What does 'he ascended' mean except that he also descended to the lower, earthly regions? He who descended is the very one who ascended higher than all the heavens, in order to fill the whole universe."

Psalm 107:10-14: "Some sat in darkness, in utter darkness, prisoners suffering in iron chains, because they rebelled against God's commands and despised the plans of the Most High. So he subjected them to bitter labor; they stumbled, and there was no one to help. Then they cried to the Lord in their trouble, and he saved them from their distress. He brought them out of darkness, the utter darkness, and broke away their chains."

Matthew 12:40: "For as Jonah was three days and three nights in the belly of the whale, so will the Son of Man be three days and three nights in the heart of the earth."

In the above verse in Matthew, Jesus' Harrowing of Hell is compared to the Hebrew myth of Jonah. According to the myth, Jonah was swallowed by a whale and lived in its belly for three days until being spit out. However, it is impossible for a whale to swallow something as large as a man because whales only eat plankton. And although their mouths are cavernous, their throats are only a few inches wide. So like other Hebrew myths, there must be a higher spiritual interpretation to the story of Jonah. This myth was not limited to the Hebrews either. The story is important in Islam as well. The myth of Jonah has an astrological and a spiritual interpretation. The Semitic translation for the name "Jonah" is "sun". This international myth refers to the sun as it "dies" for three days on December 22nd, the winter solstice. When the sun stops in its movement south, it is "born again" or "resurrected" on December 25th when it resumes its movement north. Because Jesus himself referred to this myth when referring to his three-day Harrowing of Hell after his death, it is worth examining the myth as described in the Book of Jonah:

Jonah 2:1-6: "From inside the fish Jonah prayed to the Lord his God. He said: 'In my distress I called to the Lord, and he answered me. From deep in the realm of the dead I called for help, and you listened to my cry. You hurled me into the depths, into the very heart of the seas, and the currents swirled about me; all your waves and breakers swept over me. I said, 'I have been banished from your sight; yet I will look again toward your holy temple.' The engulfing waters threatened me, the deep surrounded me; seaweed was wrapped around my head. To the roots of the mountains I sank down; the Earth beneath barred me in forever. But you, Lord my God, brought my life up from the pit."

We can now see how the myth of Jonah, when applied to the human soul in general, is a metaphor for the soul rising to heaven after death and reincarnating to life. It also nullifies the idea of people resting in Abraham's bosom until a corpse resurrection day at the end times. All of the above Bible verses refer to the same event: souls (angels) who are liberated from hell. And because these references of freeing of souls from hell is past tense, it means the event has already occurred. The conclusion is "judgment day" for these souls has already happened. This is incompatible with corpse resurrection, but compatible with reincarnation. Souls being liberated from hell - even by Jesus - is a familiar motif in NDE studies such as that of Howard Storm's NDE.

E. The Nation of Israel Reincarnated

The Book of Ezekiel contains in detail those elements necessary for the reincarnation of the spirit. Until Aristotle (384-322 BC), the ancients believed emotional functions took place in the heart where the soul is located. The understanding of emotional functions being carried out in the brain is relatively modern. Because of this, whenever the prophet Ezekiel (622-570 BC) refers to the "heart" he is really referring to the soul. For this reason, when Ezekiel described how a person is given a new life, he not only receives a new spirit (ruach) but also a new soul (nephesh):

Ezekiel 11:14-19: "The word of the Lord came to me: 'Son of man, the people of Jerusalem have said of your fellow exiles and all the other Israelites, 'They are far away from the Lord; this land was given to us as our possession.' 'Therefore say: 'This is what the Sovereign Lord says: Although I sent them far away among the nations and scattered them among the countries, yet for a little while I have been a sanctuary for them in the countries where they have gone. Therefore say: 'This is what the Sovereign Lord says: I will gather you from the nations and bring you back from the countries where you have been scattered, and I will give you back the land of Israel again. They will return to it and remove all its vile images and detestable idols. I will give them an undivided heart and put a new spirit in them; I will remove from them their heart of stone and give them a heart of flesh."

Ezekiel 18:31: "Rid yourselves of all the offenses you have

committed, and get a new heart and a new spirit. Why will you die, people of Israel?"

Ezekiel 36:26-27; 31: "I will give you a new heart and put a new spirit in you; I will remove from you your heart of stone and give you a heart of flesh. And I will put my Spirit in you and move you to follow my decrees and be careful to keep my laws... Then you will remember your evil ways and wicked deeds, and you will loathe yourselves for your sins and detestable practices."

In the following Bible verse, Hosea's prophecy to redeem Israel from the grave is associated with childbirth implying reincarnation:

Hosea 13:9-14: "You are destroyed, Israel, because you are against me, against your helper... The guilt of Ephraim is stored up, his sins are kept on record. Pains as of a woman in childbirth come to him, but he is a child without wisdom; when the time arrives, he doesn't have the sense to come out of the womb. I will deliver this people from the power of the grave; I will redeem them from death. Where, O death, are your plagues? Where, O grave, is your destruction?"

The prophet Isaiah gave a similar prophecy associating childbirth with reincarnation:

Isaiah 26:18-19: "We were with child, we writhed in labor, but we gave birth to wind. We have not brought salvation to the Earth, and the people of the world have not come to life. But your dead will live, Lord; their bodies will rise - let those who dwell in the dust wake up and shout for joy - your dew is like the dew of the morning; the Earth will give birth to her dead."

In the next Bible verse, Jeremiah's prophecy compared a potter, reshaping a pot from a marred lump of clay and then reforming it to another pot, to what God does to the people of Israel which has reincarnation implications:

Jeremiah 18:1-6: "This is the word that came to Jeremiah from the Lord: 'Go down to the potter's house, and there I will give you my message.' So I went down to the potter's house, and I saw him working at the wheel. But the pot he was shaping from the clay was marred in his hands; so the potter formed it into another pot, shaping it as seemed best to him. Then the word of the Lord came to me. He said, 'Can I not do with you, Israel, as this potter does?' declares the Lord. 'Like clay in the hand of the potter, so are you in my hand, Israel.'"

In NDE and reincarnation studies, a person's spirit is their immortal, eternal part of God, also known as the "higher self," the "higher consciousness," or "Holy Spirit" when enlightened. A person's soul is mental body and memories of a person's experience of a single lifetime on Earth which is a single "expression" of the spirit - much like the single facet of a diamond. The soul is also known as the "astral body," the "collective unconscious," the subconscious mind, and the psyche. After death, the soul body is absorbed into the spirit body. Before reincarnation, another three-dimensional person is created when another aspect of the spirit body becomes a person's new soul for a new experience in a new conscious physical body.

The next chapter, Ezekiel 37, is the famous passage about the "Valley of the Dry Bones," a metaphorical event which has been taken in its most literal sense by Christian theologians. The clue to the interpretation of this metaphor is in the description of the bones that "they were very dry" (verse 2) which is repeated to leave no doubt as to the meaning: from "the dust of the ground," as understood in the Book of Genesis:

Genesis 2:7: "Then the Lord God formed a man from the dust of the ground and breathed into his nostrils the breath of life, and the man became a living being"

Genesis 3:19: "By the sweat of your brow you will eat your food until you return to the ground, since from it you were taken; for dust you are and to dust you will return."

When Ezekiel followed God's orders speaking to the dry bones, he is in fact telling them from dust they will sprout flesh again in order to be finally endowed with spirit. The ancient prophet ignored what we know now as the "chain of life," a modern expression describing the cycle of recovery of the organic matter to give new material life where nothing is wasted. Everything finally returns to life - all matter to matter. And concerning the "great chain of being," the spirit returns to God to eventually reincarnate in new bodies. The key verse in Ezekiel 37 is here:

Ezekiel 37:13-14: "Then you, my people, will know that I am the Lord, when I open your graves and bring you up from them. I will put my Spirit in you and you will live, and I will settle you in your own land."

Because Israel did indeed return to their homeland after exile in Babylon, the only way the above verse could have occurred is through reincarnation. Notice also this negates a final end time corpse resurrection.

F. The Reincarnation of the Apostle John

The Bible describes the final missions of the apostles John and Peter. Jesus told Peter he was to follow him and be crucified:

John 21:18-19: "'Very truly I tell you, when you were younger you dressed yourself and went where you wanted; but when you are old you will stretch out your hands, and someone else will dress you and lead you where you do not want to go.' Jesus said this to indicate the kind of death by which Peter would glorify God. Then he said to him, 'Follow me!'"

Jesus told John he would be alive to see his return:

John 21:21-23: "When Peter saw him, he asked, 'Lord, what about him?' Jesus answered, 'If I want him to remain alive until I return, what is that to you? You must follow me.' Because of this, the rumor spread among the believers that this disciple would not die. But Jesus did not say that he would not die; he only said, 'If I want him to remain alive until I return, what is that to you?'"

In one of his letters, Peter mentioned a mission he would perform after his death:

2 Peter 1:13-15: "I think it is right to refresh your memory as long as I live in the tent of this body, because I know that I will soon put it aside, as our Lord Jesus Christ has made clear to me. And I will make every effort to see that after my departure you will always be able to remember these things."

Jesus' prophecies of the final missions of the apostles John and Peter did indeed come true. According to Christian tradition, sometime between 64 and 68 AD, the apostle Peter was crucified in Rome under Emperor Nero (54-68 AD). The apostle John was banished to the island of Patmos (off the coast of Turkey) during the reign of the Emperor Domitian (81-96 AD) for "the testimony of Jesus" where he received visions of Jesus' Second Coming of which he wrote in the Book of Revelation. One event described in the Book of Revelation appears to be a fulfillment of Peter's after-death mission described in 2 Peter 1:13-15. In the Book of Revelation, after the fall of "Babylon" and a three-fold Hallelujah by a great multitude in heaven, John encountered an "angel" whose testimony revealed the angel's identity was very likely the apostle Peter in heaven:

Revelation 19:9-10: "Then the angel said to me, 'Write this: Blessed are those who are invited to the wedding supper of the Lamb!' And he added, 'These are the true words of God.' At this I fell at his feet to worship him. But he said to me, 'Don't do that! I am a fellow servant with you and with your brothers and sisters who hold to the testimony of Jesus. Worship God! For it is the Spirit of prophecy who bears testimony to Jesus.'"

Immediately after this event, John describes Jesus appearing on a white horse and the Second Coming of Christ occurring. The evidence for the "angel's" identity as Peter seems strong. Although John did not recognize the transfigured Peter in heaven, it is probably the same reason Mary Magdalene and others did not recognize the transfigured Jesus after his death (John 20:11-17).

Revelation 19 is also a fulfillment of Jesus' prophecy concerning the apostle John:

John 21:23: "I want him (John) to remain alive until I return."

But Jesus' prophecy concerning John has a more deeper spiritual meaning - one involving reincarnation. In Revelation 10, an angel gave John a book and a heavenly voice uttered a mysterious message which John was initially forbidden to record. Later the message was revealed to John: he "must prophesy again about many peoples, nations, languages and kings." In other words, he must reincarnate and prophecy until Jesus returns:

Revelation 10:1-11: "Then I saw another mighty angel coming down from heaven.... He was holding a little scroll, which lay open in his hand. He planted his right foot on the sea and his left foot on the land, and he gave a loud shout like the roar of a lion. When he shouted, the voices of the seven thunders spoke. And when the seven thunders spoke, I was about to write; but I heard a voice from heaven say, 'Seal up what the seven thunders have said and do not write it down.' Then the angel I had seen standing on the sea and on the land raised his right hand to heaven... and said, 'There will be no more delay! But in the days when the seventh angel is about to sound his trumpet, the mystery of God will be accomplished, just as he announced to his servants the prophets.' Then the voice that I had heard from heaven spoke to me once more: 'Go, take the scroll that lies open in the hand of the angel who is standing on the sea and on the land.' So I went to the angel and asked him to give me the little scroll. He said to me, 'Take it and eat it. It will turn your stomach sour, but 'in your mouth it will be as sweet as honey.' I took the little scroll from the angel's hand and ate it. It tasted as sweet as honey in my mouth, but when I had eaten it, my stomach turned sour. Then I was told, 'You must prophesy again about many peoples, nations, languages and kings.'"

So now John 21:23 can be seen in a whole new light when Jesus told John: "I want him (John) to remain alive until I return." So Revelation 10:1-11 can be summarized in this way:

A great angel announced that he was about to give John a little scroll containing "a mystery of God" to be accomplished. In response, the seven thunders uttered a message to the angel. John began to record this message; but, another voice, a voice from heaven, said to John, "Seal up the message and do not write it down."

"Why should there be any more delay?" replied the angel; so he interceded and by saying something like this: "It has been agreed that in the days of the voice of the seventh angel, the mystery of God should be accomplished!"

Author's Note: According to Revelation 11:15-19, at the sound of the seventh angel, Jesus will reign for ever and ever (Revelation 11:15). Jesus will take his great power and rule the world (Revelation 11:17). He will reward the righteous, and judge the dead (Revelation 11:18). So, according to Revelation 10:7, this is the "mystery of God" to be accomplished at the sound of the seventh angel.

The voice from heaven agreed with the angel and said to John, "All right, get the scroll from the angel and eat it. But it will be sweet in your mouth but bitter in your belly!" So, it was agreed upon: They would give the "mystery of God" straight to John.

So John was given the message. He took the scroll and ate it. It was indeed sweet in his mouth and bitter in his belly. Why was it so sweet in his mouth and so bitter in his belly? The answer is found in verse 11: John was to "prophesy again about many peoples, nations, languages and kings." In other words, he was to reincarnate to prophesy before many peoples, nations, languages and kings. And as Jesus said in John 21:23, John would have to reincarnate ("remain alive") until Jesus returns to Earth.

So the above analysis of Revelation 10:1-11 reveals John was to become what Buddhists call a "bodhisattva" - a person who has attained liberation from reincarnation, but has taken a vow to reincarnate to help everyone else attain liberation. And if reincarnating until Christ returns is a part of John's mission, it should not be surprising that it should be a part of every Christian's mission.

G. The Reincarnation of the Apostle Paul

The apostle Paul, a Pharisee, studied under Gamaliel (Acts 22:3). Gamaliel was the grandson of one of the most famous Jewish religious leaders and co-founders of rabbinic Judaism, Hillel the Elder (110 BC -10 AD), who taught reincarnation as understood in the Bible and and the traditions of Judaism including "Merkabah mystery teachings." Paul evidently knew and believed these teachings because of his Biblical references to out-of-body experiences (2 Corinthians 12:2-4), becoming "one" with Christ (Philippians 2:1) and affirming the teachings of reincarnation (Romans 11:25-32) as one of the hidden mysteries given as an oral tradition only to those Christian initiates worthy of them. In Romans 7, Paul mentioned a time when he was not under God's law:

Romans 7:9-10: "I was once alive apart from the law, but when the commandment came, sin revived and I died, and the very commandment that promised life proved to be death to me."

Given the fact of Paul being born a Jew, an Israelite, born under the law of Moses, a descendant of Abraham from the tribe of Benjamin (Romans 11:1); the question is this: at what time was Paul "alive without the law?" He could only have been referring to a past life when he was not a Jew subjected to the law of Moses. Paul said he was alive "when the commandment came" which is a reference to being alive during the time of Moses. He said, at that time, "sin revived" and he suffered spiritual death. This makes sense only in terms of reincarnation. The Christian Gnostics understood Paul's statement as a reference to reincarnation. The "sin" is "revived" can be understood as a "revival" of old deeds in the form of karma in a new incarnation. Origen said the Christian Gnostics interpreted Romans 7:9 in this sense:

Origen: "The Apostle said, 'I lived without a law once,' that is, before I came into this body, I lived in such a form of body as was not under a law, that of a beast namely, or a bird." (Hort, Fenton John Anthony (1911). "Basilides, Gnostic sect founder". In Wace, Henry; Piercy, William C. Dictionary of Christian Biography and

Literature to the End of the Sixth Century (third ed.). London: John Murray.)

Paul affirmed the teaching of reincarnation to be one of the mysteries in Romans 11 when he described how all of Israel will be saved and how God shows mercy to everyone:

Romans 11:25-32: "I do not want you to be ignorant of this mystery, brothers and sisters, so that you may not be conceited: Israel has experienced a hardening in part until the full number of the Gentiles has come in, and in this way all Israel will be saved. As it is written: 'The deliverer will come from Zion; he will turn godlessness away from Jacob. And this is my covenant with them when I take away their sins.' As far as the gospel is concerned, they are enemies for your sake; but as far as election is concerned, they are loved on account of the patriarchs, for God's gifts and his call are irrevocable. Just as you who were at one time disobedient to God have now received mercy as a result of their disobedience, so they too have now become disobedient in order that they too may now receive mercy as a result of God's mercy to you. For God has bound everyone over to disobedience so that he may have mercy on them all."

In the above verse, Paul affirmed God's covenant with Israel has not been abrogated; and all of Israel will be saved. This is a reference to the universal salvation of all the people of Israel as promised by God in the Hebrew Bible. This includes every unrighteous and evil Israelite who ever lived. And this can only occur if God has a plan of salvation for the unrighteous after death - such as reincarnation. Not only that, Paul declared how:

Romans 11:32: "God has bound everyone over to disobedience so that he may have mercy on them all."

The above verse is a reference to the universal salvation of everyone and makes sense if reincarnation is a part of God's plan of salvation.

In two of Paul's epistles, he reveals a mystery that he (and the Christians to whom he wrote) would be alive when Christ returns and the beginning of the resurrection of the dead. But because Christ did not return when they were alive, we can assume they will be reincarnated and alive on Earth when Christ does return:

1 Corinthians 15:51-52: "Behold, I show you a mystery: We shall not all sleep (die), but we shall all be changed, In a moment, in the

twinkling of an eye, at the last trump: for the trumpet shall sound, and the dead shall be raised incorruptible, and we shall be changed."

1 Thessalonians 4:16-17: "For the Lord himself will come down from heaven, with a loud command, with the voice of the archangel and with the trumpet call of God, and the dead in Christ will rise first. After that, we who are still alive and are left will be caught up together with them in the clouds to meet the Lord in the air. And so we will be with the Lord forever."

Concerning the "dead in Christ", as Jesus explained to the Sadducees, this is a reference to the resurrection of the dead to life - reincarnation:

Matthew 22:31-32: "But about the resurrection of the dead - have you not read what God said to you, 'I am the God of Abraham, the God of Isaac, and the God of Jacob'? He is not the God of the dead but of the living."

H. Summary

The Bible refers to angels as humans, humans as angels, and spirits who "fell from heaven" long ago and are currently on a path back to God through reincarnation. The Bible mentions angels in "prisons" which is a Christian Gnostic metaphor meaning "flesh". The soul must free itself from the "prison" of flesh by following Christ in taking up its own cross. The Bible also uses "prison" as a metaphor for hell. Both angels and humans are described in the Bible as being rescued from hell. The Bible mentions the entire nation of Israel reincarnating. The Bible mentions the apostles John and Paul reincarnating. For all these reasons and more, reincarnation must now become an official doctrine of Christianity.

2. Dead Bodies Coming Out of Tombs Versus Live Babies Coming Out of Womb

A. The Case Against Resting In Peace Until the Night of the Living Dead

As previously mentioned in this article, traditional Christian eschatology holds that the Resurrection of the Dead is the doctrine of the soul after death immediately facing a particular judgment resulting in the soul either resting in peace or in torments in Hades (Greek for the Hebrew concept of Sheol) as an intermediate state until the end times when all corpses are resurrected and reunited with the soul for the Last Judgment. Accordingly, the Last Judgment then determines the soul's final destiny - either heaven (Paradise) or hell (Gehenna). However, there are serious problems with this doctrine. The doctrine was developed at a time when early influential Christians were looking for the return of Christ and an imminent end of the world. Many of them had little interest in an intermediate state between death and resurrection. But when it became apparent that Christ was not going to return anytime soon, the idea of "resting in peace", or "soul sleep" (Christian mortalism) became less appealing. The Catholic Church finally declared "soul sleep" a heresy at the Fifth Council of the Lateran (1512–1517 AD). Seven months after the closing of the council, Martin Luther posted his 95 theses against the Catholic Church thereby starting the Protestant Reformation which reinstated soul sleep. So the idea of Christians going immediately to heaven after death is a relatively new doctrine; but is supported by scripture and NDE studies. The following Bible verses suggest the soul immediately goes to heaven after death:

Luke 23:42-43: "Then he (the thief on the cross) said, 'Jesus, remember me when you come into your kingdom.' Jesus answered him, 'Truly I tell you, today you will be with me in paradise.'"

2 Corinthians 5:6-8: "Therefore we are always confident and know that as long as we are at home in the body we are away from the Lord. For we live by faith, not by sight. We are confident, I say, and would prefer to be away from the body and at home with the Lord."

Philippians 1:21-23: "For to me, to live is Christ and to die is gain. If I am to go on living in the body, this will mean fruitful labor for me. Yet what shall I choose? I do not know! I am torn between the two: I desire to depart and be with Christ, which is better by far."

The following verse is often used to refute reincarnation; but instead refutes the traditional concept of resurrection:

Hebrews 9:27-28: "Just as people are destined to die once, and after that to face judgment, so Christ was sacrificed once to take away the sins of many; and he will appear a second time, not to bear sin, but to bring salvation to those who are waiting for him."

This verse has historically been interpreted as people dying only once, then immediately facing a particular judgment, and then either "resting in peace" or in torment in Hades until the body is resurrected at the end times. But this verse simply declares a "one life, one death, one judgment" principle which doesn't refute reincarnation. According to reincarnation, a person's body dies once, never to be inhabited again; and then the soul immediately faces judgment resulting in it inhabiting either a heavenly realm, a hellish realm, or a realm in between. Later, if the soul chooses to reincarnate, it inhabits a new body having a new life subjected to a new death and new judgment. Therefore, reincarnation upholds the principle of "one life, one death, one judgment." But the above verse does not, in fact, support corpse resurrection. Corpse resurrection is the reanimation of a dead body, which happened to Lazarus and many other people in the Bible. All such people (with the exception of Christ) experienced death not once, but twice, violating the "one life, one death, one judgment" principle. Other people in the Bible, such as Enoch, Elijah and Melchizedek, supposedly did not die at all. And the Book of Revelation even mentions a second death (Revelation 2:11, Revelation 20:6, Revelation 20:14, Revelation 21:8).

A look at the original Greek translation of the word "judgment" in Strong's Bible Concordance (2920) yields even more information. The word "judgment" comes from the Greek word "krisis" which is one of the most misunderstood words in the entire Bible. The King James version rendered the word as: "accusation, condemnation, damnation, and judgment." But these words all have diverse meanings, and none of them are an exact translation. The modern English word "crisis", which is derived from the Greek word "krisis", is a more accurate rendering than the Bible translations. The actual Greek word "krisis" implies a decision that brings correction. If it is used in connection with the word "judgment" the idea of a corrective judgment is implied. The word "krisis" is used in another very interesting Bible verse:

John 5:28-29: "The hour is coming, in the which all that are in the graves shall hear his voice, and shall come forth; they that have done good, unto the resurrection of life; and they that have done evil, unto the resurrection of damnation (krisis)."

First of all, notice how the above verse appears to support corpse resurrection from graves. Jesus mentioned that someday "all that are in the graves" will hear his voice and "come forth." But as previously mentioned in Part 1 of this article, both Jews and Christians believed in an intermediate state called Sheol (Hebrew) which translated into Hades (Greek) where both the righteous and unrighteous go. So Jesus is referring to souls in Hades who will hear his voice and come forth to appear before God's Judgment Seat, and not literally corpses "in their graves" resurrecting to Earth.

Secondly, notice how in the above verse in John 5:28-29, Jesus mentions two types of resurrections:

Two Types of Resurrections

(1) The resurrection of life: For those who have done good.

(2) The resurrection of "krisis": For those who have done evil.

So a resurrection of "damnation" is an incorrect word for translators to use. The resurrection of "krisis" should more appropriately be called "the resurrection of correction" or "the resurrection which forces correct decisions." Such a "resurrection" would be a reincarnation into a lifetime involving the person's karma. For example, if the person "lived by the sword" in their previous lifetime and did not "die by the sword" nor repent, then they could reincarnate into a lifetime where they would "die by the sword" and be given the opportunity to pay their karmic debt, repent and be saved.

Anti-reincarnationalists have trouble explaining the justification of the injustice of a particular situation where a mass murderer, such as Hitler, could repent and accept Jesus at the last moment of his life and be guaranteed a "ticket" to heaven. While it is true that Christ paid the price for all sin for which God has forgiven all of humanity of sin; and therefore nobody will perish or suffer for eternity in hell - and everyone will eventually be saved - this event occurred almost 2,000 years ago and all of humanity has stood redeemed ever since. So, all of humanity technically stands on good grace with God. But karma, on the other hand, is God's divine law which governs the relationships of humans between humans. It is one thing for God to forgive a murderer for killing someone, it is another thing for the murderer's victim to forgive the murderer. This is where karma comes in. Murdering someone is a sin against both God and the victim. The murderer must seek forgiveness from both God and the victim. Having God forgive a murderer of murdering someone does not free the murderer of the obligation of seeking forgiveness from the victim. Then there also is the issue of restitution to the victim. On top of that, there is karma for starting the whole cycle to begin with. So it is not enough to accept Christ's sacrifice on the cross for our sins. Jesus said, "Whoever does not take up their cross and follow me is not worthy of me." (Matthew 10:38) And "Whoever wants to be my disciple must deny themselves and take up their cross and follow me." (Mark 8:34) Karma is reincarnation: "Live by the sword, die by the sword." "Eye for eye, tooth for tooth" and "Whoever sheds human blood, by humans shall their blood be shed." (Genesis 9:6) So karma allows a murderer to reincarnate, to be put in a position of possibly being murdered with the opportunity to instead be forgiven by his murderer and avoid being murdered himself. Jesus' payment of Adam's karmic debt allowed God to forgive all humanity (1 Corinthians 15:22;45). Karma permits humans to forgive each other. Jesus explained this principle perfectly in Matthew 5 where he taught how God's perfect Law is not abrogated:

Matthew 5:17-20: "Do not think that I have come to abolish the Law or the Prophets; I have not come to abolish them but to fulfill them. For truly I tell you, until heaven and Earth disappear, not the smallest letter, not the least stroke of a pen, will by any means disappear from the Law until everything is accomplished. Therefore anyone who sets aside one of the least of these commands and teaches others accordingly will be called least in the kingdom of heaven, but whoever practices and teaches these commands will be called great in the kingdom of heaven. For I tell you that unless your righteousness surpasses that of the Pharisees and the teachers of the law, you will certainly not enter the kingdom of heaven."

Then, later in the same chapter, Jesus taught why we must overcome the consequences of God's perfect Law:

Matthew 5:21-26: "You have heard that it was said to the people long ago, 'You shall not murder, and anyone who murders will be subject to judgment.' But I tell you that anyone who is angry with a brother or sister will be subject to judgment. Again, anyone who says to a brother or sister, 'Raca,' is answerable to the court. And anyone who says, 'You fool!' will be in danger of the fire of hell. Therefore, if you are offering your gift at the altar and there remember that your brother or sister has something against you, leave your gift there in front of the altar. First go and be reconciled to them; then come and offer your gift. Settle matters quickly with your adversary who is taking you to court. Do it while you are still together on the way, or your adversary may hand you over to the judge, and the judge may hand you over to the officer, and you may be thrown into prison. Truly I tell you, you will not get out until you have paid the last penny."

Jesus doesn't say "Truly I tell you, you will not get out at all, forever, eternal damnation." He said "until you have paid the last penny" suggesting limited punishment. It also invalidates the popular Christian notion of eternal hell, fire and brimstone as in the graphic on the left.

So, a "correcting judgment" implied with a "reincarnation of correction" doesn't nullify salvation by grace as some anti-reincarnationalist assume. The idea that reincarnation is contrary to the concept of salvation through grace is based upon an inadequate understanding of the nature of reincarnation and its biblical application. Such misunderstanding completely misses the point of God's judgment as a "correcting judgment" and Christ's status as spiritual "counselor" and "advocate." It also fails to understand that karma and reincarnation are the very instruments of implementing God's grace. In fact, the opposite interpretation - a resurrection of "damnation" - limits God's grace by requiring God to pronounce judgment of horrible eternal consequences because of a single earthly life lived under conditions of apparent unjust inequity among human beings. The damnation principle also creates spiritual laziness by lulling the Christian into believing one life is enough to attain spiritual perfection in Christ. The damnation principle also allows for immoral behavior by suggesting that people can avoid their transgressions against others by simply "accepting Christ" without realizing that no one who truly accepts Christ can escape seeking forgiveness and paying restitution to those they have wronged. And as previously mentioned in Part 4, the NDE "life review" is evidence of the corrective judgment mentioned in the Bible.

The following is another interesting Bible verse supporting reincarnation as "resurrection":

John 5:21: "For just as the Father raises the dead and gives them life, even so the Son gives life to whom he is pleased to give it."

In the above verse, Jesus plainly says how, in the same way that the Father "raises the dead to life," so does Jesus "give life" to whomever he pleases. Notice Jesus used the present tense to say the equivalent of: "The Father is currently raising the dead and giving them life, even as I am currently giving life to whomever I please." If the Father is currently "raising the dead" before the end times, then this is a reference to reincarnation and not an end time corpse resurrection. And the "life" Jesus is giving to whomever he pleases must then refer to spiritual "resurrection" - regeneration by the Holy Spirit.

Another fact contradicting the Hebrews 9:27-28 misinterpretation of "people are destined to die only once" is the mentioning of the "second death" described in Revelation 20:14-15 when those who are judged to be "damned" must suffer a second and final death again. More will be said about "the damned" this later in this article.

Paul also contradicts the idea of "resting in peace" until a final corpse resurrection in his Second Epistle to the Corinthians:

2 Corinthians 5:1: "For we know that if the earthly tent we live in is destroyed, we have a building from God, an eternal house in heaven, not built by human hands."

2 Corinthians 5:8: "We are confident, I say, and would prefer to be away from the body and at home with the Lord."

2 Corinthians 12:2-4: "I know a man in Christ who fourteen years ago was caught up to the third heaven. Whether it was in the body or out of the body I do not know - God knows. And I know that this man - whether in the body or apart from the body I do not know, but God knows - was caught up to paradise and heard inexpressible things, things that no one is permitted to tell."

Paul used the idiom "I know a man" out of modesty because he is referring to himself. In Acts 14:19 Paul is described as being stoned and left for dead. This may be when Paul experienced his NDE. Nevertheless, the man who was "caught up to the third heaven" did so during an out-of-body experience and certainly an NDE. The fact that the man went straight to heaven after death also contradicts the idea of the soul resting in Hades until an end time corpse resurrection. Perhaps this is why Paul could confidently say:

Philippians 1:21: "For to me, to live is Christ and to die is gain."

Evidence against soul sleep until the end times is supported by multitudes of people who have had an NDE where they describe traveling immediately into the afterlife after death with the possibility of returning to reincarnate later. In fact, NDE studies reveal how believing in soul sleep until a corpse resurrection can even be dangerous. The following is an excerpt from the NDE testimony of Dr. George Ritchie when he was given a guided tour of the afterlife by Jesus:

Dr. George Ritchie: "One of the places we observed seemed to be a receiving station. Beings would arrive here oftentimes in a deep hypnotic sleep. I call it hypnotic because I realized they had put themselves in this state by their beliefs. Here were what I would call angels working with them trying to arouse them and help them realize God is truly a God of the living and that they did not have to lie around sleeping until Gabriel or someone came along blowing on a horn."

The dangers of believing in "resting in peace" until a "corpse resurrection" is also affirmed by others NDE experiencers:

Arthur Yensen: "Things change little in the hereafter. Suppose we have the fixed idea that we'll sleep till the resurrection of the body. Then suppose there isn't a resurrection of the body. We might sleep a very long time."

P.M.H. Atwater: "Those that died believing they would sleep until awakened by Gabriel, reported a black darkness, a feeling of being trapped and alone, stranded. What I've finally come to realize is we truly and most literally create our own realities. When we die, the reality we created is where we will live and what we will become."

Betty Bethards: "If you don't believe in God or an afterlife, you will probably be kept in a sleep state for the first two to three day period. You will wake up in a beautiful meadow or some other calm and peaceful place where you can reconcile the transition from the death state to the continuous life. You are given teachings in the hope that you do not refuse to believe that you are dead."

Ruth Montgomery: "He (the atheist) expects to find nothing when he passes through the door called "death", and for a long time that is usually what he finds - nothing. He is in a state like unto death for a goodly while, until at last something arouses him."

Another Bible verse appears to suggest corpses are indeed resurrected at the end of time. The passage about the resurrection of Lazarus is one of them:

John 11:23-26: "Jesus said to her, 'Your brother will rise again.'

Martha answered, 'I know he will rise again in the resurrection at the last day.' Jesus said to her, 'I am the resurrection and the life. The one who believes in me will live, even though they die; and whoever lives by believing in me will never die. Do you believe this?'"

But in the above verse, Jesus corrected Martha about how Lazarus would "rise" again - a word that also applied to reincarnating prophets and others in Biblical times

Matthew 11:11: "Truly I tell you, among those born of women there has not risen anyone greater than John the Baptist; yet whoever is least in the kingdom of heaven is greater than he."

Isaiah 45:13: "I will raise up Cyrus to fulfill my righteous purpose, and I will guide his actions. He will restore my city and free my captive people - without seeking a reward! I, the Lord of Heaven's Armies, have spoken!"

Zechariah 11:16: "For I am going to raise up a shepherd over the land who will not care for the lost, or seek the young, or heal the injured, or feed the healthy, but will eat the meat of the choice sheep, tearing off their hooves."

Jeremiah 29:15: "You may say, 'The Lord has raised up prophets for us in Babylon.'"

In reply to Jesus telling Martha that Lazarus would rise again, Martha expressed her confusion of believing Lazarus' corpse would rise out of his grave on the "Last Day." But by literally raising several people from the dead, and teaching the correct concept of both spiritual "resurrection" (regeneration by the Holy Spirit) and bodily "resurrection" (reincarnation), Jesus demonstrated that there is no final resurrection of corpses at the Last Day. Jesus corrected Martha by revealing to her the real meaning of "resurrection" - that it doesn't involve the dead, but the living. By stating, "I am the resurrection and the life," Jesus informed Martha that he the living example of the "true resurrection" which is of the Holy Spirit and not the body. Jesus taught how people don't have to wait until the "Last Day" to have this new, spiritually "resurrected" life. To emphasize his point, Jesus miraculously raised Lazarus from death - something that astonished even his religious enemies (John 12:9-11).

During reported NDEs involving Jesus, it is very common for Jesus to help near-death experiencers rise from their dead bodies to heaven during their NDEs. Some NDEs involve Jesus freeing people from hell, such as the NDE of Howard Storm, proving that the "Harrowing of Hell" by Jesus continues to occur. NDE testimonies alone are evidence against a final resurrection of corpses. NDEs also show that reincarnation is a part of God's plan. And as previously mentioned in Part 4 of this article, according to NDE studies, God's judgment on "Judgment Day" is actually a "life review" which occurs immediately after death which results in determining the next stage in the life of the soul in the next afterlife realm. Time in the afterlife is also different than we experience on Earth according to NDEs. And the idea of a literal 24-hour "Last Day" time period when corpses are reanimated for Jesus to judge can be refuted with the following Bible verse: "With the Lord a day is like a thousand years, and a thousand years are like a day" (2 Peter 3:8).

B. Paul and the Reincarnation of the Spirit

In Chapter 15 of Paul's First Epistle to the Corinthians, he described the mystery of the renewal of man through the sacrifice of Christ and the resurrection. From 1 Corinthians 15:1-34, Paul discussed the resurrection of Christ which has historically been interpreted to mean a resurrection of Christ's corpse. However, the Christian Universalist scholar, Ken R. Vincent, Ph.D., submitted two scholarly peer-reviewed papers[1] [2] showing how the resurrection appearances of Christ could have been apparitional experiences of Christ as opposed to corpse resurrection appearances - relegating what exactly happened to Christ's corpse to be a mystery. Modern parapsychological research is familiar with the phenomenon of "after-death communications" which includes full-body apparitions of the recently deceased appearing to grieving loved ones to comfort them. The author's website has several examples.

After speaking of Christ's resurrection, Paul began his description of the nature of the "resurrection body" starting from verse 1 Corinthians 15:35 by discarding in verse 37 the idea of the spirit incarnating into the reanimation of a corpse:

1 Corinthians 15:35-38: "But someone will ask, 'How are the dead raised? With what kind of body will they come?' How foolish! What you sow does not come to life unless it dies. When you sow, you do not plant the body that will be, but just a seed, perhaps of wheat or of something else. But God gives it a body as he has determined, and

to each kind of seed he gives its own body."

Jesus also affirmed this "same old spirit, new body" concept in the Gospel of Matthew in his Parable of the New Wine into Old Wineskins:

Matthew 9:14-17: "Then John's disciples came and asked him, 'How is it that we and the Pharisees fast often, but your disciples do not fast?' Jesus answered, 'How can the guests of the bridegroom mourn while he is with them? The time will come when the bridegroom will be taken from them; then they will fast. No one sews a patch of unshrunk cloth on an old garment, for the patch will pull away from the garment, making the tear worse. Neither do people pour new wine into old wineskins. If they do, the skins will burst; the wine will run out and the wineskins will be ruined. No, they pour new wine into new wineskins, and both are preserved.'"

The central point of Jesus' parable seems to be that one shouldn't try to fit new concepts to old ways of thinking. As applied to fasting, Jesus didn't want his "new wine" (disciples) to be exposed to "old wineskins" (the harsh, old tradition of fasting) while they were about to experience the grief of his death. It would have been too much suffering for them. As applied to corpse resurrection, one doesn't put "new wine" (the spirit) into "old wineskins" (a corpse). In the same way that it is best to use new cloth to patch new clothing, store new wine into new wineskins, and have the disciples rejoice while they still have Jesus - so it is best that the spirit incarnate into a new body. Like taking off your old clothes and putting on new clothes, when a person enters a new life on Earth the spirit receives a new body and gives up the old and useless one. It's a more natural solution and the parable fits perfectly with the idea of reincarnation and the continuity of life.

Then in 1 Corinthians 15:39-40, Paul continued to clarify, contrary to what some eastern religions believe, the human spirit does not reincarnate into animals. He even gives the reasons for this:

(1) 1 Corinthians 15:39-41: "Not all flesh is the same: People have one kind of flesh, animals have another, birds another and fish another. There are also heavenly bodies and there are earthly bodies; but the splendor of the heavenly bodies is one kind, and the splendor of the earthly bodies is another. The sun has one kind of splendor, the moon another and the stars another; and star differs from star in

splendor."

(2) 1 Corinthians 15:44: "It is sown a natural body, it is raised a spiritual body. If there is a natural body, there is also a spiritual body."

(3) 1 Corinthians 15:50: "I declare to you, brothers and sisters, that flesh and blood cannot inherit the kingdom of God, nor does the perishable inherit the imperishable."

So, according to Paul, the "resurrection of the dead" involves the raising of the spirit to heaven at the time of death because: "What you sow does not come to life unless it dies" (verse 36). And we know after his resurrection, Christ descended into the intermediate regions of the afterlife - into Hades - to free the souls captive there; thereby disproving the notion of resting in peace until an end time corpse resurrection day.

C. An Immortal and Indestructible Soul Implies Reincarnation

Jesus taught, "The Kingdom of God is within you" (Luke 17:20-21) which implies divinity within humanity. The Hebrew words used to describe the soul and spirit are "nephesh" (literally "living being"), "ruach" (literally "wind"), "neshama" (literally "breath"), "chaya" (literally "life") and "yechidah" (literally "singularity"). In Judaism the soul is believed to be given by God to a person as mentioned in Genesis:

Genesis 2:7: "And the Lord God formed man of the dust of the ground, and breathed into his nostrils the breath of life; and man became a living soul."

Judaism equates the quality of one's soul to one's performance of the commandments, mitzvot, and reaching higher levels of understanding, and thus closeness to God. A person with such closeness is called a "tzadik" - a righteous one. Therefore, Judaism embraces the commemoration of the day of one's death - "Yahrtzeit" - and not the birthday as a festivity of remembrance, for only toward the end of life's struggles, tests and challenges could human souls be judged and credited for righteousness and holiness. Judaism places great importance on the study of souls.

The Kabbalah and other religious traditions go into greater detail into the nature of the soul. The Kabbalah separates the soul into five elements, corresponding to the five worlds:

(1) "nephesh" which is related to natural instinct.
(2) "ruach" which is related to emotion and morality.
(3) "neshamah" which is related to intellect and the awareness of God.
(4) "chayah" which is considered a part of God.
(5) "yechidah" which is also termed the "pintele Yid" (the "essential [inner] Jew"). This aspect is essentially one with God. Kabbalah also proposed a concept of reincarnation, the gilgul. See also "nefesh habehamit" - the "animal soul".

The Greek New Testament counterpart to the Hebrew Old Testament word for soul (nephesh) is "psyche". The Greek New Testament counterpart to the Hebrew Old Testament word for spirit (ruach) is "pneuma". In the New Testament the words for soul and spirit carry a similar "range of meanings" and both can designate the person or the person's life as a whole. According to early Christian writers, towards the end of the 2nd century, psyche had begun to be understood in a more Greek than a Hebrew way, contrasted with the body. By the 3rd century, with the influence of Origen, the traditions of the inherent immortality of the soul and its divine nature were established. Inherent immortality of the soul was accepted among western and eastern theologians throughout the Middle Ages, and after the Reformation.

Next to Paul, the first Church Father Origen is one of the most influential figures in early Christianity because of his Greek scholarship, asceticism and his prolific writings in multiple branches of Christian theology, including textual criticism, biblical exegesis and hermeneutics, philosophical theology, preaching, and spirituality. Origen's cosmology of humanity begins with the preexistence of all spirits in heaven. Before the known world was created, God created all immortal spiritual intelligences - none have been created since then. At first devoted to the contemplation and love of their Creator, a large number of these intelligences eventually grew bored of contemplating God, their love for God grew cold, and they left their former habitations. This resulted in the creation of the physical universe. Those spirits whose love for God diminished the most became what is known as "demons." Those spirits whose love diminished moderately became human souls and eventually began to incarnate in fleshly bodies. Those spirits whose love diminished the least remained as angels. One spirit, however, who remained perfectly devoted to God became, through love, one with the Word (Logos) of God. The Logos ultimately took on flesh and was born of Mary, becoming Jesus the Christ.

The diverse conditions in which human beings are born is dependent upon what their souls did in this preexistent state and in previous lifetimes. For this reason what apparently seems unfair, that some souls are born into families with few resources while other souls are born into families with many resources; some souls are born into unhealthy lives while others are born healthy; and so forth, is as Origen insists, actually a by-product of the free will of souls. The return of the fallen condition of the cosmos to its original state through divine reason is the object of the entire cosmic process. Through reincarnation, all souls will eventually return to Paradise - the "apocatastasis". God so ordered the universe, all individual acts work freely together toward one cosmic end which culminates in returning to God as co-creators. Humanity, conceived in the image of God with an eternal soul (spirit), and is able by imitating God in good works to become like Christ - the perfect image of God within a human being. The following Bible verses support this:

Genesis 1:26: "Then God said, 'Let us make mankind in our image, in our likeness.'"

2 Corinthians 4:18: "So we fix our eyes not on what is seen, but on what is unseen, since what is seen is temporary, but what is unseen is eternal."

Luke 17:20-21: "Now when He was asked by the Pharisees when the kingdom of God would come, He answered them and said, 'The kingdom of God does not come with observation; nor will they say, 'See here!' or 'See there!' For indeed, the kingdom of God is within you.'"

John 10:30-36: "'I and the Father are one.' Again his Jewish opponents picked up stones to stone him, but Jesus said to them, 'I have shown you many good works from the Father. For which of these do you stone me?' 'We are not stoning you for any good work,' they replied, 'but for blasphemy, because you, a mere man, claim to be God.' Jesus answered them, 'Is it not written in your Law, 'I have said you are gods? If he called them gods, to whom the word of God came - and Scripture cannot be set aside - what about the one whom the Father set apart as his very own and sent into the world? Why then do you accuse me of blasphemy because I said, 'I am God's Son'?"

Psalm 82:6: "I (God) said, 'You are gods; you are all sons of the Most High.'"

John 1:12-13: "But as many as received him, to them gave he power to become the sons of God, even to them that believe on his name: Which were born, not of blood, nor of the will of the flesh, nor of the will of man, but of God."

Matthew 23:9: "And do not call anyone on Earth 'father,' for you have one Father, and he is in heaven."

D: Thy Kingdom Come Through Reincarnation

In the Book of Acts of the Apostles, as Jesus was about to ascend to heaven, the disciples learned how Jesus will return to Earth in his heavenly body to establish the Kingdom of Heaven:

Acts 1:6-11: "Then they gathered around him and asked him, 'Lord, are you at this time going to restore the kingdom to Israel?' He said to them: 'It is not for you to know the times or dates the Father has set by his own authority. But you will receive power when the Holy Spirit comes on you; and you will be my witnesses in Jerusalem, and in all Judea and Samaria, and to the ends of the Earth.' After he said this, he was taken up before their very eyes, and a cloud hid him from their sight. They were looking intently up into the sky as he was going, when suddenly two men dressed in white stood beside them. 'Men of Galilee,' they said, 'why do you stand here looking into the sky? This same Jesus, who has been taken from you into heaven, will come back in the same way you have seen him go into heaven.'"

Notice how Jesus' followers expected the Kingdom of Heaven to be established on Earth when Jesus was about to ascend to heaven. But Jesus told them they would first have to personally be witnesses "to the ends of the Earth." The only logical way for them to do so is through reincarnation. Christ's prophecy of his disciples being witnesses "to the ends of the Earth" has indeed been fulfilled. As of 2012, Christianity has the largest number of adherents in the world with 2.2 billion adherents or 31.5%, Islam with 1.6 billion adherents or 22.32%; non-religious or atheist with 1.1 billion adherents or 15.35%; and Hinduism with 1 billion adherents or 13.95%. The influence Christianity has had upon the world throughout history, both good and bad (but especially good), certainly cannot be denied. So Jesus' prophecy of the worldwide spread of his teachings have certainly come true. The idea of Christians reincarnating and spreading Christianity to the entire world until Christ returns is similar to the central point of Jesus' Parable of the Weeds in Matthew 13:

Matthew 13:24-30: "Jesus told them another parable: 'The kingdom of heaven is like a man who sowed good seed in his field. But while everyone was sleeping, his enemy came and sowed weeds among the wheat, and went away. When the wheat sprouted and formed heads, then the weeds also appeared. The owner's servants came to him and said, 'Sir, didn't you sow good seed in your field? Where then did the weeds come from?' 'An enemy did this,' he replied. The servants asked him, 'Do you want us to go and pull them up?' 'No,' he answered, 'because while you are pulling the weeds, you may uproot the wheat with them. Let both grow together until the harvest. At that time I will tell the harvesters: First collect the weeds and tie them in bundles to be burned; then gather the wheat and bring it into my barn."

Jesus' notion of wheat and weeds growing in a field until the harvest is an ideal metaphor for Christians reincarnating until they have spread Christianity to the entire world. Like the good seed being planted, the good soul is born into the world. Likewise, the weed seed being planted, the bad soul is born into the world. Then the seeds "die" (i.e., germinate, see 1 Corinthians 15:35-37) and plants begin to sprout. Throughout a plant's morphology, as the plant matures, it will bud many times. In the same way, as the same soul matures it will reincarnate many times. Finally, as with the soul, when the plant has reached full maturity it is ready for the harvest - the Kingdom of God.

Paul described how our spiritual "resurrection" - regeneration by the Holy Spirit - allows God to show his grace in the "ages to come." The assumption is God shows his grace in the "ages to come" until the arrival of the Kingdom on Earth through bodily "resurrection" (reincarnation):

Ephesians 2:6-7: "[God] raised us up with him (Christ) and seated us with him in the heavenly places in Christ Jesus, so that in the ages to come he might show the immeasurable riches of his grace in kindness toward us in Christ Jesus."

E. The Book of Revelation and Reincarnation

The Book of Revelation occupies a central place in Christian eschatology. It's the only apocalyptic document in the New Testament canon although there are short apocalyptic passages in various places in the Gospels and the Epistles. The author, assumed to be the apostle John, describes a series of prophetic visions, including figures such as the "Whore of Babylon" and "the Beast", culminating in the Second Coming of Jesus and the establishment of the Kingdom of Heaven on Earth and eventual a new heaven and a new Earth. Wikipedia has an excellent chronological list of events in the Book of Revelation and an outline of the book. The obscure and extravagant imagery has led to a wide variety of Christian interpretations. Historicist interpretations view Revelation as a broad view of history. Preterist interpretations view Revelation as mostly referring to the events of the apostolic era (1st century), or, at the latest, the fall of the Roman Empire. Futurist interpretations view Revelation describing future events. Idealist or symbolic interpretations of Revelation refers to, not only actual people or events, but also as an allegory of the spiritual path and the ongoing struggle between good and evil both within individual human beings and within humanity in general. The famous Christian psychic and near-death experiencer, Edgar Cayce (1877-1945), gave an idealist, dream interpretation to the Book of Revelation by which he unlocked all of its metaphorical symbols. Some of these interpretations, both literal and symbolic, also involve reincarnation. A similar symbolic Christian Gnostic interpretation of the Book of Revelation was provided by James M. Pryse in his 1910, free, 244-page work, "The Apocalypse Unsealed."

Through his thousands of documented out-of-body journeys to heavenly realms, Cayce received information which discovered the Bible to be the symbolic account of the Fall of the human soul from its divine origins, as symbolically described in the Book of Genesis, culminating symbolically with the restoration of the human soul to heaven in the Book of Revelation. Cayce was an expert in dream interpretation and he believed the key to unlocking the mysteries of the Book of Revelation was through dream interpretation. The apostle John received his visions through deep meditation and prayer which is obvious because his visions contain a tremendous amount of dream symbolism - some of which can be found in the prophet Daniel's dreams and the prophet Ezekiel's spiritual visions. All Biblical dreams, such as those of Joseph, Gideon, Daniel, Paul, and Peter, are highly symbolic and have a deeper spiritual interpretation. Such symbolism, as in the Book of Revelation, must be viewed as dream symbols rather than literal symbols to be interpreted - although more than one interpretation (historic, preterist, futurist, or idealist) can exist.

F. The Dream Interpretation of the End Times in the Book of Revelation

Literal Interpretation: In chapters 15-18 of the Book of Revelation, the apostle John is shown seven angels each of whom holds a vial containing a plague which they pour upon the Earth one at a time. John then saw a prostitute sitting on a seven-headed beast with ten horns. She wore on her forehead the name "Mystery, Babylon the Great, the Mother of Harlots and Abominations of the Earth." John is told the seven heads symbolizes the seven mountains on which the woman sits; and the ten horns symbolizes ten kings. These make war against the lamb and the lamb conquered.

Cayce interpretation: John saw within the "body of humanity" (the "Earth") being purified and tested on seven spiritual centers of the human body (the "chakras", endocrine glands) symbolized by the seven plagues (karmic tribulation of purification) being poured out by the seven angels (spiritual influences on the spiritual centers of the body). The "prostitute" riding "a beast" symbolizes humanity's lust for riches and gratification of the flesh. The beast it rides on are the unevolved animalistic influence within human beings stemming from self-gratification. John is told these influences had taken control of the seven spiritual centers of the human body, thereby becoming possessed and ruled. However, because the highest forces of evolved humanity (the "lamb", Christ Consciousness) overcame the forces of self, even the ten basic urges of the body symbolized by the ten horns, these same forces will in time fulfill the divine pattern (the "Logos", the Word of God). As the divine nature in humanity become less realized, society is destroyed (Armageddon) by its own hand through self-gratification.

Literal Interpretation: In chapter 19 of the Book of Revelation, John saw a great multitude of people in heaven praising God for the fall of Babylon. Then the "wedding supper of the Lamb" was announced. Christ returned to Earth with his "armies of heaven" and cast the "beast" and the "false prophet" into the Lake of Fire.

Cayce interpretation: John witnessed the final salvation of the bodily, mental, and spiritual forces taken place in himself and collective humanity. This is the "Wedding of the Lamb" - the union of the body and mind with the Christ Consciousness. When humanity recognizes the divinity within them as the controlling force in the world, and turns away from their own selfish pattern of living for self alone, the old pattern will disappear and the Christ pattern will emerge. The "Bride" is the body raised as a new being. The merging of the evolved self with the divine superconscious (Holy Spirit), which has taken place in John, must also take place in all humanity (verse 7). The "false prophet" symbolizes self-delusion. The "Lake of Fire" symbolizes self-judgment, self-condemnation, the repressed area of the subconscious mind.

Literal Interpretation: In chapter 20 of the Book of Revelation, an angel seizes Satan and imprisons him into the Abyss for a thousand years. Then the first resurrection of God's holy people occurs including those martyred because of the Word of God. They live and reign with Christ for a thousand years. Afterward, Satan is released from the Abyss and he then tries to deceive the nations. He gathers them for battle against the holy city. Satan makes war against God's people, but is defeated and cast into the Lake of Fire. The Last Judgment of the dead occurs. Anyone not found in the book of life, along with death and Hades, are cast into the Lake of Fire which is the second death.

Cayce interpretation: "Satan" symbolizes the "fallen" spiritual nature in humanity (as opposed to the spirit of truth): the spirit of hate, contention, strife, faultfinding, lovers of self, lovers of praise, etc. The "thousand year reign of Christ" is the literal thousand year reign of Christ and Christ Consciousness on Earth - the coming golden age predicted in the Bible. The "first resurrection" is the reincarnation of only advanced souls to Earth during the thousand years. "Satan imprisoned into the Abyss" is the prevention of souls from the lower afterlife realms from reincarnating to Earth during those thousand years. "Satan released from the Abyss" symbolizes the permission of souls from the lower afterlife realms to reincarnate to the Earth once again after the thousand years is over. During the thousand years of peace, the planet will be healed. Great spiritual schools will be developed. Great institutions and organizations will be established, all by spiritually enlightened human beings to help those unenlightened souls when they are once again allowed to reincarnate. When the remaining souls from the lower afterlife realms begin to reincarnate, bringing with them their unsatisfied ambitions and desires, this will attempt to bring about the former conditions of imbalance (wars, plagues, Armageddon). These conditions, all man-made, will then be themselves eliminated and all mental forms and patterns not formed by divine will are purged. The "dead in judgment" symbolizes reincarnating souls. The "Book of Life" is a person's "akashic records" - all the memories and knowledge of the soul's experience in time. "Hell" and "fire and brimstone" represents purification. The "second death" is the destruction of all man-made unevolved conditions of the soul.

Literal Interpretation: In chapter 21 of the Book of Revelation, the "first heaven" and the "first Earth" is replaced with a new heaven and new Earth. Then God comes to dwell with humanity in the "New Jerusalem" where there is no more suffering or death.

Cayce interpretation: Along with a literal interpretation, Cayce interpreted the "new heaven and new Earth" that John saw as a metaphor of humanity's perfected state of consciousness and regenerated body. Humanity at this point is now one with the divine in the perfection of control and is free from outside limitations. The human mind merges with the Spirit. The "New Jerusalem" is the spirit awakened in oneness with divinity. The "Temple of God" is the human being with the Christ consciousness. These verses also imply hell itself will be judged and cast into the "Lake of Fire" for purification (verses 6-8). They also indicate there is not just one heaven, for it states the "first heaven" would pass away and the "holy city" would come down out of heaven (presumably from another heaven). Note that the Bible mentions three heavens. In the New Testament Apocrypha (the Apocalypse of Paul), it not only mentions a total of ten heavens, it mentions a soul being punished by having to reincarnate to Earth.

God creating a new heaven and a new Earth is interesting because it exactly matches a reference to reincarnation presented earlier in this article, Ecclesiastes 1:1-11, which speaks of the cycles of nature and peoples not having memories of prior lifetimes (verse 11), and also specifically echoes Isaiah 65:17:

Revelation 21:1: "Then I saw a new heaven and a new Earth, for the first heaven and the first Earth had passed away, and there was no longer any sea."

Isaiah 65:17: "See, I will create new heavens and a new Earth. The former things will not be remembered, nor will they come to mind."

Ecclesiastes 1:11: "No one remembers the former generations, and even those yet to come will not be remembered by those who follow them."

Apparently, there is a good reason for God to create a new heaven and a new Earth. This will allow the people in the first heaven to transfer to the second heaven. God's people on the old Earth can transfer to the new first heaven. This is the fulfillment of reincarnation allowing souls to work their way through the afterlife realms immediately after death to attain higher heavens. Those people who are purified in the lower "Lake of Fire" (or "Gehenna" as Jesus taught) can then eventually reincarnate to the new Earth where there will be "no remembrance of former things."

In chapter 22 of the Book of Revelation, John saw the Garden of Eden restored on Earth. He is shown the "river of Water of Life" and the "Tree of Life" which is for the healing of the nations and peoples. The curse of sin has ended. The Book of Revelation also reveals the Kingdom of Heaven is here and growing now - within us and around us - just as is the "resurrection" (reincarnation) has been constantly occurring here and now:

2 Corinthians 6:2: "For he says, 'In the time of my favor I heard you, and in the day of salvation I helped you.' I tell you, now is the time of God's favor, now is the day of salvation."

Isaiah 49:8: "This is what the Lord says: 'In the time of my favor I will answer you, and in the day of salvation I will help you; I will keep you and will make you to be a covenant for the people, to restore the land and to reassign its desolate inheritances.'"

G. The Lake of Fire as the Purification of Reincarnation

So the "Lake of Fire" is not a resurrection of "eternal damnation," rather it is the purification of reincarnation. Most translations of Revelation 20:10 render "forever and ever" (in Greek "aionas ton aionon") to mean eternity, perpetuity or everlasting - such as the New Revised Standard Version (NRSV) translation:

Revelation 20:10: "And the devil who had deceived them was thrown into the lake of fire and sulfur, where the beast and the false prophet were, and they will be tormented day and night forever and ever (aionas ton aionon)."

However, the correct translation of "aionas ton aionon" is "ages of the ages" as found in Young's Literal Translation (YLT):

Revelation 20:10, YLT: "And the Devil, who is leading them astray, was cast into the lake of fire and brimstone, where are the beast and the false prophet, and they shall be tormented day and night - to the ages of the ages (aionas ton aionon)."

The Greek word "aion" is English for "age." In the context of Biblical Hebrew cosmology, "age" refers to an astrological age which is one of twelve astrological ages corresponding to the twelve zodiacal signs of the Zodiac ("Mazzaroth" in Hebrew). The length of one astrological age is approximately 2,160 years. As of 2017, humanity is transitioning from the Age of Pisces (the fish, the Church Age) to the Age of Aquarius (the water-bearer, the Christ Age). So in some Bible translations, they make a reference to the end of "the world" (instead of "age") or about "eternal" (instead of "age-enduring") punishment while in other translations the reference has a much different translation and meaning. Compare the following small selection of verses from Matthews gospel which speak of the "ages," and see how much it changes the meaning. The first translation is the King James Version (KJV):

Matthew 12:32; 24:3; 25:46; 28:20, KJV: "And whosoever speaketh a word against the Son of man, it shall be forgiven him: but whosoever speaketh against the Holy Ghost, it shall not be forgiven him, neither in this world, neither in the world to come ... And as he sat upon the mount of Olives, the disciples came unto him privately, saying, 'Tell us, when shall these things be? and what shall be the sign of thy coming, and of the end of the world?' ... And these shall go away into everlasting punishment: but the righteous into life eternal ... Teaching them to observe all things whatsoever I have commanded you: and, lo, I am with you always, even unto the end of the world. Amen."

Now compare the above King James Bible verses with the same Bible verses in the New International Version of the Bible:

Matthew 12:32; 24:3; 25:46; 28:20, NIV: "Anyone who speaks a word against the Son of Man will be forgiven, but anyone who speaks against the Holy Spirit will not be forgiven, either in this age or in the age to come ... As Jesus was sitting on the Mount of Olives, the disciples came to him privately. 'Tell us,' they said, 'when will this happen, and what will be the sign of your coming and of the end of the age?'... Then they will go away to eternal (age-enduring) punishment, but the righteous to eternal (age-enduring) life ... and teaching them to obey everything I have commanded you. And surely I am with you always, to the very end of the age."

Notice how the correct interpretation shows the so-called "unforgivable sin" of blasphemy against the Holy Spirit proves to be forgivable after several lifetimes (the "age" to come) and proves that all sins have been forgiven by Christ at the cross as mentioned in other Bible verses (1 John 1:7, Colossians 2:13). Notice also how Christ's return is not the "end of the world", but the beginning of a new "age". Notice also how those judged unrighteous do not go to "eternal" punishment, but a very long punishment (as one day in the afterlife can seem like an eternity).

Also, the Greek word "aion" is the root for the English word "eon" or "aeon" which means a very long - not eternal - finite amount of time. So the idiom "ages of the ages" ("aionas ton aionon"), mistranslated as "forever and ever," should never be literally translated as an infinite amount of time. Here are a few articles explaining why all Biblical references for "eternity" and "forever" instead mean a finite amount of time:

http://www.tentmaker.org/FAQ/forever_eternity.html
http://www.tentmaker.org/articles/aionole.htm
http://www.tentmaker.org/tracts/ShortOneAion.html
http://www.tentmaker.org/articles/comparative_concordance_aion.html

A common Christian belief is that people first undergo a preliminary judgment after death and then go immediately to heaven or to hell according to how the dead conducted their life. Those who hold this belief consider such a judgment a preliminary one because they also expect an end time worldwide resurrection of corpses and a "Last" or "Final Judgment" for everybody. In effect, the "Last Judgment" is only a confirmation of the preliminary judgment. However, this type of cosmology doesn't make clear how Christians are supposed to understand notions of "heaven" or "hell" because these concepts are not specifically defined in the Bible as we know it. For example, there are a variety of Christian views on heaven, a variety of Christian views on hell, and a variety of Christian views on Hades. However, there were texts excluded from the final New Testament canon that did have detailed descriptions of heaven and hell. The Apocalypse of Peter is one of them and was mentioned in the Muratorian fragment - the oldest surviving list of New Testament books. Another book is the Apocalypse of Paul which was cited as scripture by early Christians and is now part of the New Testament Apocrypha.

The Book of Revelation describes the final judgment of death, hell, and the "wicked":

Revelation 20:14-15: "Then death and Hades were thrown into the lake of fire. The lake of fire is the second death. Anyone whose name was not found written in the book of life was thrown into the lake of fire."

First of all, this verse contradicts the dogma of eternal damnation in hell because hell itself is thrown into the "Lake of Fire" with implications for purification. Concerning the "second death," death is never the end of life. The immortal soul cannot be destroyed. The spirit cannot be punished forever as an image of God. Eternal damnation contradicts everything presented in this article as biblically true. And ever since this verse in Revelation was first recorded, the souls of humanity have in the meantime had thousands of years time - and an unknown amount of time in the future - to reincarnate repeatedly. In verse 15 of Revelation 20, anyone not found in the Book of Life is cast into the "Lake of Fire." But considering all the Bible verses dealing with universal salvation (Part 3 of this article), reincarnation, and the eternal divine nature of the human soul/spirit (Part 5), verse 15 can only be interpreted as a metaphor for judgment, purification, and reincarnation. And there is scriptural support for this. Fire is a metaphor used in the Bible to describe God and manifestations of God through the metaphor of purifying fire:

Hebrews 12:29: "Our God is a consuming fire."

1 Thessalonians 5:19: "Do not put out the Spirit's fire."

Matthew 3:11: "He will baptize you with the Holy Spirit and with fire."

Luke 12:49: "I (Jesus) have come to bring fire on the Earth, and how I wish it were already kindled!"

Isaiah 4:4: "He will cleanse the bloodstains from Jerusalem by a spirit of judgment and a spirit of fire."

Fire is a metaphor used in the Bible to describe the purification of people on Earth such as the following verses:

1 Peter 1:7: "These have come so that your faith - of greater worth than gold, which perishes even though refined by fire - may be proved genuine and may result in praise, glory and honor when Jesus Christ is revealed."

Revelation 3:18-19: "I counsel you to buy from me gold refined in the fire, so you can become rich; and white clothes to wear, so you can cover your shameful nakedness; and salve to put on your eyes, so you can see. Those whom I love I rebuke and discipline."

1 Corinthians 3:11-15: "For no one can lay any foundation other than the one already laid, which is Jesus Christ. If any man builds on this foundation using gold, silver, costly stones, wood, hay or straw, his work will be shown for what it is, because the Day will bring it to light. It will be revealed with fire, and the fire will test the quality of each man's work. If what he has built survives, he will receive his reward. If it is burned up, he will suffer loss; he himself will be saved, but only as one escaping through the flames."

Malachi 3:2-3: "But who can endure the day of his coming? Who can stand when he appears? For he will be like a refiner's fire or a launderer's soap. He will sit as a refiner and purifier of silver; he will purify the Levites and refine them like gold and silver."

One can suppose hell to be any place of torment such as the tortured mind, a prison, skid row, a lonely palace, a disembodied realm. So even here on Earth, there are conditions and situations which can only be described as "a living hell" and places of purification. All Bible verses referring to "purification" through trials and tribulations in this world supports this:

1 Peter 1:6-7: "In all this you greatly rejoice, though now for a little while you may have had to suffer grief in all kinds of trials. These have come so that the proven genuineness of your faith - of greater worth than gold, which perishes even though refined by fire - may result in praise, glory and honor when Jesus Christ is revealed."

Revelation 7:14: "'I answered, 'Sir, you know.' And he said, "These are they who have come out of the great tribulation; they have washed their robes and made them white in the blood of the Lamb."

James 1:2-4: "Consider it pure joy, my brothers and sisters, whenever you face trials of many kinds, because you know that the testing of your faith produces perseverance. Let perseverance finish its work so that you may be mature and complete, not lacking anything."

Hebrews 1:3: "The Son is the radiance of God's glory and the exact representation of his being, sustaining all things by his powerful word. After he had provided purification for sins, he sat down at the right hand of the Majesty in heaven."

H. Gregory of Nyssa's Reasons Why the Church Rejected Reincarnation

Gregory, the Bishop of Nyssa (335-395 AD), a believer in reincarnation and venerated as a saint, gave five reasons why the Christian Church regarded belief in reincarnation as heresy:

Why the Church Rejected Reincarnation

(1) Claim: Reincarnation seems to minimize Christian salvation.

Argument: Reincarnation does minimize salvation based solely upon by merely giving verbal and/or mental assent to the idea of "Jesus is Lord" or "Jesus is God" or "Jesus is Savior." It also minimizes the idea of salvation based upon accepting the cross of Christ without taking up one's own cross. Reincarnation minimizes the idea of God giving people only one lifetime (one opportunity) - and sometimes a short life - at salvation. Reincarnation minimizes the idea of sanctification being a process involving only one lifetime rather than many lifetimes. Reincarnation also minimizes the idea of salvation being exclusively the work of God.

(2) Claim: Reincarnation is in conflict with the resurrection of the body.

Argument: This is true. The idea of a worldwide reanimation of corpses coming out of their graves all at once is preposterous, repulsive, unnatural and contrary to all scientific knowledge. On the other hand, reincarnation does have a scientific basis in fact. I hope this article has also shown corpse resurrection to be unbiblical as well.

(3) Claim: Reincarnation creates an unnatural separation between body and soul.

Argument: This is also true. The early Church mistakenly believed the body and soul were "of one substance" because of their misunderstanding of the mystery of God in humanity - specifically - of God in Christ. See Part 5 of this article.

(4) Claim: Reincarnation is built on a much too speculative use of Christian scriptures.

Argument: You must be the judge whether or not this article is too speculative when it comes to supporting reincarnation or its alternative - the reanimation of corpses. I believe that on the basis of Jesus' teaching of John the Baptist as the reincarnation of Elijah the Prophet alone is sufficient biblical proof of the reality of reincarnation. See Part 1 of this article.

(5) Claim: There is no recollection of previous lives.

Argument: Generally this is true. However, many people do have recollection of past lives - including Biblical personalities such as Jesus:
John 8:56: "Your father Abraham rejoiced at the thought of seeing my day; he saw it and was glad."
There is a good reason why God doesn't allow the recollection of previous lives in general. Imagine having a past-life memory of being Adolf Hitler: assuming you reincarnated with Hitler's spirit and had a

186

normal functioning brain to remember anything because of his tremendous amount of bad karma. How would you be able to live with yourself or live a normal lifetime? Or imagine having a past-life memory of being a murderer. It's the same thing only on a smaller scale. The purpose behind not recollecting past lives is out of God's mercy. When it comes to memory of past lives, God gives people a "clean slate" to work with each lifetime. Otherwise, it would be like a teacher giving students the answers to a test they are about to take. And NDE and reincarnation studies do show that Earth is a school of "Hard Knocks," life is indeed "a test" for which we learn and are "graded" after completing. With each test (lifetime) there is spiritual growth carried over from one lifetime to the next. Our higher consciousness (soul and spirit) remembers the lessons and we grow on a soul and spiritual level. But on a conscious level, we cannot remember our past lives.

I. Summary

Biblical evidence reveals "resurrection" means "live babies coming out of wombs" instead of "dead bodies coming out of tombs". Although "sleep" is a common metaphor in the Bible for "death", the idea of "soul sleep" and "corpse resurrection" did not originate with Judaism or Christianity, but with the Persian religion of Zoroastrianism. The few instances recorded in the Bible where corpses were reanimated were miracles. Doctors today bring people back from the dead with modern technology as evidenced by NDEs. A preexistent, eternal, divine soul (or spirit) does not sleep after death nor can it be extinguished. Only by overcoming the flesh through spiritual regeneration and overcoming karma can the eternal soul no longer be subjected to the cycle of birth-death-rebirth and attain eternal life for the soul once again. The Book of Revelation is the story of humanity's final conquering of reincarnation and the reestablishment of the Garden of Eden through the Second Coming of Christ. On a metaphorical level, the Book of Revelation is also the story of how a person can overcome reincarnation through the spiritual regeneration of the Spirit of Christ within. The Book of Revelation describes a new heaven and Earth being created; and hell and "the wicked" being thrown into the "Lake of Fire" as a place of purification, not punishment. After the thousand year reign of Christ on Earth, God's people will dwell in the new "first heaven" created. Those in the Lake of Fire can then reincarnate to the new Earth for more perfecting. Biblical references to the "end of the world" and "eternal" punishment are mistranslations of Greek and misunderstandings of Hebrew cosmology. Reincarnation is supported by other Christian doctrines such as God's law of divine justice, karma, universal salvation, Christian perfection, preexistence, the indwelling immortal spirit, divinization, salvation and judgment according to works, all of which is mentioned many times throughout the Bible. All the evidence in this article, taken together as a whole, shows the "Kingdom of Heaven" is here and now - within you and among you. The "resurrection" is also happening here and now - within you and outside you. So now is the day of God's salvation. We don't have to wait until after death for it to happen. The concept of reincarnation is supported by many NDEs including those where Jesus appears. For these reasons and more, reincarnation is a doctrine which can be accepted by every follower of Christ and should be a part of orthodox Christian doctrine.

CHAPTER 7:
REINCARNATION IN THE BIBLE (PART 7)

1. The Past Lives of Jesus Christ

A. King David as a Past Life of Jesus Christ

(1) Who Do People Say Jesus Was in a Past Life?

Jesus asked his disciples the following question: "Who do people say the Son of Man is?" (Matthew 16:13-16)

The disciples' reply was that people were saying he was one of the Old Testament prophets such as Elijah or Jeremiah. The nature of Jesus' question, and his disciples' reply, reveals the question was assumed to be one about who the people were saying Jesus was in a past life. His disciples knew this and so they gave a reincarnational answer. And Jesus made no comment against the popular belief in reincarnation and his question sealed it with his approval. Belief in reincarnation during the time of Jesus was almost universal including in all the so-called pagan religions. Nowhere in the New Testament is reincarnation denied, disputed or questioned. If reincarnation was a false doctrine it would almost certainly have been denounced in the same harshest terms as idolatry, sorcery and evil throughout the entire Bible. Instead, as we have seen, reincarnation is referenced throughout the Bible and taught by Jesus.

More evidence of reincarnation as a teaching of Jesus can be found in the belief systems of the early Judeo-Christians. One group, known as the Ebionites, believed the Holy Spirit had incarnated first as Adam and later as Jesus. Other early Judeo-Christians, such as the Elkasaites and Nazarenes, also believed this. In the Clementine Homilies, an early Judeo-Christian document, also taught of Jesus having many previous incarnations. The Jewish sect of Samaritans in Jesus' day, believed the spirit of Adam had reincarnated as Seth, Noah, Abraham, and Moses. Even today, Orthodox Judaism teaches reincarnation (gilgul).

As was discussed in Part 4 of this article, all human beings are participating in an evolving, reincarnational, perfecting process toward sanctification and holiness. In the Epistle to the Hebrews, it states that Jesus himself, as a human being, also needed perfecting and it was through his suffering on the cross which accomplished this (Hebrews 2:10, Hebrews 5:9). This implies Jesus himself had enduring the perfecting process of past lives, and the biblical evidence shows this. One of those past lives is King David (1000 BC) who was anointed the king of Israel and Judah. David conquered Jerusalem, took the Ark of the Covenant into the city, and established the Kingdom there. David is mentioned in the prophetic Hebrew literature as an ideal king and Messiah. The Hebrew word translated as "Messiah" comes from the Hebrew noun meaning "the anointed one." In the First Book of Samuel, the young shepherd David is anointed King ("Messiah") of Israel (1 Samuel 16:1,10-13). In the Second Book of Samuel, the dying King David is called "the anointed ("Messiah") of the God of Jacob (2 Samuel 23:1). As we will see, the Hebrew Bible is filled with references of David as God's first Messiah and references of Jesus as the reincarnation of David.

(2) Whose Son is the Messiah?

Jewish eschatology, the Messiah also came to refer to a future Jewish king from the Davidic line who will be the king of God's kingdom and rule the Jewish people during the Messianic Age. In Judaism, he is referred to as "Messiah ben David," which means "Messiah, son of David." Belief in the eventual coming of a future Messiah is a fundamental part of Judaism and Christianity. The early Church believed the life of David foreshadowed the life of Christ; Bethlehem is the birthplace of both; the shepherd life of David points out Christ the Good Shepherd; the five stones chosen to slay

Goliath are typical of the five wounds on Christ; the betrayal by his trusted counselor, Achitophel, and the passage over the Cedron remind us of Christ's sacred Passion. Many of the Davidic Psalms, as we learn from the New Testament, are clear references to Jesus. In the Gospel of Luke, the archangel Gabriel informs the Virgin Mary she will give birth to Jesus whom God will give the throne of "his father David."

Luke 1:31–33: "You will conceive and give birth to a son, and you are to call him Jesus. He will be great and will be called the Son of the Most High. The Lord God will give him the throne of his father David, and he will reign over Jacob's descendants forever; his kingdom will never end."

The "Son of David" is a clear title of the Messiah is the New Testament (See Luke 1:31–33; Matthew 1:1; Matthew 15:22; Mark 10:47). Jesus confounded the religious leaders who were persecuting him by asking them a question about the son of David:

Matthew 22:41-45, Mark 12:35-37, and Luke 20:41-44: "While the Pharisees were gathered together, Jesus asked them, 'What do you think about the Messiah? Whose son is he?' 'The son of David,' they replied. He said to them, 'How is it then that David, speaking by the Spirit, calls him 'Lord'? For he says, 'The Lord said to my Lord: 'Sit at my right hand until I put your enemies under your feet.' If then David calls him 'Lord,' how can he be his son?' No one could say a word in reply, and from that day on no one dared to ask him any more questions."

In the above verse, Jesus references David's Psalm 110: "The Lord says to my lord: 'Sit at my right hand until I make your enemies a footstool for your feet.'" (Psalm 110:1)

Although Jesus doesn't give us the answer to his question on how the Messiah can be David's son when David calls him "lord," we already know the answer. Jesus knew that he himself, as the Messiah, was not a genetic son of David because he was the only "begotten son of God" - the title given to the soul whom God first gave to David:

David as God's only begotten son: "I will declare the decree: The Lord has said to me, 'You are my son, today I have begotten you.'" (Psalm 2:7)

Jesus as God's only begotten son: "For God so loved the world that He gave His only begotten son, that whoever believes in Him should not perish but have everlasting life." (John 3:16)

Jesus' human father, Joseph, was a genetic descendant of David; but because Jesus was not a genetic descendant of Joseph - and therefore not of David - the only way he could be the "son of David," David's "lord," and God's "only begotten son" would be if David's soul was a past life soul of Jesus.

(3) David and Jesus as Firstborn, Seed, Root, Melchizedek, Savior

And as the "only begotten son," both David and Jesus are said to be the "firstborn" of God:

David as firstborn of God: "I have found My servant David; with My holy oil I have anointed him, with whom My hand shall be established; also My arm shall strengthen him... He will call out to me, 'You are my Father, my God, the Rock my Savior.' And I will appoint him to be My firstborn, the most exalted of the kings of the earth." (Psalm 89:20, 26-27)

Jesus as firstborn of God: "And again, when God brings his firstborn into the world, he says, 'Let all God's angels worship him.'" (Hebrews 1:6; See also Romans 8:29, Colossians 1:15-18, Hebrews 12:22-23, Revelation 1:5)

In the gospels and in Paul's epistles, the soul (spirit) is metaphorically referred to as a "seed" (See Matthew 13:24-30; 1 Peter 1:23). God promised David that his "seed" and throne would be established forever to all generations suggesting his "seed" would be his reincarnation:

The seed of David established with David: "I have made a covenant with My chosen, I have sworn to my servant David: 'Your seed I will establish forever, and build up your throne to all generations.'" (Psalm 89:3-4)

The seed of David established with Jesus: "Has not the Scripture said that the Christ comes from the seed of David and from the town of Bethlehem, where David was?" (John 7:42)

An even more direct reference to the soul of Jesus as a reincarnation of the soul of David is the Messianic title "Root of Jesse." Jesse was the father of David and a direct descendant from Judah, Jacob, Isaac and Abraham. So "Root of Jesse" is the literal son of Jesse, who is David himself. Isaiah the prophet, whose ministry was active hundreds of years after David's death from 740 BC to 698

BC, prophesied of a "Branch" which will rise from the "Root of Jesse" (David) of whom "the Spirit of the Lord will rest on him" during a time when "the wolf will live with the lamb." The apostle Paul confirms that Isaiah's prophesy applies to Jesus:

Root of Jesse anointed Messiah: "Now the Lord said to Samuel, "How long will you mourn for Saul, seeing I have rejected him from reigning over Israel? Fill your horn with oil, and go; I am sending you to Jesse the Bethlehemite. For I have provided Myself a king (David) among his sons." (1 Samuel 16:1)

Messiah as Branch from "Root of Jesse": "A shoot will come up from the stump of Jesse; from his roots a Branch will bear fruit... In that day the Root of Jesse (David) will stand as a banner for the peoples; the nations will rally to him, and his resting place will be glorious." (Isaiah 11:1,10)

Jesus as One from the "Root of Jesse": "And again, Isaiah says, 'The Root of Jesse (David) will spring up, one who will arise to rule over the nations; in him the Gentiles will hope.'" (Romans 15:12)

Again, because Jesus was not the genetic descendant of David, he could only be the "Root of Jesse" if his soul was a reincarnation of David who WAS a genetic descendant of Jesse. And genetic ancestry is critical in Judaism. In the Book of Revelation, Jesus is also referred to as the "Root of David" (Revelation 5:5) which is also a Messianic title. Concerning the "shoot" and "Branch" rising from the "Root of Jesse," as previously mentioned, the gospels and epistles use the metaphor of a "seed" for the soul (Matthew 13:24-30; 1 Peter 1:23). From the seed arises the "shoot" - the "resurrected" body - which we've already made the case is the reincarnated soul in a new body (a fetus). The prophet Jeremiah, whose ministry was active from 626 BC until 587 BC, like the prophet Isaiah, also prophesied of a future "Branch" - another Messianic reference to Jesus - whom God will one day "raise up" (reincarnate) as King to rule after the Jews are brought back to their homeland from all the nations:

Jeremiah 23:5: "'The days are coming,' declares the Lord, 'when I will raise up for David a righteous Branch, a King who will reign wisely and do what is just and right in the land."

Another connection between David and Jesus is their "Priesthood of Melchizedek." Melchizedek was a king and priest appearing in the Book of Genesis whose name means "King of Righteousness" - a name echoing kingly and priestly functions. He is the first individual to be given the title of "priest" in the Hebrew Bible. The majority of Chazalic literature attributes the primary character of the following Psalm as King David who was a "righteous king" of Salem (Jerusalem) and, like Melchizedek, had certain priest-like responsibilities:

David as "priest of Melchizedek": "The Lord has sworn and will not change his mind: 'You (David) are a priest forever, in the order of Melchizedek.'" (Psalm 110:4)

Jesus as "priest of Melchizedek": "We have this hope as an anchor for the soul, firm and secure. It enters the inner sanctuary behind the curtain, where our forerunner, Jesus, has entered on our behalf. He has become a high priest forever, in the order of Melchizedek." (Hebrews 6:19-20)

As we will also see, there is also biblical evidence of Jesus, and therefore David, as having a past life as Melchizedek. Other Messianic titles shared between David and Jesus include "King of Israel," "King of Righteous," "Servant of the Lord," and "Shepherd." In Psalm 22, David also demonstrated his ability as a prophet when describing - in uncanny detail - the experience of Jesus on the cross:

Psalm 22:1-24: "My God, my God, why have you forsaken me?... (v.1) But I am a worm and not a man, scorned by everyone despised by the people... (v.6) All who see me mock me; they hurl insults... (v.7) 'He trusts in the Lord,' they say, 'let the Lord rescue him'... (v.8) From birth I was cast on you; from my mother's womb you have been my God... (v.10) Many bulls surround me; strong bulls of Bashan encircle me... (v.12) I am poured out like water, and all my bones are out of joint... (v.14) My heart has turned to wax; it has melted within me... (v.14) My mouth is dried up like a potsherd, and my tongue sticks to the roof of my mouth... (v.15) You lay me in the dust of death... (v.15) Dogs surround me, a pack of villains encircles me... (v.16) They pierce my hands and my feet... (v.16) All my bones are on display... (v.17) People stare and gloat over me... (v.17) They divide my clothes among them and cast lots for my garment... (v.18) For he (God) has not despised or scorned the suffering of the afflicted one... (v.24) He has not hidden his face from him but has listened to his cry for help (v.24)

(4) David Will Be Reincarnated in the Last Days

The prophet Hosea's ministry was active just before the destruction of Israel in 722 BC - several hundred years after the death of King David. Hosea prophesied that "in the last days" Israel will be restored and King David himself will rule over them:

Hosea 3:4-5: "For the Israelites will live many days without king or prince, without sacrifice or sacred stones, without ephod or household gods. Afterward the Israelites will return and seek the Lord their God and David their King. They will come trembling to the Lord and to his blessings in the last days."

Note that Israel was established as a Jewish nation in 1948, and they are still awaiting their Messiah - as Christians are awaiting the return of Christ. The implication is that Jesus, as the reincarnation of David, will rule at that time.

The prophet Ezekiel (622-570 BC) prophesied incessantly for five years and acted out the destruction of Jerusalem and its temple several hundred years after the death of David. Like Hosea, Ezekiel prophesied the future return of the Jews to Israel and the reincarnation of David himself to rule them:

Ezekiel 34:13, 23-24: "I will bring them out from the nations and gather them from the countries, and I will bring them into their own land... I will place over them one shepherd, My servant David, and he will tend them; he will tend them and be their shepherd. I the Lord will be their God, and My servant David will be prince among them. I the Lord have spoken."

In Part 6 of this article, in Ezekiel's "vision of the Valley of the Dry Bones" in Chapter 37, Ezekiel described the entire nation of Israel reincarnating in the last days and King David himself reincarnating to rule over them:

Ezekiel 37:22-24: "I will make them one nation in the land, on the mountains of Israel. There will be one king over all of them and they will never again be two nations or be divided into two kingdoms. They will no longer defile themselves with their idols and vile images or with any of their offenses, for I will save them from all their sinful backsliding, and I will cleanse them. They will be my people, and I will be their God. My servant David will be king over them, and they will all have one shepherd. They will follow my laws and be careful to keep my decrees."

The prophet Jeremiah was a contemporary of Ezekiel whose prophetic ministry was active from 626 BC until after the fall of

195

Jerusalem and the destruction of Solomon's Temple in 587 BC. During that time, Babylon conquered Jerusalem and began taking Jews as captives to Babylon. Jeremiah prophesied that the Jews would be scattered from their homeland and persecuted; but God would protect them from total destruction and one day return to their homeland. He also prophesied a day when Israel will no longer be enslaved by foreigners and God would "raise up" King David himself to rule over them:

Jeremiah 30:1-3; 8-9: "This is the word that came to Jeremiah from the Lord: 'This is what the Lord, the God of Israel, says: 'Write in a book all the words I have spoken to you. 'The days are coming,' declares the Lord, 'when I will bring my people Israel and Judah back from captivity and restore them to the land I gave their ancestors to possess... In that day,' declares the Lord Almighty, 'I will break the yoke off their necks and will tear off their bonds; no longer will foreigners enslave them. Instead, they will serve the Lord their God and David their king, whom I will raise up for them.'"

Notice also Jeremiah 30:9 states that King David himself will be "raised up" (reincarnated) sometime after Israel is restored. As previously mentioned, "raised up" is a reference to reincarnation. Notice also that even if we assume a corpse resurrection interpretation, Jeremiah says it will be King David himself who will be "raised up." From this information, we can conclude that the so-called "Second Coming" of Jesus will actually be the "Third Coming" of King David assuming Jesus and King David were the same soul. See also Jeremiah 23:5-6 and Jeremiah 33:15-16 for more support.

The prophet Zechariah began his ministry in the second year of Darius, king of Persia (520 BC), about sixteen years after the beginning of the Jews returning to Israel from their Babylonian exile and hundreds of years after the death of David. Jeremiah prophesied of a future time when all the nations of the world will be against Jerusalem causing God to destroy all Israel's enemies and establish the House of David (the Davidic line of kingship):.

Zechariah 12:2-3;8-10: "I am going to make Jerusalem a cup that sends all the surrounding peoples reeling. Judah will be besieged as well as Jerusalem. On that day, when all the nations of the earth are gathered against her, I will make Jerusalem an immovable rock for all the nations. All who try to move it will injure themselves... On that day the Lord will shield those who live in Jerusalem, so that the feeblest among them will be like David, and the house of David will be like God, like the angel of the Lord going before them. On that day I will set out to destroy all the nations that attack Jerusalem. And I will pour out on the house of David and the inhabitants of Jerusalem a spirit of grace and supplication. They will look on me, the one they have pierced, and they will mourn for him as one mourns for an only child, and grieve bitterly for him as one grieves for a firstborn son."

The "Angel of the Lord" (in Hebrew "Messenger of Yahweh") is an entity appearing 65 times in the Old Testament on behalf of God (Yahweh). In some instances it is made clear that the reference is to an appearance of Yahweh himself rather than a separate entity acting on his behalf. The Angel of the Lord is identified by the early Church Fathers, such as Justin Martyr and Tertullian, as the pre-incarnate Christ whose appearance is recorded in the Old Testament. Zechariah's prophecy reveals it will be a reincarnation of the "house of David" (David himself) - the Angel of the Lord (Jesus), the one who was pierced, who will save Israel in the latter days.

(5) More Evidence of David as a Past Life of Jesus

The following biblical comparisons show David and Jesus as having the same identity. Both are "the most exalted king of the Earth":

David as the most exalted king of the Earth: "I have found My servant David; with My holy oil I have anointed him, with whom My hand shall be established; also My arm shall strengthen him.... He will call out to me, 'You are my Father, my God, the Rock my Savior.' And I will appoint him to be My firstborn, the most exalted of the kings of the Earth." (Psalm 89:20, 26-27)

Jesus as the most exalted king of the Earth: "On his robe and on his thigh he has this name written: King of Kings and Lord of Lords." (Revelation 19:16)

Both David and Jesus are "the Holy One", the Messiah:

David as the "Holy One": "For our shield belongs to the Lord, and our king to the Holy One of Israel. Then You spoke in a vision to your Holy One, and said: 'I have given help to one who is mighty; I have exalted one chosen from the people. I have found My servant David; with My holy oil I have anointed him". (Psalm 89:18-20)

Jesus as the "Holy One": "Simon Peter answered him, 'Lord, to whom shall we go? You have the words of eternal life. We have come to believe and to know that you are the Holy One of God.'" (John 6:68-69) (See also Mark 1:24; Luke 4:34)

David said God would not leave his soul in Sheol, nor allow God's "Holy One" to see corruption:

Psalm 16:8-10: "I have set the Lord always before me; because He is at my right hand I shall not be moved. Therefore my heart is glad, and my glory rejoices; my flesh also will rest in hope. for you will not leave my (David's) soul in Sheol, nor will You allow your Holy One (Messiah) to see corruption."

The above Psalm of David corresponds with the Acts of the Apostles where Peter revealed Jesus to be a past life of David during his sermon at Pentecost when he explained how Jesus fulfilled the prophecy of David concerning how God would not leave David's soul, as Jesus, in Sheol:

Acts 2:25-31: "For David says concerning him (Jesus): 'I foresaw the Lord always before my face, for He is at my right hand, that I may not be shaken. Therefore my heart rejoiced, and my tongue was glad; moreover my flesh also will rest in hope. For you will not leave my soul in Hades, nor will you allow your Holy One to see corruption. You have made known to me the ways of life; You will make me full of joy in Your presence.' Men and brethren, let me speak freely to you of the patriarch David, that he is both dead and buried, and his tomb is with us to this day. Therefore, being a prophet, and knowing that God had sworn with an oath to him that of the fruit of his body, according to the flesh, he would raise up the Christ to sit on his throne, he, foreseeing this, spoke concerning the resurrection of the Christ, that his (Jesus') soul was not left in Hades, nor did his flesh see corruption."

In the above verse, Peter equated David mentioning his soul would not be allowed to be left in Hades (Sheol) with Jesus' soul not allowed to be left in Hades.

In the next verse, James (the brother of Jesus) quotes an end time prophecy in Amos 9:9-12 concerning David's fallen "tent" being restored as a metaphor for the resurrection of Jesus' "body" which implies David and Jesus were the same soul:

Acts 15:12-19: "The whole assembly became silent as they listened to Barnabas and Paul telling about the signs and wonders God had done among the Gentiles through them. When they finished, James spoke up. 'Brothers,' he said, 'listen to me. Simon has described to us how God first intervened to choose a people for his name from the Gentiles. The words of the prophets are in agreement with this, as it is written: 'After this I will return and rebuild David's fallen tent. Its ruins I will rebuild, and I will restore it, that the rest of mankind may seek the Lord, even all the Gentiles who bear my name, says the Lord, who does these things' - things known from long ago. It is my judgment, therefore, that we should not make it difficult for the Gentiles who are turning to God."

In the Bible, the word "tent" is used as a metaphor for the physical body, such as in the New Testament, by both the apostles Paul and Peter for example:

2 Corinthians 5:1: "For we know that if the earthly tent we live in is destroyed, we have a building from God, an eternal house in heaven, not built by human hands."

2 Peter 1:12-13: "So I will always remind you of these things, even though you know them and are firmly established in the truth you now have. I think it is right to refresh your memory as long as I live in the tent of this body."

B. Melchizedek as a Past Life of Jesus Christ

As we have seen in Part 1 of this article with the case of John the Baptist as the reincarnation of Elijah the Prophet, events in one lifetime often repeat in another lifetime for a variety of reasons, such as the fact that life is a cycle (Ecclesiastes 3:15), bad karma extending into future lifetimes (Numbers 14:18), personality traits transferring from one lifetime to other lifetimes, etc. For these reasons, we can find biblical parallels between one biblical personality and another.

Such careful examination of the evidence reveals another past life of Jesus is the Old Testament figure known as Melchizedek, the High Priest and King of Salem (Jerusalem). It is clear from the Book of Hebrews that Melchizedek was not an ordinary man, assuming he even was a man, "without father or mother, without genealogy, without beginning of days or end of life" (Hebrews 7:2-3). There are strong parallels between Melchizedek as you can see in the chart below. Besides the Biblical evidence, there exists evidence from the discoveries of early Christian texts in 1945 and the Dead Sea Scrolls in 1947. There is also extra-Biblical revelations supporting this Melchizedek-Jesus connection. You can read the entire article of evidence here. Below is a summary of the biblical evidence:

Biblical Parallels of Melchizedek and Jesus

(1) Identical Sonship: "Son of God"

Melchizedek: "Without father or mother, without genealogy, without beginning of days or end of life, resembling the Son of God, he remains a priest forever." (Hebrews 7:3).
Jesus: "The beginning of the good news about Jesus the Messiah, the Son of God" (Mark 1:1).

(2) Identical Order of High Priesthood: "Melchizedek"

Melchizedek: "Then Melchizedek king of Salem brought out bread and wine. He was priest of God Most High." (Genesis 14:18).
Jesus: "And he says in another place, 'You are a priest forever, in the order of Melchizedek.'" (Hebrews 5:6).

(3) Identical Symbol of Rule: "King of Righteousness"

Melchizedek: "Abraham gave him a tenth of everything. First, the name Melchizedek means "king of righteousness"; then also, "king of Salem" means "king of peace."" (Hebrews 7:2).
Jesus: "But of the Son he says, 'Your throne, O God, is forever and ever, and the righteous scepter is the scepter of your kingdom.'" (Hebrews 1:8).

(4) Identical Right to Rule: Appointed by God:

Melchizedek: "Then Melchizedek king of Salem brought out bread and wine. He was priest of God Most High" (Genesis 14:18).
Jesus: "For it is clear that our Lord descended from Judah, and in regard to that tribe Moses said nothing about priests." (Hebrews 7:14)

(5) Identical Title: King "of Peace":

Melchizedek: "Abraham gave him a tenth of everything. First, the name Melchizedek means "king of righteousness"; then also, "king of Salem" means "king of peace."" (Hebrews 7:2).

Jesus: "For to us a child is born, to us a son is given, and the government will be on his shoulders. And he will be called Wonderful Counselor, Mighty God, Everlasting Father, Prince of Peace." (Isaiah 9:6).

(6) Identical Term of Priesthood: Eternal

Melchizedek: "Without father or mother, without genealogy, without beginning of days or end of life, resembling the Son of God, he remains a priest forever." (Hebrews 7:3).

Jesus: "And he says in another place, "You are a priest forever, in the order of Melchizedek." (Hebrews 5:6).

(7) Identical in Likeness: Priest

Melchizedek: "Then Melchizedek king of Salem brought out bread and wine. He was priest of God Most High." (Genesis 14:18)

Jesus: "And what we have said is even more clear if another priest like Melchizedek appears, one who has become a priest not on the basis of a regulation as to his ancestry but on the basis of the power of an indestructible life." (Hebrews 7:15-16).

(8) Identical Age: Pre-Existent

Melchizedek: "Without father or mother, without genealogy, without beginning of days or end of life, resembling the Son of God, he remains a priest forever." (Hebrews 7:3)

Jesus: "In the beginning was the Word, and the Word was with God, and the Word was God. He was with God in the beginning." (John 1:1-2).

(9) Identical Association with: Abraham

Melchizedek: "Then Melchizedek king of Salem brought out bread and wine. He was priest of God Most High, and he blessed Abram, saying, 'Blessed be Abram by God Most High, Creator of heaven and earth." (Genesis 14:18-19)

Jesus: "'Your father Abraham rejoiced at the thought of seeing my day; he saw it and was glad.' 'You are not yet fifty years old," they said to him, "and you have seen Abraham!' 'Very truly I tell you,' Jesus answered, 'before Abraham was born, I am!' At this, they picked up stones to stone him, but Jesus hid himself, slipping away from the temple grounds." (John 8:56-59).

(10) Identical Use of Ritualistic Symbols: Bread and Wine

Melchizedek: "Then Melchizedek king of Salem brought out bread and wine. He was priest of God Most High" (Genesis 14:18).

Jesus: "While they were eating, Jesus took bread, and when he had given thanks, he broke it and gave it to his disciples, saying, 'Take and eat; this is my body.' Then he took a cup, and when he had given thanks, he gave it to them, saying, 'Drink from it, all of you. This is my blood of the[a] covenant, which is poured out for many for the forgiveness of sins. I tell you, I will not drink from this fruit of the vine from now on until that day when I drink it new with you in my Father's kingdom.'" (Matthew 26:26-29).

C. Joseph as a Past Life of Jesus Christ

Another past life of Jesus apparently is Joseph, the son of Jacob and Rachel in the Old Testament. Joseph is an important figure in the Book of Genesis and also in Islam's Quran. Joseph's father was Jacob, the grandson of Abraham. Jacob fathered twelve sons from whom have sprung the Twelve Tribes of Israel. Because of this, Jacob's name was later changed to Israel. Joseph was Rachel's firstborn and Jacob's eleventh son. Of all the sons, Joseph was preferred by his father, and this is represented by a "long coat of many colors." When Joseph was seventeen years old he had two dreams that made his brothers plot his demise. In the first dream, Joseph and his brothers gathered bundles of grain, of which those his brothers gathered, bowed to his own. In the second dream, the sun (father), the moon (mother), and eleven stars (brothers) bowed to Joseph himself. These dreams, implying Joseph's supremacy, angered his brothers who sold him into slavery. But Joseph rose to become the second most powerful man in Egypt next to Pharaoh, where his presence and office caused Israel to leave Canaan and settle in Egypt. Joseph, the Hebrew Prince of Egypt, has some of the most interesting parallels to the life of Jesus suggesting Joseph was a previous incarnation of Jesus. In Judaism, the Messiah was thought of as the "son of Joseph" (Messiah ben Joseph) as well the "son of David."

Jewish tradition actually alludes to four messianic figures. Called "the Four Craftsmen" discussed in Babylonian Talmud, each will be involved in ushering in the Messianic age. They are mentioned in the Talmud and the Book of Zechariah (Zechariah 2:1-17). Rabbi Shlomo Yitzchaki (aka "Rashi") in his commentary on the Talmud gives more details. His commentary which covers nearly all of the Babylonian Talmud has been included in every edition of the Talmud since its first printing. Rashi explains that Messiah ben Joseph is called a craftsman because he will help rebuild the temple. Nahmanides also commented on Messiah ben Joseph's rebuilding of the temple. The roles of the Four Craftsmen are as follows. Elijah will be the herald of Jewish eschatology. If necessary, Messiah ben Joseph will wage war against the evil forces and die in combat with the enemies of God and Israel. According to Saadia Gaon the need for his appearance will depend on the spiritual condition of the Jewish people. In the Sefer Zerubbabel and later writings, after his death a period of great calamities will befall Israel. God will then "resurrect the dead" and usher in the Messianic Era of universal peace. Messiah ben David will reign as a Jewish king during the period when God will resurrect the dead. With the ascendancy of Rabbinic Judaism the Righteous Priest (Melchizedek) has largely not been the subject of Jewish messianic speculation. Most Jews believe that the Third Temple will be built during this era.

You can read the entire article of evidence here. Below is a summary of the biblical evidence:

Biblical Parallels of Joseph and Jesus

1. Both were miraculously born. Joseph: (Genesis 30:22-24); Jesus: (Matthew 1:18-23).

2. Both were a shepherd of his father's sheep. Joseph: (Genesis 37:2);

Jesus: (John 10:11-14).

3. Both were most beloved sons. Joseph: (Genesis 37:3); Jesus: (Matthew 3:17).

4. Both were hated for no good reason. Joseph: (Genesis 37:4); Jesus: (John 15:25).

5. Both had brothers who rejected him. Joseph: (Genesis 37:5-8); Jesus: (John 7:4-5).

6. Both were given visions of the future. Joseph: (Genesis 37:6-7): Jesus: (Matthew 24:3).

7. Both were hated for their teachings. Joseph (Genesis 37:8): Jesus: (John 7:7).

8. Both were rebuked by their earthly parents because they didn't understand why they treated their parents the way they did. Joseph: (Genesis 37:10): Jesus: (Luke 2:48-50).

9. Both were hated because of their brothers' jealousy. Joseph: (Genesis 37:11); Jesus: (Matthew 27:17-20).

10. Both were stripped of their robes. Joseph: (Genesis 37:23); Jesus: (Matthew 27:28).

11. Both descended into a pit. Joseph: (Genesis 37:24); Jesus: (Matthew 12:40).

12. Both were betrayed by the advice of Judah (Judas), one of the Twelve. Joseph: (Genesis 37:26-27); Jesus: (Matthew 26:14).

13. Both were betrayed for the price of a slave in silver. Joseph: (Genesis 37:28); Jesus: (Matthew 26:15).

14. Both were taken into Egypt to avoid being killed. Joseph (Genesis 37:28); Jesus: (Matthew 2:13).

15. Both gained the confidence of others quickly. Joseph: (Genesis 39:3); Jesus: (Matthew 8:8).

16. Both became a servant. Joseph: (Genesis 39:4); Jesus: (Philippians 2:6-7).

17. Both resisted the most difficult temptations. Joseph: (Genesis 39:6-9); Jesus: (Hebrews 4:15).

18. Both were persecuted because of false witnesses. Joseph: (Genesis 39:14-19); Jesus: (Matthew 26:60-62).

19. Both were silent before their accusers. Joseph: (Genesis 39:20-21); Jesus: (Mark 15:4-5).

20. Both were condemned with two other prisoners. Joseph: (Genesis 40:1-3); Jesus: (Luke 23:32).

21. Both received the same punishment as the two other prisoners. Joseph: (Genesis 40:2-4); Jesus: (Luke 23:33).

22. Joseph asked one of the other prisoners to "remember him" when he is released and reinstated to Pharaoh. Jesus had one of the other prisoners ask to "remember him" when he is released and reinstated to the Kingdom of God. Joseph: (Genesis 40:12-14); Jesus: (Luke 23:42).

23. Both had one of the two other prisoners with them released and exalted. Joseph: (Genesis 40:20-22); Jesus: (Luke 23:39-43).

24. Both of their lives were changed by the power of dreams. Joseph: (Genesis 41:15); Jesus: (Matthew 2:19-20).

25. Both were taught by God. Joseph: (Genesis 41:15-16); Jesus: (John 5:19).

26. Both miraculously gave bread to hungry people who came to him. Joseph: (Genesis 41:17-36); Jesus: (Mark 6:41).

27. Both were filled with the Spirit of God. Joseph: (Genesis 41:38); Jesus: (Luke 4:1).

28. Both became exalted by God for their great suffering. Joseph: (Genesis 41:39-40); Jesus: (Matthew 28:18).

29. Both arose into a new life. Joseph: (Genesis 41:41); Jesus: (Mark 16:6).

30. Both began their ministry at the age of thirty. Joseph: (Genesis 41:46); Jesus: (Luke 3:23).

31. Both were not recognized by their own brothers. Joseph: (Genesis 42.8); Jesus: (Luke 24:36-37).

32. Both tested people to reveal their true nature. Joseph: (Genesis 42:8-17); Jesus: (Mark 11:28-30).

33. Both forgave the people who wanted to kill them. Joseph: (Genesis 45:3-14); Jesus: (Luke 23:34).

34. Both loved people unconditionally. Joseph: (Genesis 45:15); Jesus: (Matthew 5:43-45).

35. Both had people who refused to believe they were not dead. Joseph: (Genesis 45:26); Jesus: (Luke 24:9-11).

36. Both returned to their father. Joseph: (Genesis 46:29); Jesus: (Mark 16:19).

37. Both had someone state they could die now that they saw them. Joseph: (Genesis 46:30); Jesus: (Luke 2:25-32).

38. Both arose victorious to be great princes. Joseph: (Genesis 49:26); Jesus: (Isaiah 9:6).

39. Both returned good for evil. Joseph: (Genesis 50:17-20); Jesus: (Luke 6:27).

40. Both of their families were called out of Egypt and back to Israel as an act of salvation. Joseph: (Hosea 11:1); Jesus: (Matthew 2:14-15).

D. Adam as a Past Life of Jesus Christ

Judaism, Christianity and Islam all accept the account of Adam and Eve as part of their religion. The Bible gave the distinct title of "Son of God" to only four personalities in the entire Bible: Adam, Melchizedek, David and Jesus. So, it should not be surprising that these four personalities have a connection that goes well beyond coincidence. This connection is proof that these personalities were indeed the same soul appearing in different incarnations. This evidence shows how the Bible is the story of the sojourn of the "Son of God" beginning with humanity in Paradise lost and ending with Paradise restored by the same "Son of God." The following information describes this Adam-Jesus connection. You can read the entire article of evidence here. Below is a summary of the biblical evidence:

Biblical Parallels of Adam and Jesus

1. Identical Title: "Son of Man": Adam: "Adam Kadmon"; Jesus: (Matthew 16:13).

2. Identical Title: "Son of God": Adam: (Luke 3:38); Jesus: (John 11:27).

3. Identical Birth Order: "firstborn of every creature": Adam: (Genesis 2:7); Jesus: (Colossians 1:15).

4. Identical Rule: "ruler of God's creation": Adam: (Genesis 1:28); Jesus: (Revelation 3:14).

5. Identical Parent: "father of the human race": Adam: (Isaiah 43:27); Jesus: (Isaiah 9:6).

6. Identical Essence: "human-divine" unity": Adam: (Genesis 1:26); Jesus: (1 Corinthians 15:47-49).

7. Identical Pattern: "image" and "copy": Adam: (Genesis 1:26); Jesus: (Romans 5:14).

8. Identical Positions: "first and last": Adam: (1 Corinthians 15:45); Jesus: (Revelation 1:17).

9. Identical Immortality: immortal from the beginning: Adam: (Genesis 2:15-17); Jesus: (John 1:1-2).

10. Identical Origins: "beginning" and "end": Adam: (Mark 10:6); Jesus: (Revelation 21:6).

11. Identical Title: Logos: Adam: "Genesis 1:26); Jesus: (John 1:1-2).

12. Identical Nature: "Image of God": Adam: (Genesis 1:26); Jesus: (2 Corinthians 4:4).

13. Identical Sacrificial Result: "first" and "last sacrifice": Adam: (Genesis 3:21); Jesus: (Hebrews 7:27-28).

14. Identical Association: Tree of Life: Adam: (Genesis 3:22-24); Jesus: (Revelation 2:7).

15. Identical Karma: Required to pay for Original Sin: Adam: (Genesis 3:13-15); Jesus: (Romans 5:19).

2. Final Summary of This Article

Part 1 of this article is an introduction to reincarnation in Christian history including the biblical evidence of John the Baptist as the reincarnation of Elijah the Prophet.

The religious concept of the "Resurrection of the Dead," a massive worldwide reanimation of corpses at the end of time, is a foreign concept originating from ancient Persia - not Judaism or Christianity. The few instances recorded in the Bible where corpses were reanimated were "miracles". A massive worldwide reanimation of corpses is bizarre, repulsive, unnatural, and against science.

In many documented near-death experiences (NDEs), doctors bring people back from the dead with modern technology. In many

NDEs involving Jesus, the concept of reincarnation appears such as with Sandra Rogers and Jeanie Dicus. NDE and reincarnation studies support the scientific reality of reincarnation.

All Hebrew, Judeo-Christian and Gnostic scriptures support reincarnation: the Bible, the Dead Sea Scrolls, the Christian Gnostic gospels, the Hebrew Apocrypha, the New Testament Apocrypha, the Kabbalah and Zohar, and other Judeo-Christian texts.

Reincarnation was widely believed by the people of Israel in the days of Jesus, the Roman Empire, Hellenistic culture, and by people all around the world. Reincarnation was also a Christian salvation "mystery" teaching and oral tradition handed down from the apostles only to those initiated into the Christian mysteries.

Reincarnation has been a tenet in Orthodox Judaism for thousands of years and continues to this day.

The doctrines of preexistence and reincarnation championed by Origen of Alexandria (184-253 AD) were eventually declared a heresy by the Roman Church in 553 A.D at the Second Council of Constantinople.

The mystery of reincarnation in Christianity was mostly hidden for almost two thousand years until the 1945 discovery of the lost Christian Gnostic writings in northern Egypt and the 1946 discovery of the Dead Sea Scrolls around the time of the "rebirth" of the nation of Israel in 1948 which was a great fulfillment of Bible prophecy.

For thousands of years, traditional Christianity has taught that when a person dies their soul rests in peace until a final resurrection of the dead and the Last Judgment - a doctrine based upon the unusual notion that the soul is inseparable from the physical body.

Many of the Biblical references to "resurrection" refer to spiritual regeneration of the Holy Spirit to people already alive instead of the reanimation of corpses on the so-called "Last Day."

Biblical reincarnation is shown to be God's design for the soul, through good works, to "work its way up" through the afterlife realms immediately after death with the goal of becoming permanent citizens in God's Kingdom in heaven.

Based upon the biblical evidence of John the Baptist as the reincarnation of Elijah alone, it can be easily declared that Jesus taught reincarnation. John had both the spirit and power of Elijah - meaning he was the reincarnation of Elijah.

All skeptical objections to Elijah's reincarnation as John have been debunked.

John and Elijah shared many similarities suggestive of reincarnation including appearance, diet, personality, relationships, life situations, ministry, locations inhabited throughout in Israel, and karma.

If John was not the reincarnation of Elijah as prophecy foretold, then Jesus was not the Messiah as prophecy foretold.

Elijah and Moses appeared transfigured with Christ at his First Coming. The Bible shows Elijah and Moses reincarnating for Christ's Second Coming.

Part 2 of this article described more biblical reincarnating prophets and other holy people; also Jesus' teachings on bodily and spiritual rebirth.

Throughout the Bible is the expression of a common knowledge among God's people that God occasionally reincarnates prophets to warn the people of Israel.

The Bible describes God taking the dead from Sheol (Hades) and bringing them up, and bringing those in heaven back down to Earth - a perfect description of reincarnation - and a contradiction of an end time corpse resurrection.

Jesus taught his followers that they would be alive on Earth at his Second Coming which could only occur through reincarnation. Jesus promised reincarnation and "good karma" to those who have forsaken everything to follow him. Jesus taught his followers they must spread the gospel throughout the entire world before he returns implying their reincarnation.

The New Testament describes people who had an opportunity to return to Earth after death and describes women receiving their dead - "raised to life again" - which cannot be a reference to corpse resurrection because the verse also mentions people refusing to die so they can live longer to do good works so they may obtain more favorable conditions in their next reincarnation - a "better resurrection."

The Book of Ecclesiastes describes life as a cycle and teaches reincarnation. In the Book of James, there is a reference to this cycle as the "wheel of birth" which is another clear reference to reincarnation.

In the Book of Job, Job wondered if he will live again after death. He answered his own question by saying he will live again at the time of his "renewal." According to the Hebrew dictionary, the word translated "renewal" is "chaliyphah" (pronounced "khal-ee-faw") which is an obvious reference to a "change in body" as a "change in garments" as in reincarnation.

Jesus taught Nicodemus that, "You must be born again," which has a literal meaning of bodily "rebirth" (reincarnation), but is also used metaphorically to mean spiritual "rebirth" (regeneration) by the Holy Spirit. So "born again" has a reincarnational meaning and a spiritual "resurrection" meaning - not a corpse resurrection meaning.

Because the phrase "born again" literally means "reincarnation," there is nothing in the Bible to warrant putting only a metaphorical interpretation on the phrase "you must be born again" although we know Jesus meant it to be understood both metaphorically and literally.

The Bible also contains many references to "born again" (reincarnation), baptism, and Christ's resurrection as metaphors for the transformation from spiritual death to spiritual rebirth by the Holy Spirit.

According to Strong's Concordance, the phrase "rise again" is translated "egeirontai" which means repeated embodiments which also negates a one-time resurrection.

In all the verses in the New Testament where the word "resurrection" is a translation of the Greek word "anastasis" - according to Strong's Concordance - the word can mean either a one-time "resurrection" or repeated embodiments of "rising again."

Jesus taught the Sadducees how "resurrection" involves living souls becoming "like angels" and then as "children of the resurrection" such as the children of Abraham, Isaac, and Jacob.

Part 3 of this article proves it is God's will that everyone is saved which can only realistically occur through reincarnation. Part 3 also describes how God's law of divine justice (also known universally as "karma") is the same as the law of reincarnation

Throughout the Bible are declarations that it is God's will that everyone is saved. Because God wills everyone to be saved - and nobody can thwart the will of God - then everyone will be saved. Universal salvation implies the reality of reincarnation. There are numerous Bible verses mentioning the salvation of all humanity.

Universal salvation, like preexistence and reincarnation, was widely believed by Christians and Jews during the first 500 years of

Christianity and was championed by the early Church Father Origen.

Several of Jesus' parables declare how a person will not get out of "prison" (hell) until their "debt" (transgressions) has been paid in full which falsifies eternal punishment. Because these parables imply people getting out of hell, one wonders where they would go? It would be reasonable to assume they would be reincarnated. The New Testament Apocrypha states that this is exactly what happens.

Paul mentioned a time of "universal reconciliation" in his letter to the Colossians. In the Book of Acts, Peter mentioned a time of "universal restoration" or "apokatastasis" in Greek which refers to the thousand year reign of Christ on Earth and the universal salvation of all souls resulting from it mentioned in the Book of Revelation.

God's law of divine justice of "an eye for an eye," also known as "karma," is the law of reincarnation and is mentioned throughout the Old and New Testaments, the gospels, Jesus' parables, and the Epistles.

According to the biblical concept of "original sin," Adam's sin created "bad karma" for himself and for his descendants - spiritual death - which was "paid" by Christ at the cross (1 Corinthians 15:22). However, Christ's atonement for sins and the redemption of sinners of original sin does not nullify karma.

Karmic debts against other people are separate from our karmic debts to God for sin because God's law was not nullified at the cross (Matthew 5:17-20). God may forgive a man for killing another man; but God's forgiveness of his sins doesn't nullify the murderer's obligation to seek forgiveness, pay restitution, and restore the karmic "balance" with his victims.

The Christian "mystery" of reincarnation is that a person's accumulation of "bad" and "good" karma determines which level of heaven or hell in God's hierarchy of afterlife realms they dwell in between earth lifetimes.

Jesus taught people how to overcome and reverse the cycle of bad karma when it happens to them by "turning the other check when slapped" for example, and through good karma or good works, and through the greater divine laws of love, forgiveness, and grace.

Part 4 of this article describes the biblical case of how God's demand for human perfection and holiness can only realistically occur through reincarnation. Part 4 also describes how God's salvation and judgment "according to works" also can only realistically occur through reincarnation.

In the Book of Revelation, Jesus said that once a person overcomes the world, they will never "again" have to leave heaven which means they will never again have to reincarnate.

Paul said the sanctification process continues until the Second Coming of Christ implying reincarnation.

Sanctification is the perfecting process by the Holy Spirit working together with the soul of the person toward becoming transformed into Christ's image. It is self-evident that this perfection process is much more than a single lifetime process to accomplish.

The belief in the soul "resting in peace" until a final corpse resurrection at the end times makes any personal identity of the soul, salvation, and personal spiritual growth after death impossible. However, the Bible mentions Jesus descended to Hades to preach to the "imprisoned spirits" for their possible salvation after his death, an event called "the Harrowing of Hell" - an event which supports reincarnation.

All Bible verses about people being judged and "saved according to their works" proves God's law (the Ten Commandments) remains in effect and has not been abrogated. Such verses also support the existence of a perfecting sanctification process involved in God's plan of salvation which implies reincarnation.

According to numerous Bible verses, everyone is judged according to God's law, according to their works both good and bad. It is self-evident that if everyone, without exception, is judged according to their works, and a perfecting process in salvation exists, then this is a very high standard for attaining entrance into God's Kingdom in heaven, and this can only realistically occur through reincarnation. Perhaps this is why Jesus said the way to heaven is narrow.

At this point, the idea of God giving a person only one chance at salvation in one very short life needs to be forever abandoned.

In the Bible, a Greek word "palingenesía" is sometimes translated "regeneration" but is a word the Greeks used when referring to reincarnation.

The "life review" undergone by people who have an NDE resembles God's judgment "according to works" as mentioned in the Bible requiring them to return from their NDE which also supports reincarnation.

Part 5 of this article describes the biblical doctrines of the preexistence of the soul and the Christian "mystery" of God within human beings as important principles involving Christian reincarnation.

Preexistence is the doctrine of the soul/spirit not being created at birth; but rather having existed before birth in past lives on Earth and in afterlife realms. All Bible verses referring to reincarnation assumes the reality of the preexistence of the soul. All Bible verses referring to preexistence of the soul implies the reality of reincarnation.

Both concepts of reincarnation and preexistence are inseparable and both concepts were common knowledge in Jesus' day.

The disciples asked Jesus if a man committed a sin causing him to be born blind. Given the fact the man was blind since birth, this was an unusual question to ask unless they believed in preexistence and reincarnation.

The Bible affirms the preexistence of Adam, Jacob and Esau, Jeremiah, Jesus, John the Baptist, and all of humanity.

The biblical doctrines of predestination, election, calling, and God's foreknowledge also implies the reality of preexistence and reincarnation.

The nature of an eternal, immortal, and indestructible human soul/spirit shows that all human beings partake in the divine spirit as Jesus did. Jesus taught, "the Kingdom of God is within you" (Luke 17:20-21) which implies divinity within humanity. An immortal human soul/spirit makes reincarnation a necessity.

Because the human spirit is a part of God, it cannot be destroyed nor can it suffer eternally in hell. It is the spirit - the "spark" of the divine - within human beings that is reincarnated.

It is the flesh which must be overcome, and through reincarnation, this becomes possible. As co-heirs with Christ, humans can attain at-onement with God as Jesus did. It is self-evident that this requires more than one lifetime and this implies the necessity of reincarnation.

The Bible describes a "Trinity" (the Father, Son, and Holy Spirit), three parts of Christ (the Mind of Christ, the Body of Christ, and the Spirit of Christ), and three dimensions of God (light, life, and love) which the three-dimensional enlightened Christian shares (mind, body, and spirit). So the mystery of God in man defines all of humanity created with a spirit in the image and likeness of God's Spirit which is immortal and indestructible and refutes eternal damnation or destruction.

Because of the fallen nature of the preexistent human spirit from the highest heaven created before the world began, the human spirit is "trapped in flesh" and subjected to reincarnation which, like Jesus himself, is the way for the soul to regain the highest heaven through soul growth according to good works.

The mystery of God in man is the reality of human beings evolving into the image of Christ. In Christian theology, the Greek word "theosis" is translated divinization (deification, making divine) and is the perfecting effect of divine grace by the atonement of Christ and spiritual regeneration by the Holy Spirit.

Divinization mean exactly what Jesus and the Bible says, humans can become "gods" or "godlings" - not "Gods" - but "sons" of God, "children" of God, an "image" of God, like "the Logos," like Christ, a "part" of God, a "thought" within the Mind of God.

According to NDE studies, everyone is born into this world with a "mission" from God - lessons in life to learn toward spiritual growth and perfection. The life review also affirms reincarnation and often reveals how one lifetime is not enough to accomplish all a person must accomplish on Earth including the process of spiritual growth.

Part 6 of this article describes more reincarnating biblical personalities including fallen angels as reincarnating human beings. The dream interpretation of the end times in the Book of Revelation is described as having a reincarnation interpretation.

Fallen angels reincarnating as human beings, including Satan and the "fallen" human soul, are described in the Bible, the Book of Enoch, the Book of Jubilees, and the New Testament Apocrypha.

The story of "Jacob's Ladder" in Genesis describes "angels" ascending and "angels" descending a heavenly "stairway." Ascending this stairway implies death and going to heaven. Descending this stairway implies returning to Earth and reincarnation.

The idea of a "stairway to heaven" is also a useful metaphor for the near-death experience (NDE) tunnel which so many NDE experiencers travel through during their NDEs.

Another example of angels reincarnating as humans can be found in the story of the Nephilim ("fallen" angels). The "Nephilim" is a metaphor for "fallen" souls from heaven because angels don't have genitals and cannot have sex, neither do they marry according to

Jesus.

According to the cosmology of Christian Gnosticism and Jewish mystery teachings, God's plan for the fallen human souls was a limited series of reincarnations with periods in between of dwelling in other heavenly dimensions (afterlife realms) where increasingly righteous souls dwell in higher afterlife realms and increasingly unrighteous souls dwell in lower afterlife realms. Reincarnation continues until the soul completes its plan originally laid out for the soul toward a human-divine unity.

The Christian psychic, Edgar Cayce, confirmed the evidence from early Christian Gnostic writings which shows that humanity, as preexistent souls, had fallen from the highest spiritual realm before the creation of the physical realm (a lower realm). The Bible allegorically refers to this event as "the Fall" in the Garden of Eden in the Book of Genesis and "the revolt of the angels" in the Book of Revelation.

The Bible refers to the entire nation of Israel reincarnating and holy men reincarnating such as the apostles John and Paul.

The case was made against a resurrection interpretation of "dead bodies coming out of tombs" and in favor of a reincarnation interpretation of "live babies coming out of wombs." It is a case against "resting in peace" until a final "night of the living dead" of a worldwide corpse resurrection.

A verse in Hebrews 9:27-28 is often used to refute reincarnation; but instead refutes the traditional concept of resurrection that "people are destined to die once, and after that to face judgment." This verse has historically been interpreted to mean people die only once, then they rest in peace in Abraham's bosom until the body is resurrected at the end times to face judgment. But this verse simply declares a "one life, one death, one judgment" principle which doesn't refute reincarnation. According to reincarnation, a person's body dies once, never to be inhabited again. Then the spirit immediately faces judgment. Later, if a person chooses to reincarnate, a different body having a different life is subjected to a different death and judgment. Therefore, reincarnation upholds the principle of "one life, one death, one judgment." But this verse in Hebrews 9 does not, in fact, support corpse resurrection. Corpse resurrection is the reanimation of a dead body, which happened to Lazarus and many other people in the Bible. All such people experienced death not once, but twice, violating the "one life, one death, one judgment" principle. Corpse resurrection also contradicts the doctrine of the "second death" mentioned in the Bible. And this verse in Hebrews implies judgment occurs immediately after death which also refutes the idea of resting in peace until an end time corpse resurrection Judgment Day.

The original Greek translation of the word "judgment" in Strong's Bible Concordance comes from the Greek word "krisis" which is one of the most misunderstood words in the entire Bible. The King James version rendered the word as: "accusation, condemnation, damnation, and judgment." But the actual Greek word "krisis" implies a decision that brings correction. The resurrection of "krisis" should more appropriately be called "the resurrection of correction" or "the resurrection which forces correct decisions." Such a "resurrection" would be a reincarnation into a lifetime involving a "reincarnation of correction."

A "resurrection of damnation" limits God's grace by requiring God to pronounce judgment of horrible eternal consequences because of a short, single, earthly life lived under conditions of apparent unjust inequity among human beings.

The traditional doctrine of salvation of "faith alone" involving only one lifetime creates spiritual laziness by lulling the Christian into believing one life is enough to attain spiritual perfection in Christ. It also allows for immoral behavior by suggesting that people can avoid the consequences of their transgressions against others by simply "accepting Christ" without realizing that no one who truly accepts Christ can escape seeking forgiveness and paying restitution to those they have transgressed.

The return of the fallen condition of the cosmos to its original state is the object of the entire cosmic process. Through reincarnation, all souls will eventually return to Paradise - a process which the Bible refers to as the "apocatastasis." God created the universe in which all individual acts work freely together toward one cosmic end which culminates in returning all souls to God as co-creators.

Humanity, conceived in the image of God with an eternal soul (spirit), is able by imitating Christ in good works to become like Christ - the perfect image of God in man - refutes eternal damnation and supports reincarnation.

Symbolic interpretations of the Book of Revelation refers to - not only actual people and events - but also an allegory of the spiritual path through reincarnation and the ongoing struggle between good and evil both within individual human beings and within humanity as a whole.

The Christian psychic, Edgar Cayce, gave an idealist dream interpretation of the Book of Revelation by which he unlocked all of its religious symbolism. Cayce revealed the Bible to be the symbolic account of the Fall of the human soul from its divine origins, as symbolically described in the Book of Genesis, culminating with the restoration of the human soul to heaven symbolically described in the Book of Revelation. The literal "thousand year reign of Christ" in the Book of Revelation is the future "golden age of humanity" predicted in the Bible.

Later in the Book of Revelation, it describes how the "first heaven" and the "first Earth" is replaced with a new heaven and new Earth. God's people on the old Earth can rise to the new first heaven. The people who are purified in the lower "Lake of Fire" (or "Gehenna" as Jesus taught) can then eventually reincarnate to the new Earth where there will be "no remembrance of former things" mentioned in Revelation.

Concerning a person's citizenship in Gehenna, most biblical translations render the Greek "aionas ton aionon" to mean "forever and ever." However, the correct translation of "aionas ton aionon" is "ages of the ages." The Greek word "aion" is English for "age." In the context of Biblical Hebrew cosmology, "age" refers to an astrological age which is one of twelve astrological ages corresponding to the twelve zodiacal signs of the Zodiac ("Mazzaroth" in Hebrew). The Greek word "aion" is also the root word for "eon" which is a finite, long period of time.

In the final chapter of the Book of Revelation, John foresaw the "Garden of Eden" restored on Earth. The Book of Revelation reveals the Kingdom of Heaven is here and growing now - within us and around us - just as is the "resurrection" (reincarnation) has been constantly occurring here and now.

The Book of Revelation describes the final judgment as the unrighteous, death, and Hades being thrown into the "Lake of Fire" which is called the "second death." Revelation states that anyone whose name is not found written in the "Book of Life" was thrown into the "Lake of Fire." This event in Revelation contradicts the dogma of eternal damnation in hell because hell itself is thrown into the "Lake of Fire" which implies purification. Death is never the end of life. The immortal soul cannot be destroyed. The spirit cannot be punished forever as an image of God. Eternal damnation contradicts everything presented in this article as biblically true.

Fire is a metaphor used in the Bible to describe God and manifestations of God through the metaphor of purifying fire. Fire is also a metaphor used in the Bible to describe the purification of people on Earth through tribulation. According to NDE studies, God's judgment on "Judgment Day" is actually a "life review" which occurs immediately after death which results in determining the next stage in the life of the soul or the next afterlife realm.

The idea of a literal 24-hour "Last Day" time period when corpses are reanimated for Jesus to judge them can be refuted with the following Bible verse: "With the Lord a day is like a thousand years, and a thousand years are like a day." (2 Peter 3:8). The evidence shows today is the day of salvation, now is the "resurrection" occurring and the "harvest" of the Kingdom of Heaven on Earth growing, and the "day of the Lord" is approaching.

Part 7 of this article describes the biblical case for the past lives of Jesus Christ as King David, Melchizedek, Joseph, and Adam. Part 7 includes a final summary of this article and a final conclusion by Kevin Williams.

The Biblical case was made for David as a past life of Jesus. Both David and Jesus share titles such as: the anointed one (Messiah), the Holy One, only begotten son, firstborn, Root of Jesse, priest of Melchizedek, and most exalted king of the Earth. The Bible clearly states that David himself will be reincarnated in the Last Days (Hosea 3:4-5; Ezekiel 34:13-24; Ezekiel 37:22-24; Jeremiah 30:1-9). In Acts 15:12-19, the apostle Peter equated rebuilding "David's fallen tent" with the resurrection of Jesus' body. In the Bible, "tent" is a metaphor for the human body (2 Corinthians 5:1; 2 Peter 1:12-13).

The Biblical case was made for Melchizedek as a past life of Jesus. Both Melchizedek and Jesus share titles such as: Son of God, King of Righteousness, King of Peace, of the order of Melchizedek high priesthood, appointed by God, an eternal priesthood, preexistent, personally associated with Abraham, who used ritualistic symbols of bread and wine.

The Biblical case was made for Joseph as a past life of Jesus. Both Joseph and Jesus were miraculously born; were taken into Egypt to avoid being killed; whose families were called out of Egypt and back to Israel as an act of salvation; began their ministry at the age of thirty; became a humble servant; were hated for their teachings; miraculously gave bread to hungry people who came to him; were betrayed by the advice of Judah (Judas), one of the Twelve; were betrayed for the price of a slave in silver; were persecuted because of false witnesses; were condemned with two other prisoners; had one of the prisoners released and exalted with him; were stripped of their robes; forgave the people who wanted to kill them; descended into a pit; arose victorious to be great princes; and had people who refused to believe they were not dead.

The Biblical case was made for Adam as a past life of Jesus. Both Adam and Jesus shared titles such as: Son of God, Son of Man, "firstborn" of every creature, an immortal soul from the beginning, the "Image" of God, the "human-divine" unity, "father" of the human race, "ruler" of God's creation, the "first" and "last" sacrifice, the "Alpha" and "Omega", associated with the Tree of Life, and having identical karma which required them to pay for Original sin.

Part 8 of this article provides references, resources, and links related to reincarnation and Christian reincarnation in particular. Internet links to websites provided include reincarnation main websites, researchers, case studies, news, YouTube videos, articles, Wikipedia and Psi Encyclopedia references.

3. Conclusion by Kevin Williams

The Biblical evidence of John the Baptist as the reincarnation of Elijah the Prophet should be enough proof to the Christian for the reality of reincarnation. Also is the fact that if reincarnation was a false doctrine it would almost certainly have been denounced in the same harshest terms as idolatry, sorcery and evil throughout the entire Bible. Instead, as we have seen, reincarnation is referenced throughout the Bible and taught by Jesus. By studying the historical records and allowing NDE concepts to guide me, I reached the same conclusion many others have which is that reincarnation is actually a gift from God allowing humans to have as many opportunities as necessary to become permanent residents of God's highest heaven.

"Hell" means having to dwell in lower, hellish afterlife realms, then reincarnating to be subjected to the cycle of life and death repeatedly until eternal life in heaven is attained. These hidden mysteries of Jesus were not limited to Jesus or to Judeo-Christianity. Examples of these mystery teachings of attaining a human-divine unity can also be found in the Perennial Philosophy and the more modern school of psychology called Transpersonal Psychology which includes NDE studies. All assume the same goal which is the liberation of the soul from the lower, animalistic nature of the flesh through the awakening of the spirit within - our higher nature. Reincarnation is to the soul, what evolution is to the body. And for scientists who are skeptical of reincarnation, there is the reincarnation and NDE research of Dr. Ian Stevenson whose 40+ years of research yielded much scientific evidence suggestive of reincarnation. Dr. Kenneth Ring also studied reincarnation in NDE studies. Then there is my own reincarnation research where I provide evidence for the reincarnation of Abraham Lincoln and in my own NDE studies. From all that has been presented in this article, it must be admitted by the open mind that Christianity originally began with reincarnation as an assumed teaching and special doctrine, and that reincarnation should be a doctrine preached from the pulpits of every Christian Church.

REINCARNATION 8:
REINCARNATION IN THE BIBLE (PART 8)

1. References

Atkinson, William Walker (1908). Reincarnation and the law of karma. YOGeBooks.

Besant, Annie (1920). The necessity for reincarnation. The Theosophical Publishing House. Download from website.

Burke, Abbot George (2016). May a Christian believe in reincarnation? Light of The Spirit Press..

Cooper, Irving S. (1959). Reincarnation: A hope of the world. The Theosophical Press..

Cronshaw Jr., Allan (2008). Reincarnation: The key to Christianity. Ebionite.com. Accessed on 05-15-2017.

Cunningham, Michael J. (2014). A connected life: Mystical Christianity for today. Don Bosco Publications

Cutler, Geoff (2011). Is reincarnation an illusion? Lulu Publications..

Foster, Brian (2014). The case for reincarnation: Your path to perfection. CreateSpace Independent Publishing..

Hall, Manly P. (1993). Reincarnation: The cycle of necessity. The Philosophical Research Society..

Hoover, D. M. (2014). Edgar Cayce on Biblical Reincarnations and the Essenes. Edgar Cayce Foundation..

House, H. Wayne (1991). Resurrection, reincarnation, and humanness. Bibliotheca Sacra, Vol. 148, No. 590 (April 91):132.

Accessed 05-15-2017.

Howe Jr., Quincy (1974). Reincarnation for the Christian. The Theosophical Publishing House..

Katsunoff, Robert G. (2009). Does the Bible Teach Reincarnation and Karma. The Theosophical Publishing House.

Lampe, Stephen M. (2009). The Christian and reincarnation. Millennium Press..

Lewis, H. Spencer (1986). Mansions of the soul. Amorc..

Luz, Angel (2013). John 16:12-13: The teachings of Jesus Christ clarified and made plain. Amazon Digital Services LLC..

Macchio, Joseph P. (2010). The Orthodox Christian Conspiracy: How Church Fathers suppressed original Gnostic Christianity. Infinity Publishing..

MacGregor, Donald (2014). Christian Reincarnation? CANA Publications. Download from website.

Martin, Stephen H. (2015). Reincarnation: Good news for open-minded Christians and other truth-seekers. Publisher..

Myers, Katie (2014). Reincarnation in the Bible (Yes, It's There!). CreateSpace Independent Publishing..

Pandarakalam, James P. (2010). The Biblical Reincarnation. Royal College of Psychiatrists. Download from website.

Peterson, Doug (2013). Resurrecting Reincarnation? Millennium Publications.

Pradeep, Charles (2011). Karma in Christianity. Cinnamon Teal..

Prophet, Elizabeth Clare (1997). Reincarnation: The missing link in Christianity. Summit University Press..

Pryse, James M. (1904). Reincarnation in the New Testament. Kessinger Publishing..

Puryear, Herbert B. (2002). Why Jesus taught reincarnation: A better news gospel. New Paradigm Press..

Sigdell, Jan Erik (2014). Reincarnation, Christianity and the dogma of the Church: Unmasking the myth that the reincarnation doctrine would be unChristian. Jan Erik Sigdell. Download from website.

Van Auken, John (1989). Born again and again: How reincarnation occurs and what it means to you. A.R.E. Press.

VanHoose, L. Edward (2013). The Bible Reveals Reincarnation. CreateSpace Independent Publishing..

Varady, Luis (2014). The wheel of birth: Reincarnation in early Gnostic Christianity. Amazon Digital Services LLC.

Zumtaugwald, Claudia (2006). Teaching of reincarnation and the 5th Council of 553 in Constantinopel. Advo-Kanzlei.ch.

2. Resources and Links

A. Reincarnation eBooks

Near-Death.com eBook Library: VII. Reincarnation eBooks - https://www.near-death.com/library/reincarnation-ebooks.html

Reincarnation And Christianity, by Geoffrey Hodson - https://www.theosophical.org/files/resources/articles/Reincarnatio nChristianity.pdf

Reincarnation - A Study in Human Evolution, by Dr. Théophile Pascal - https://cdn.website-editor.net/e4d6563c50794969b714ab70457d9761/files/uploaded/Re incarnation_DrTPascal.pdf

Reincarnation in the New Testament, by James M. Pryce - https://cdn.website-editor.net/e4d6563c50794969b714ab70457d9761/files/uploaded/Re incarnationInTheNewTestament_JMPryce.pdf

B. Reincarnation Websites

(1) Reincarnation Researchers

Dr. Ian Stevenson's Reincarnation Research - https://www.near-death.com/reincarnation/research/ian-stevenson.html

Scientific Proof of Reincarnation: Dr. Ian Stevenson's Life Work - http://reluctant-messenger.com/reincarnation-proof.htm

Jim B. Tucker, M.D. Official Site - http://www.jimbtucker.com/

Dr. Erlendur Haraldsson, University of Iceland Faculty Site - https://notendur.hi.is/~erlendur/english/index.html

Dr. Satwant Pasricha, Parapsychology Foundation -
http://www.pflyceum.org/49.html

Carol Bowman, M.S. Official Site - http://www.carolbowman.com/

Walter Semkiw, M.D., Institute for the Integration of Science,
Intuition and Spirit - http://www.iisis.net/index.php?page=semkiw-
reincarnation-past-lives-principles

James G. Matlock, Ph.D., Signs of Reincarnation -
http://jamesgmatlock.net/

Paul Von Ward, Ph.D., The Reincarnation Experiment -
http://www.reincarnationexperiment.org/

Rob Schwartz, PLSRt, BLSRt, Your Soul's Plan -
http://yoursoulsplan.com/

Brian L. Weiss, M.D. Official Site - http://www.brianweiss.com/

Dr. Bruce Goldberg, Past & Future Life Hypnotherapy -
http://www.drbrucegoldberg.com/

Kevin Williams, B.Sc., Reincarnation Evidence of the Afterlife -
https://www.near-death.com/reincarnation.html

(2) Reincarnation Main Websites

Division of Perceptual Studies, Psychiatry and Neurobehavioral
Sciences, University of Virginia -
https://med.virginia.edu/perceptual-studies/research-area/children-
who-report-memories-of-previous-lives/

Reincarnation Research - http://reincarnationresearch.com/

Edgar Cayce's Association for Research and Enlightenment -
https://www.edgarcayce.org/the-readings/philosophy-
reincarnation/

Institute for the Integration of Science, Intuition and Spirit - http://www.iisis.net/

Resurrection as the Lost Christian Doctrine of Reincarnation - https://www.near-death.com/reincarnation/history.html

In Another Life: Reincarnation In America - http://www.ial.goldthread.com/

Skeptiko Podcast, Past Live Archives - http://skeptiko.com/tag/past-lives/

Crystalinks: Reincarnation - http://www.crystalinks.com/reincarnation.html

Victor Zammit, A Lawyer Presents the Case for the Afterlife: Reincarnation - http://www.victorzammit.com/book/4thedition/chapter24.html

The Newton Institute for Life Between Lives Hypnotherapy - http://newtoninstitute.org/

3. Article References

Reincarnation Evidence of the Afterlife - https://www.near-death.com/reincarnation.html

Part 1: Reincarnation in the Bible - https://www.near-death.com/reincarnation/history/bible-01.html

Part 2: Reincarnation in the Bible - https://www.near-death.com/reincarnation/history/bible-02.html

Part 3: Reincarnation in the Bible - https://www.near-death.com/reincarnation/history/bible-03.html

Part 4: Reincarnation in the Bible - https://www.near-death.com/reincarnation/history/bible-04.html

Part 5: Reincarnation in the Bible - https://www.near-death.com/reincarnation/history/bible-05.html

Part 6: Reincarnation in the Bible - https://www.near-death.com/reincarnation/history/bible-06.html

Part 7: Reincarnation in the Bible - https://www.near-death.com/reincarnation/history/bible-07.html

Part 8: Reincarnation in the Bible - https://www.near-death.com/reincarnation/history/bible-08.html

4. About The Author

Kevin R. Williams is a computer programmer with a Bachelor of Science degree in Computer Science. He is the webmaster of the website "Near-Death Experiences and the Afterlife" at www.near-death.com. The website is one the most comprehensive website on the internet about near-death experiences. He is an active member of IANDS, the International Association for Near-Death Studies. His interests also include metaphysics, early Christian history, and comparative religions.

Williams believes his mission in life is to bring information about the NDE to the internet. He states, "My mission is to magnify the truth and to shine a light in this world of darkness. I seek to end the ignorance and fear of death and to plant seeds of more spiritual love and light within my fellow human beings. I wish everyone could find the enormous love and the great light I have discovered in meditating on the profound truths revealed in the NDE. This is my mission in this life and my love."

Williams currently lives near Sacramento, California, where he continues to write and maintain his website.

Printed in Great Britain
by Amazon

26753747R00138